ESCAPE TO FREEDOM

Sometimes I feel like sitting some place very quiet, and taking my hat off, and thinking the biggest thoughts I can think about Frederick Douglass—such a giant of a person was he, both in his own life and in the history of black people. Fred—were he alive today—would be about one hundred and sixty-two years old; but he is still one of the most modern and up-to-date Americans I know . . . my hero . . . my role model.

A man's books are not altogether unlike children. He brings them forth, tries to give them character and substance and personality—to make them as important to his readers as to himself; yet in the end, a book has to live its own life. Once Papa has launched it out into the mainstream, he can only stand on the sidelines, keep track, and wish it well. *Escape to Freedom*, the story of the boyhood of Frederick Douglass, has already made me proud and fatherly. And the fact that it now goes into a second printing indicates that there are others out there who have the same bubbling-up feelings I have about Frederick Douglass; how he swapped bread with little white boys, because he was hungry for what was more important—the knowledge in their schoolbooks. How, in spite of the fact that it was against the law, he sneaked behind the backs of the people who owned him, and taught himself to read and write. How knowledge made Fred rebellious, and he was sent to a special plantation to be broken and tamed like a mule; but where—risking his life—he battled the vicious slave breaker blow for blow, and finally whipped him! And how, after forging his own pass, and pretending to be a sailor, he got on the train as bold as you please and made his escape from Baltimore to freedom. This has to be one of the most exciting stories an American boy or girl could read—and every word of it true!

If Frederick Douglass were alive today I am sure the president would appoint him head of all the boards of education in the country, especially the drop out department. I have no doubt, drawing on his own childhood, he would talk to the students as only one of America's greatest orators could talk—weaving such magnificent stories, right out of his own life—that they would sit there—as completely caught as I am, even now, whenever I think about the man; for they, too, would see what an exciting, hair-raising, breathtaking, high-flying adventure getting an education can be! If, with this book I can share with them the smallest part of what I felt when I was a boy, and first read about Fred, and his fantastic escape to freedom, and how it opened a whole new universe for me, then . . . WOW!

Ossie Davis
New Rochelle, New York
July 1989

Escape to Freedom

Escape to Freedom

A PLAY ABOUT
YOUNG FREDERICK DOUGLASS

OSSIE DAVIS

Copyright © 1976 by Ossie Davis.
Cover illustration copyright © 1976 by Jerry Pinkney.
All rights reserved. Published by Scholastic Inc., 557 Broadway, New York, NY 10012, by arrangement with Penguin Group (USA) Inc..
Printed in the U.S.A.

ISBN-13: 978-0-590-29983-1
ISBN-10: 0-590-29983-2

7 8 9 10   23   14 13 12

Escape to Freedom, by Ossie Davis, directed by Robbie McCauley, with musical arrangements and direction by Harrison Fisher, was first presented by Performing Arts Repertory Theatre (P.A.R.T.) at Town Hall, New York City, on March 8, 1976.

CAST

Frederick Douglass	*Jesse Goins*
Black Boy	*Myles McMillan*
Black Man	*John Henry Redwood*
Black Woman	*Mimi Ayers*
White Woman	*Lynn Kearney*
White Boy	*Stephen Scott*
White Man	*John McNamara*

Prologue

[*Curtain rises to reveal entire cast on stage as song begins.*]

COMPANY

> I'm on my way (*my way*)
> To the freedom land (*freedom land*)
> I'm on my way, great God
> I'm on my way
> I'm on my way
> To the freedom land

[COMPANY *hums melody under narration.*]

FRED   [*To audience*] My name is Frederick Douglass. I was born a slave, near Easton, in Talbot County, Maryland, in 1817 or 1818—I never knew which.

BLACK WOMAN   This book—a narrative of the life of Frederick Douglass—this little book, and the man who wrote it, helped millions of Americans to make up their minds that it was an evil thing to hold black people—or any people—in slavery.

[BLACK WOMAN *exits.*]

WHITE BOY   To tell our story, each of us will change his costume from time to time ...

BLACK MAN   And become different characters when it is necessary.

[WHITE BOY *and* BLACK MAN *exit.*]

WHITE MAN   All except one—the young man who will play the part of Frederick Douglass.

[WHITE MAN, WHITE WOMAN, *and* BLACK BOY *exit.* FRED *crosses to center stage as the rest of the stage lights fade to half.*]

Scene One

[*A slave cabin. Behind* FRED, *we see* BLACK WOMAN *enter with candle and kneel beside a dummy baby—young* FRED—*wrapped in a gunny sack and lying on the floor.*]

FRED [*To audience*] My mother's name was Harriet Bailey. I took the name Douglass later in my life. I never saw my mother more than four or five times in my life, and each time was very brief—and always at night.

[BLACK WOMAN *picks up baby and begins singing softly as she rocks it to sleep.* FRED *continues narration under song.*]

BLACK WOMAN

> Black sheep, black sheep
> Where'd you lose your lamb?

> *Way down in the valley*
> *The birds and the butterflies*
> *Are picking out its eyes*
> *Poor little thing crying mammy*
> *Go and tell Aunt Susie*
> *Go and tell Aunt Susie*
> *Go and tell Aunt Susie*
> *The old gray goose is dead.*

FRED She did not live with me, but was hired out by my master to a man who lived about twelve miles down the road, which she had to walk, at night, after she was through working, in order to see me at all. She couldn't stay long, being a field hand—the penalty for not showing up in the fields at sunrise was a severe whipping. It was whispered that my master was my father, but my mother, in the few times I ever got to see her, never told me one way or another.

[BLACK WOMAN *puts baby back on the floor, covers it with a gunny sack, takes one last look, and exits.*]

FRED Long before I waked she would be gone. After my mother died I was sent to live with my Aunt Jenny, but we had almost no time at all to be together. I was one of three or four hundred slaves who lived on the plantation. I was not old enough to work in the fields —I was only about seven at the time. I had no bed, no regular place to sleep, and would probably have died from hunger and cold, except that on the coldest nights I would steal a sack that was used for carrying corn to the mill, and crawl into it, and go to sleep on the cold, damp floor.

[FRED *finds a gunny sack, crawls into it, and tries to cover up for the night, but he is too tall and his feet stick out of the bottom. He tries to find a more comfortable position and finally goes to sleep. A beat, to indicate passage of time. A sudden noise and a light bursting through the door bring* FRED *awake.* WHITE BOY, *as overseer, bursts in, followed by* BLACK BOY, *as a very frightened young slave.* WHITE BOY, *seeing* FRED *asleep, pushes him with his foot.*]

WHITE BOY   Where is she, boy—where is your Aunt Jenny?

FRED   [*Scared out of his wits, trying to pull himself together, trying to wake up*] Where is who, sir?

WHITE BOY   [*Snatching* FRED *to his feet*] Don't mess with me, boy, you know who I mean! I'm talking about your Aunt Jenny—now, where did she go when she left here last night?

FRED   [*Completely in the dark*] My Aunt Jenny wasn't here last night—

[WHITE BOY *turns to* BLACK BOY, *standing nearby, as* WHITE MAN *and* BLACK WOMAN *enter.*]

BLACK BOY   That's what she told us when she left the cabin last night, Mr. Gore—said she was coming over here to say good night to Frederick, her nephew—

FRED   I ain't seen my Aunt Jenny since a long, long time ago—

WHITE BOY   You lie to me, boy, and I'll break your neck.

FRED   I ain't lying, Mr. Gore, I ain't lying!

WHITE MAN   [*As Colonel Lloyd, to* BLACK BOY] You know what happens to darkies who try to escape from me, don't you?

BLACK BOY   Yessir—

WHITE MAN   Was your Aunt Jenny in here to see you last night? Tell me the truth—

FRED   I am telling the truth, Colonel Lloyd—my Aunt Jenny wasn't here last night.

[WHITE MAN, *satisfied, turns from* FRED. WHITE BOY, *not to be outdone, turns to the other slaves.*]

WHITE BOY   Well, if she didn't come here, she must have run away, and if she ran away, she must have had some help—now, who did it? Which one of you lazy, shiftless no-goods helped Jenny escape?

[BLACK WOMAN *and* BLACK BOY, *afraid of what they know is coming, ad-lib their earnest denials.*]

BLACK WOMAN *and* **BLACK BOY**   Please, sir, Mr. Gore, we ain't done nothing! It wasn't me, sir! We don't know nothing!

[BLACK MAN *hurries in.*]

BLACK MAN   Colonel Lloyd! Colonel Lloyd, sir—

WHITE MAN   What is it, Jethro?

BLACK MAN   It's Uncle Noah, sir—

WHITE MAN   Uncle Noah? What about him?

BLACK MAN   Uncle Noah's done escaped, too!

WHITE BOY   Oh, my God! They're running off together!

[WHITE BOY *and* WHITE MAN *race off. The three blacks wait until they are sure they are not being observed, then they jump up and down in glee as they celebrate the fact.* FRED *watches, not fully understanding, until he finally manages to get* BLACK MAN's *attention.*]

FRED   Uncle Jethro! Uncle Jethro—why you-all dancing?

BLACK MAN   [*Trying to keep his voice down*] We celebrating the escape! Jenny and Noah, they done escaped —and we celebrating! If they makes it and don't get caught, it means they *free!* No more having to call some mean old white man your master—

[BLACK MAN *looks around and is suddenly aware that* WHITE MAN *and* WHITE BOY *are at the door and within earshot.* BLACK MAN *grabs* FRED *by the head and pushes him to his knees.* BLACK BOY *and* BLACK WOMAN, *catching on, sink to their knees also.* BLACK MAN *looks upward to heaven as if what follows were a continuation of heartfelt prayer.*]

BLACK MAN   Master, master, oh, gracious master, look down from your throne of grace and mercy and catch ol' Noah and Jenny by the scruffs of their no-good necks—

WHITE BOY   All right, that's enough of that bull—

BLACK MAN   I was just trying to help Colonel Lloyd in this deep, dark hour of his distress—

WHITE BOY   Enough, I say—and get out of here, the lot of you, and get into them fields and get to work—now! [*Indicating* FRED] Not you, boy.

[BLACK MAN, BLACK WOMAN, *and* BLACK BOY *hurry out.* WHITE BOY *turns to* WHITE MAN, *indicating* FRED.]

WHITE BOY   Colonel, you want me to send this boy to the fields with the rest of them?

WHITE MAN   No. All I want from Fred is that he looks after my yard—my flowers, my trees, and my fruit—right, boy?

FRED   Yes, sir.

[WHITE MAN *and* WHITE BOY *exit.* FRED *is left alone.* BLACK BOY *and* WHITE WOMAN *enter, as trees in the orchard. They are carrying prop trees, which* FRED *eyes hungrily.*]

FRED   [*To audience*] This garden was not the least source of trouble on the plantation. Its excellent fruit was quite a temptation to the hungry swarm of boys, as well as the older slaves. Scarcely a day passed but that some slave had to take the lash for stealing fruit.

[FRED *crosses to one tree and tries to shake loose an apple; no luck. He moves to the other tree and shakes it; an apple falls. He grabs the apple, looks around, and starts offstage as* BLACK MAN *enters and grabs him.*]

BLACK MAN   Gotcha!

FRED   [*Struggling to free himself*] Let me go—let me go!

BLACK MAN   [*Laughing, but still hanging on*] Stealing the Colonel's apples—how about that?

FRED   Please, Jethro, let me go!

[BLACK MAN *looks around to see if anyone is looking. Satisfied that the two of them are alone, he lets* FRED *loose.*]

BLACK MAN   Colonel catch you stealing his apples, he skin you, boy—

FRED   I know, Jethro, but I'm hungry—are you gonna tell?

BLACK MAN   There's only one way I know to get you out of this mess, boy, and save your thieving hide.

FRED   What's that?

BLACK MAN   Consume the evidence, boy—consume the evidence!

[BLACK MAN *takes a huge bite out of the apple and passes the remainder to* FRED.]

FRED   Where you been, Jethro?

BLACK MAN   [*Grinning as he eats*] Where you think I been, boy?

FRED   [*Excited at the prospect*] Baltimore! You been to Baltimore!

BLACK MAN   [*Pride of accomplishment*] Right! Boy, you ought to see that place!

[*An angry voice from offstage startles them.*]

BLACK WOMAN [*Offstage*] Fred! Where you at, boy?

[BLACK MAN *pulls* FRED *down and ducks himself just as* BLACK WOMAN *hurries on, carrying a clean shirt.*]

BLACK WOMAN [*Looking around*] Fred—boy, you're gonna get a whipping if you don't watch out!

[BLACK WOMAN *exits. When the coast is clear,* BLACK MAN *and* FRED *raise their heads again.*]

FRED I better git—

[FRED *starts to rise, but* BLACK MAN *pulls him back down.*]

BLACK MAN But I ain't told you what all I seen in Baltimore!

[*Much as* FRED *wants to leave, he cannot give up a chance to hear more.*]

FRED What did you see in Baltimore, Jethro?

BLACK MAN I'll tell you—but only if you promise: every time you shake down some of Colonel Lloyd's apples or oranges or whatnot, you save some for me.

FRED [*Hesitates, then takes the plunge.*] I'll do it, Jethro, I'll do it—now tell me—

BLACK MAN Well, first, there's the streets, wide, long, and all laid out—and on either side, houses to put them to shame.

FRED Do the slaves live in houses?

BLACK MAN   Of course they do! They wear shoes—

FRED   [*Astounded*] They wear shoes!

BLACK MAN   Sometimes—and warm clothes, and sometimes even hats.

FRED   Hats? Even when they work in the fields?

BLACK MAN   [*Scornful*] Ain't no fields in Baltimore, boy— Baltimore is a city, a great big city. All the slaves there work as house servants, with plenty to eat and drink all the time.

FRED   [*Dreaming*] I sure wish I could go to Baltimore!

BLACK MAN   [*Expanding*] And that ain't all. Guess what else I seen?

FRED   What, Jethro?

BLACK MAN   I seen a black man—who was free.

FRED   [*Not quite grasping the concept*] Free? You saw a black man who owned himself?

BLACK MAN   Yeah—he was a sailor.

[BLACK WOMAN *enters and spots the two.*]

BLACK WOMAN   So there you are, both of you—stealing master's fruit!

BLACK MAN   Uh. Uh! [BLACK MAN *and* FRED *jump up.*] We ain't stealing. Hard as we work for Colonel Lloyd— and for nothing—we deserve this fruit! It's part of our pay!

BLACK WOMAN   Good. I'm sure Colonel Lloyd will be glad to hear that.

BLACK MAN   [*Giving up*] Aw, woman—come on, Fred.

[BLACK MAN *and* FRED *start off.*]

BLACK WOMAN   No, you don't, Fred Bailey—I got a message from the master.

[BLACK MAN *exits.* FRED *turns to* BLACK WOMAN.]

FRED   What message?

BLACK WOMAN   First, you're to take off that filthy shirt— then you're to scrub yourself with soap and water and get into these clean clothes.

FRED   What for?

BLACK WOMAN   You're going to Baltimore—

FRED   Baltimore!

BLACK WOMAN   Master's nephew and his wife need somebody to help look after the house and their little boy. Well, don't stand there gawking, boy, get into this shirt!

[FRED *grins and starts immediately to take off his shirt as "Bright Glory" song begins offstage.*]

Scene Two

[*While singing "Bright Glory," the cast changes the set to an arrangement suggesting a neat back yard, with a white picket fence, a table, and a chair. On the table is a Bible and a plate of buttered bread.*]

COMPANY

> You don't hear me praying here
> You can't find me nowhere (*can't find me*)
> Come on up to bright glory
> I'll be waiting up there
> I'll be waiting up there, my Lord
> I'll be waiting up there (*be waiting*)
> Come on up to bright glory
> I'll be waiting up there.

[COMPANY *continues to hum melody offstage as dialogue continues.*]

[FRED *and* JETHRO *enter.* FRED *is carrying a small bundle. They cross into yard.*]

JETHRO   Well, Frederick, here we are.

FRED   [*Looking around, taking it all in*] Baltimore.

JETHRO   [*Pointing*] And that's the house, right over there. Now, remember, mind your manners; show Mr. and Mrs. Auld what a good little nigger you are—no sass, no back talk, remember your place. Keep your head bowed and your eyes on the ground—and whatever they tell you to do—do it! Right away—understand?

FRED   Yes, Jethro, but—do what?

[*Humming offstage ends.*]

JETHRO   Don't worry, they'll tell you. Now I got to be going—

FRED   But ain't you gonna take me in?

JETHRO   Look, Fred, you don't need nobody to take you in. Just obey the white folks—do whatever they tell you, and you'll be all right.

[JETHRO *exits, after a beat.* FRED *turns and takes a few tentative steps toward the house.*]

FRED   Here in Baltimore I saw what I had never seen before: it was a white face, beaming with the most kindly emotions—the face of my new mistress, Sophia Auld.

[WHITE WOMAN *enters during above. She sits at the*

table, picks up the Bible, and begins to read.]

WHITE BOY   [*Enters from house and runs to* WHITE WOMAN.]
Mother! Button up my shirt!

WHITE WOMAN   I declare, little Thomas, surely the least
you can do is button your own shirt.

WHITE BOY   I want you to button it!

[WHITE WOMAN *reluctantly puts her Bible aside and
buttons his shirt. Then she looks down.*]

WHITE WOMAN   And your shoes, Thomas, you haven't even
tied your shoes—

WHITE BOY   I want you to tie them!

[*Exasperated, she starts to reach down, but catches
sight of* FRED, *who has crossed to the back yard and
is standing nearby.*]

WHITE WOMAN   Fred?

FRED   Yes, Miz Sophia.

WHITE WOMAN   [*Relieved*] Thank God, you've come at last.
Thomas, this is Fred, your slave—your uncle sent
him to stay with us and to be your body servant—

WHITE BOY   [*Excited by the prospect*] Is he really my slave?

WHITE WOMAN   Yes.

WHITE BOY   All mine, and nobody else's?

WHITE WOMAN   Yes—until your uncle takes him back.

WHITE BOY   Good! Come, Fred—

[WHITE BOY *signals* FRED *and starts off.*]

WHITE WOMAN   Wait a minute, Thomas, where are you going?

WHITE BOY   To the dockyards, to show off my new slave. Come on, Fred—

WHITE WOMAN   No, Thomas.

WHITE BOY   We'll be right back.

WHITE WOMAN   I said no. Your father will be home in a minute, and you haven't read your Bible for today.

WHITE BOY   [*Angry*] I don't want to read the Bible for today. I want to show off my slave—

WHITE WOMAN   [*Firmly*] There'll be plenty of time for that later. Now we read from the Bible.

[WHITE WOMAN *picks up the Bible, finds the place, and hands it to* WHITE BOY.]

WHITE BOY   [*Takes the book and pretends to try, then gives up.*] I don't want to—

WHITE WOMAN   Come on, Thomas, show Freddie how well you can read.

WHITE BOY   [*Shouting*] I don't want to!

[*He flings the book down and runs into the house.*]

WHITE WOMAN   Thomas! Thomas, honey, Mother didn't mean to hurt your feelings—

[*She hurries off after him.* FRED *stands a minute; then, his curiosity getting the better of him, he picks up the Bible, opens it, trying to understand what is meant by reading.* WHITE WOMAN *re-enters, carrying a pair of sandals.* FRED *is so occupied he does not see her. She approaches and looks over his shoulder.*]

WHITE WOMAN   Fred—

FRED   [*Startled, putting the book down like a hot potato*] Yes, ma'am—[*He stands before her, guilty, his head bowed, his eyes cast down in a manner he has been taught is proper for a slave.*]

WHITE WOMAN   [*Chiding, but kindly*] No, no, Fred, you mustn't bow your head to me like that. We are all of us still God's children—nor slave nor master makes a difference to Him. It says so in the Bible—this book right here that you had in your hand.

[FRED, *remembering his guilt, casts his eyes down again.*]

FRED   I'm sorry, ma'am, I didn't mean to touch it, but—

WHITE WOMAN   Fred—

FRED   [*Still not looking up*] Yes, ma'am—

WHITE WOMAN   Here are some sandals for you to wear.

[FRED *cannot manage to speak.*]

Take them.

[*He takes them.*]

19

Put them on, they're yours.

[FRED *tries to put the sandals on but is too nervous.*]

Would you like for me to help you?

[*She kneels and puts the sandals on* FRED, *who is stunned at such kind and gentle behavior from a white person.*]

There you are—

[FRED *stands before her, dumb, his eyes cast down, unable to say a word.*]

[*Kindly, with complete understanding*] Don't you know how to say thank you?

FRED [*Not daring to look up at her, he finally manages it.*] Thank you, ma'am.

WHITE WOMAN [*Suddenly occurring to her*] My lands, child, you must be starved. Have some bread and butter.

[*She turns to the table and offers it to him.* FRED *takes it but can't seem to manage to get it into his mouth.*]

WHITE WOMAN Is something the matter?

FRED [*Quickly*] No, ma'am—it's just that—

WHITE WOMAN Yes?

[FRED *looks intently at the Bible. It is not difficult for her to read his thoughts.*]

Would you like for me to teach you to read?

FRED   Oh, yes, ma'am!

[*She picks up the Bible and hands it to him.* FRED *quickly puts his bread aside and picks up the Bible, getting great pleasure out of just being able to hold a book in his hands.*]

WHITE WOMAN   This is the Bible, and it is spelled B-I-B-L-E.

[FRED *looks at her in total confusion.*]

What I mean is: "Bible is a word—

[*She stops and studies him. It is obvious that he has absolutely no understanding of anything she is telling him. She sits and pulls him to her, takes the book into her own hands, and begins pointing out each letter.*]

—and every word is made up of letters, which we call the alphabet.

FRED   Alphabet.

WHITE WOMAN   Good. Now, the letter of the alphabet we use to begin the word "Bible" is called "B"—

FRED   "B"—

WHITE WOMAN   Very good, Fred, excellent. And this letter of the alphabet is called "I."

FRED   "I"—

[WHITE MAN, *as Hugh Auld, enters and stops, scarcely believing his eyes.*]

WHITE WOMAN   Now the third letter in the word "Bible" is

21

the same as the first letter of the word—

FRED   [*Snapping it up*] "B"!

WHITE WOMAN   [*Overjoyed at his obvious intelligence*] Excellent, Fred, excellent!

WHITE MAN   [*Shouting*] Sophia, stop!

[*He dashes over and snatches the Bible from his wife's hand.*] What are you doing?

WHITE WOMAN   I'm teaching Freddie to read—

WHITE MAN   Freddie?

WHITE WOMAN   You asked your uncle to send you a slave to be a companion to little Thomas. Freddie, this is Mr. Hugh Auld, your new master while you are in Baltimore.

[FRED *tries to find a proper response, but just at this moment* WHITE BOY *runs back on and grabs* FRED *by the arm and starts to pull.*]

WHITE BOY   Come on, Fred, I've got something to show you.

[FRED *looks to* WHITE WOMAN—*and* WHITE MAN—*for instructions.*]

Fred—I'm not ever gonna let you be my slave if you don't come on; I want to show you my new boat. Tell him, Mama—

WHITE WOMAN   [*Smiling*] It's all right, Fred.

[*A beat, then* FRED *and* WHITE BOY, *smiling at each other, run off.* WHITE MAN *watches them off, and then,*] *to make sure he will not be overheard, he takes* WHITE WOMAN *by the arm and draws her aside.*]

WHITE MAN   What on earth are you trying to do to that boy, ruin him?

WHITE WOMAN   Ruin him? I was only teaching him to read.

WHITE MAN   But you can't do that, Sophia!

WHITE WOMAN   Why not? He's a very bright boy.

WHITE MAN   He's a slave—and to teach a slave to read is not only unlawful, it's unsafe, and I forbid it.

[FRED *starts back onstage in search of the bundle he was carrying, which he has left behind, but, hearing himself being talked about, he starts back out, then stops in a spot where he will not be seen, and listens.*]

WHITE WOMAN   [*Deeply disturbed*] Forbid it? But Freddie is human, and the Bible says—

WHITE MAN   Never mind what the Bible says—and for Heaven's sakes, stop talking like an abolitionist!

WHITE WOMAN   Abolitionist?

WHITE MAN   Yes, those Yankee do-gooders, always trying to tell us Southerners that black folks are no different from the rest of us—can you imagine such nonsense? Freddie is not human, not in the ways that you and I are.

WHITE WOMAN   How can you say that of a creature that has a soul and a mind?

WHITE MAN   But, darling, Freddie hasn't got a soul—he's black; he's a slave.

WHITE WOMAN   But all the same—

WHITE MAN   Listen to me, Sophia—reading's not only no good for a black boy like Fred; it would do him harm, make him discontent, miserable, unhappy with his lot. Now, you wouldn't want that, would you?

[WHITE WOMAN *ponders a moment.*]

WHITE WOMAN   No, but—

WHITE MAN   [*As they exit*] The worst thing in the world you can do for a slave—if you want to keep him happy—is to teach that slave to read, understand?

[*From offstage we hear a low humming, which continues under the following.*]

[*When* WHITE MAN *and* WHITE WOMAN *have gone,* FRED *comes out of hiding.*]

FRED   [*To audience*] My master's words sank deep into my heart. I now understood something that had been the greatest puzzle of all to me: the white man's power to enslave the black man. Keep the black man away from the books, keep us ignorant, and we would always be his slaves! From that moment on I understood the pathway from slavery to freedom. Come hell or high water—even if it cost me my life—I was determined to read!

[*Humming ends.*]

[FRED *looks around to make sure he is not being watched, then crosses to pick up the Bible, and tries to read. He walks up and down mumbling to himself, trying to make sense out of the words on the page, but without success. So deep in his preoccupation is he that he does not see that* WHITE WOMAN *has returned and stands for a moment watching. Not until he bumps into her does he lift his eyes.*]

FRED   [*Apologetic, frightened*] Oh—Miz Sophia!

WHITE WOMAN   Fred, I made a mistake—about trying to teach you to read—it's—it's not right—it's against the law.

FRED   Why is it against the law?

WHITE WOMAN   [*Snapping, trying to steel herself for what she has to do*] Don't ask me why, it just is, that's all. And if I catch you with a book, I'll have to take it away, understand?

FRED   No, ma'am.

WHITE WOMAN   You *do* understand. You are not dumb—you have a good brain in that head of yours.

FRED   But if I do have a brain, then how—

WHITE WOMAN   And, anyway, you're my property. I own you like I own a horse or a mule. You don't *need* to read, you understand?

FRED   [*Tentative, searching, earnest, really trying*] You said that all people was equal before God—that being slave or being free didn't matter before God—

WHITE WOMAN   I am not talking about God! And anyway, what God said—about people being equal—doesn't apply to you.

FRED   Why don't it, Miz Sophia?

WHITE WOMAN   [*Growing more testy*] Because you ain't people, that's why—

FRED   But, ma'am, if I ain't people—what am I?

WHITE WOMAN   You are—some kind of animal that—that looks like people but you're not!

FRED   But I can talk—and you just said I got a good brain—

WHITE WOMAN   Don't you contradict me!

FRED   And I could read, too, if—

WHITE WOMAN   [*Shouting*] You will not read! Not in my house you won't! And if I should ever catch you—

FRED   But, please, Miz Sophia—

WHITE WOMAN   Shut your sassy, impudent mouth and get out of here! Get out of here!

[WHITE WOMAN *is disturbed by what she has just done. Clutching the Bible, she hurries off.*]

[*Humming begins offstage.*]

FRED   [*To audience*] Master Hugh wasted no time. With Miz Sophia's sudden change, I began to see that slavery was harmful to the slaveowner as well as the slave. As the months passed, if I was in a separate room for any length of time, she would search me out, sure that I had found a book—but by now it was too late. The first step had already been taken: Mistress Sophia, by teaching me what little she had, had set my feet on the highway to freedom, and I wasn't going to let her—or anybody else—turn me around.

[*Humming ends.*]

[WHITE BOY *enters, this time as a schoolboy. He is barefoot, his clothes are patched and ragged; he is obviously much worse off than* FRED. FRED *watches as* WHITE BOY *passes, drawn like a magnet by the schoolbooks he carries under his arms.* FRED *suddenly has an idea, and as* WHITE BOY *passes, he snatches up the remainder of the bread and butter on the table and runs after him.*]

FRED Hey! Hey, boy!

[WHITE BOY *does not notice him.*]

Hey, boy, wait—

[*Still no reaction*]

Hey, white boy!

WHITE BOY You calling me?

FRED Yeah, I'm calling you—what's your name?

WHITE BOY My name's Robert. What's yours?

FRED   My name's Fred. I'm a slave.

WHITE BOY   I know that—well, I gotta go.

[*He starts off, but* FRED *overtakes him.*]

FRED   Hey, does your father own slaves?

WHITE BOY   No—

FRED   Why not?

WHITE BOY   [*Embarrassed*] We're too poor. We don't even have enough to eat.

[FRED *looks at* WHITE BOY. WHITE BOY *starts off again.* FRED *conspicuously brings the bread into view.*]

FRED   Hey, you hungry?

[WHITE BOY *stops, thinks a moment, then turns just in time to see* FRED *shove a big chunk of bread into his mouth.* WHITE BOY *says nothing.* FRED, *seeing the fish is hooked, chews lustily.*]

FRED   Man, this is the best bread I ever tasted.

[FRED *breaks off a piece and holds it out.*]

Want a piece?

[WHITE BOY *hesitates a moment, then crosses over to* FRED. *He reaches for the bread, but* FRED *pulls it back.*]

First, you got to answer me a question—you go to school?

WHITE BOY   *[Eyes fastened hypnotically on the bread]* Yes.

FRED   That means you know how to read, right?

WHITE BOY   Yes—

FRED   Good.

[FRED hands WHITE BOY the remainder of the bread. WHITE BOY puts his books down, the better to deal with the bread, which he snatches and wolfs down hungrily. FRED, with equal hunger, snatches up the book and tries to read. When WHITE BOY is finished, he wipes his mouth and reaches for his book.]

WHITE BOY   Can I have my book now?

FRED   Sure, as soon as you teach me how to read.

WHITE BOY   It's against the law to teach you to read. You are a slave.

FRED   Are you a slave?

WHITE BOY   Of course I'm not a slave—I'm white—

FRED   You are white, and you will be free all your life—but I am black—

WHITE BOY   *[Thinking about it]*—which means that you will be a slave all your life.

FRED   *[Vehemently]* I don't think that's right, do you?

WHITE BOY   *[Pondering for a moment]* No!

FRED   Then teach me to read—

WHITE BOY   What?

FRED   Master Auld say, teach a slave to read and he won't
be a slave no more.

WHITE BOY   He did?

FRED   Yes—so as soon as I learn to read I'll be free, just
like you. Teach me, Robert—teach me to read from
your book—will you?

[WHITE BOY *begins to respond to* FRED's *enthusiasm.*]

WHITE BOY   [*Excited*] Of course I will.

[*They take the book between them as they sit down
on the floor—then they begin.*]

WHITE BOY   First, the alphabet—"A"—

FRED   "A"—

WHITE BOY   "B"—

FRED   "B"—

WHITE BOY   "C"—

FRED   "C"—

WHITE BOY   "D"—

FRED   "D"—

[*So caught up are they in the lesson that they do not
see that* WHITE WOMAN *has entered and is spying on
them.*]

WHITE BOY   "E"—

FRED   "E"—

WHITE BOY   "F"—

FRED   "F"—

[WHITE WOMAN *sneaks up behind the two boys on the floor.*]

WHITE BOY   "G"—

FRED   "G"—

WHITE BOY   "H"—

[WHITE WOMAN *snatches the book from* WHITE BOY'S *fingers.* FRED *and* WHITE BOY *jump up.*]

WHITE WOMAN   Caught you!

[*She tears the book up and flings the pieces to the ground.*]

WHITE BOY   Please, ma'am, we was only—

WHITE WOMAN   I know what you were doing—ruining a perfectly good slave! Now get out of here!

[*She hands broom to* FRED.]

And you get to your work!

[*She chases* WHITE BOY *offstage.*]

FRED   [*Crosses to pick up the torn pages of the book.*] From this time on she watched me like a hawk—because everything I could find with print on it I tried to read, even if I couldn't understand it all the time.

[FRED *opens the book and begins to read.*]

Escape to Freedom

[*Offstage we hear voices singing "Lord I Don't Feel No Ways Tired."*]

COMPANY

I am seeking for a city
Hallelujah
I am seeking for a city
Hallelujah
For a city into the heaven
Hallelujah
For a city into the heaven
Hallelujah

CHILDREN

Lord I don't (I don't) feel no ways tired

COMPANY

Oh glory hallelujah
For I hope to shout glory when this world is on fire

CHILDREN

Oh glory hallelujah

[*During the song* FRED, *subconsciously responding to the beat of the music, moves across the stage, reading with one eye and keeping watch with the other. He exits and immediately re-enters, this time carrying a newspaper.*]

[*The cast continues humming the melody of the song from offstage as* FRED *continues.*]

FRED   [*Reading aloud*] The general sentiment of mankind is that a man who will not fight for himself, when he has the means to do so, is not worth—

[*He throws newspaper to the ground in frustration.*]

[*The humming ends abruptly.*]

FRED   [*To audience*] As I read, I began to realize how much had been denied me as a slave. But my reading didn't show me the way to escape. I finally felt that learning to read had been not a blessing but a curse. Like Master said—the more I read, the more miserable I became.

[WHITE BOY *and* WHITE WOMAN *enter, laughing, hugging, and kissing each other. He is dressed as a sailor and she as a loose and gaudy woman of the town. They continue fondling and laughing; neither is aware that* FRED, *made somewhat bold by his anger, is watching them.*]

WHITE WOMAN   [*Finally pulling free*] I've got to go now.

WHITE BOY   I'll go with you.

WHITE WOMAN   No, you wait here, till I come back.

[*She starts off, but* WHITE BOY *pulls her back.*]

WHITE BOY   How about a little something to last me till you return?

[*She laughs as he pulls her to him.*]

WHITE WOMAN   You Yankee sailors are all devils, aren't you?

WHITE BOY   Sure are!

[*He grabs her, spins her around, and they kiss.*

Suddenly she spots FRED *and pulls free again.*]

WHITE WOMAN   What you looking at, boy?

[FRED *is still a slave, but manages, out of his anger, to stand his ground.*]

I'm talking to you, nigger!

WHITE BOY   Aw, let the fellow alone.

WHITE WOMAN   He's a slave.

WHITE BOY   So what—he's still human.

WHITE WOMAN   He's a slave, and he's got no business spying on people in a public place. He ought to be whipped!

WHITE BOY   Aw, honey, you can't mean that—he's only a kid!

WHITE WOMAN   I do mean it. I don't know how you all treat 'em up North, but down here in Maryland—

WHITE BOY   All right, all right, you run right along and I'll take care of it.

WHITE WOMAN   Ought to be whipped, that's what!

WHITE BOY   I'll take care of it—you run on along—

[*She starts offstage.*]

—and hurry back!

[WHITE WOMAN *exits. The sailor, obviously a good-natured man, chuckles as he crosses to* FRED, *who, though frightened, is determined, for the first time, to stand his ground.*]

WHITE BOY   You're the first person I ever met who was a
             slave.

FRED   Yeah, but that don't make me no different from you
        or her or anybody else.

WHITE BOY   [*Laughing*] I didn't say it did.

FRED   I got brains just like you got brains, and I can think
        just as good as you can think, and I can read just as
        good as you can read!

WHITE BOY   [*Trying to explain it, but not knowing how*]
             Look, son, I know how you feel.

FRED   How can you know how I feel? You're not black.

WHITE BOY   No, I'm not black, and I'm not a slave—but if I
             were, I'd do something about it.

FRED   [*His curiosity overcoming his feelings*] Do what?

WHITE BOY   I'd run away first chance I got.

FRED   [*Suspicious*] Why should I run away?

WHITE BOY   [*Matter-of-factly*] Why stay?

        [FRED, *not sure that this is not a trap, refuses to an-
        swer directly.*]

FRED   I knew a slave who ran away once—but they caught
        him and beat him and sold him down the river.

WHITE BOY   They might catch you—that's a chance you'll
             have to take—but if you don't take the chance, you'll
             never be free, right?

FRED   But where could I go?

WHITE BOY   You could go up north—there are people up
north doing all they can to end slavery.

FRED   What people?

WHITE BOY   Abolitionists—white people and black people,
who hate slavery as much as you do. They'd hide
you, feed you, give you clothes and money. As a matter of fact, I heard about a young fellow who dressed
himself in a sailor suit, like mine, and wrote himself
a pass.

FRED   A pass? What's that?

WHITE BOY   A pass is a little slip of paper a master gives to
a slave when he sends him on an errand by himself.

FRED   This slave you're talking about—he wrote out his
own pass, you say?

WHITE BOY   Yes, he signed his master's name to it and then
went down to the boat, and got right on, big as you
please. Anybody asked him what he was doing, he'd
show them his pass, written in his own hand, and tell
them he was traveling on business for his master.

FRED   And he got away?

WHITE BOY   All the way to New York. And if he did it, so
can you. Look—as a matter of fact—

[*He reaches into his pocket and brings out a piece of
paper and a pencil.*]—I'll show you how. Here, take
this and write down what I tell you.

[FRED *seats himself on a convenient object, takes the paper and pencil, and holds them in readiness.*]

"This pass will certify that—"

[FRED *starts to write but stops.*]

What's the matter?

FRED   [*Just discovering this fact himself*] I can't write.

WHITE BOY   Can't write? But I thought you said—

FRED   I said I could read—I taught myself how to read—but not to write.

WHITE BOY   Oh, I see.

[*Pauses a moment, then makes a decision.*]

All right, I'll teach you to write.

[*He takes pencil and paper from* FRED *and proceeds to demonstrate. Writing*] This—pass—will—certify—that—[*To* FRED] What did you say your name was?

FRED   My name is Frederick.

[*Looks up and sees* WHITE WOMAN, *who has returned and is watching.*]

WHITE WOMAN   [*Suspicious—to sailor*] What are you doing?

WHITE BOY   I was just teaching young Frederick to—

FRED   [*Rising in agitation*] No, he wasn't! He wasn't doing no such a thing!

WHITE WOMAN   Down here it's against the law to teach slaves to read and write.

WHITE BOY   [*Laughing*] Who's teaching anybody anything?

[*He rises, looking at her.*]

My, but don't you look wonderful!

[*He holds the paper and pencil behind his back and gestures for* FRED *to take them from him.*]

WHITE WOMAN   [*Eating it up*] I do? I went all the way back home just to get these earrings; I do hope you like them—

WHITE BOY   Like them? Hon, I love them!

[*Takes her by the arm and starts off.*]

Just wait till I get you downtown so the rest of the boys can see you!

[*He manages to get the pencil and paper back to* FRED *without her noticing, and then they exit.* FRED *watches after them a moment, then turns in high excitement to resume his story.*]

FRED   [*To audience*] There was no better place in all Baltimore to start the second part of my education than right where I was—in the shipyard.

[*We hear the cast humming "Lord I Don't Feel No Ways Tired" as they change the set to an arrangement suggesting a shipyard, with coils of rope, planks, etc.,*

*strewn about the stage. This continues under the fol-
lowing.*]

I remember seeing ship's carpenters at the dock cut
pieces of timber into planks—

[FRED *crosses to a plank, picks it up and examines it.*]

They would write on the plank with a piece of chalk
the part of the ship for which it was intended.

[FRED *holds the plank in such a way that we can
clearly see the letter "L" that has been handwritten
upon it.*]

"L," that's for larboard.

[FRED *takes a piece of chalk and laboriously writes
several imitations of the "L," using an appropriate
spot on the pier, or on the board, as a blackboard.
When he is satisfied, he sets the plank down and
picks up another.*]

"S," for starboard.

[FRED *repeats the previous action during the following, putting one plank down as soon as he is finished,
and picking up another.*]

"L.F.," that's for larboard forward; "S.A.," that's for
starboard aft. In a short while I could do "L," "S,"
"F," and "A" with no trouble at all.

[*He indicates his mastery with a flourish.*]

And not only planks—during this time any board

wall or brick fence or pavement that had any writing on it became my copybook.

[FRED *moves quickly from one appropriate place, construction, or object to another, copying the indicated lettering. In his movings about, he finds a half-torn book.*]

I found a Webster Spelling Book that had written script in it.

[FRED *busily copies from the book, making the lettering on every nearby object.* WHITE BOY *and* WHITE WOMAN, *as children, enter, skipping, and hand their copybooks to* FRED.]

When my little white friends finished with their lettering books at school, they gave them to me.

[FRED *takes the books, thanks* WHITE BOY *and* WHITE WOMAN, *who exit, and then* FRED *goes busily to work.*]

I copied—and copied—and copied—until I had mastered every letter of the alphabet. "Z"!

[FRED *writes a final "Z" on some appropriate surface, then stands back, in pride and satisfaction, to admire his handiwork: every place he looks, everything he sees, has some evidence of* FRED's *capacity to write.*]

I was now ready to try my hand at the most important thing of all: writing a pass.

COMPANY   [*Offstage*]
    Lord I don't (I don't) feel no ways tired

CHILDREN

Oh glory hallelujah

COMPANY

For I hope to shout glory when this world is on fire

CHILDREN

Oh glory hallelujah

FRED [*Takes out pencil and paper, reading as he writes.*] This—is—to—certify—that I—the undersigned— have given the bearer, my servant, Fred Bailey, full liberty to go to—

[FRED *looks up and sees* BLACK MAN, *as* JETHRO, *standing over him.*]

Hey, Jethro, look what I just did—

[*Something about* JETHRO's *face makes him stop.*]

JETHRO [*Sadly*] Ol' Master's dead, Fred.

FRED Dead? Colonel Lloyd?

JETHRO Yes, so all the slaves is being called back to the plantation so the property can be divided up.

FRED Jethro, I can't go back—with this pass I can get to—

JETHRO What?

FRED Never mind.

JETHRO I was sent to get you, and if you don't come, I'm in trouble, and you, too. Come on, Fred.

[JETHRO *exits.* FRED *starts to exit with him, but turns back to the audience.*]

Scene Three

[*During the following, the cast moves the set to an arrangement suggesting a rough country farm.* FRED's *demeanor is different—it is obvious that he is now involved in hard work for the first time in his entire life—work for which he is entirely unsuited.*]

FRED [*To audience*] The whole dream of my life had been to escape from slavery. Yet here I was at seventeen years of age, still a slave, back at St. Michael's on a farm, being forced to do things I had never done before: what good would my reading and writing do me now? In Baltimore with Master Hugh I had at least been fed well enough and given shoes and decent clothes—and there was always the chance that somehow I might escape! But not here at St. Michael's—Master Thomas and his wife, Rowena, not only watched me like a hawk, night and day, but also they were the meanest and stingiest people I ever saw in my life.

[WHITE MAN *enters, as Thomas Auld, dressed for church, moving across the stage. He speaks as he moves.*]

WHITE MAN   Don't just stand there gawking, boy, go hitch the horse and buggy.

FRED   Yes, sir, but first could we maybe have a little breakfast?

WHITE MAN   [*Stops and turns to* FRED.] So, looks like you've been in Baltimore too long, boy—my brother, Hugh, and that fancy wife of his have near-about ruined you, I suspect—just look at him, all fat and sassy—dressed up good as any white man—I bet you think you are as good as a white man, don't you, boy? And drop your eyes when I'm talking to you!

[FRED *does so.*]

That's better.

[WHITE MAN *turns and exits.*]

FRED   [*To audience*] And his wife, Rowena—

[WHITE WOMAN, *as Rowena Auld, enters, also dressed for church, and moves rapidly across in opposite direction.*]

WHITE WOMAN   This ain't Baltimore, boy—you heard Mr.

Thomas—get the horse and buggy. We're late already!

FRED   [*Tries to stop her*] Yes, ma'am, but we ain't had nothing to eat!

[*She exits.* FRED *shouts after her.*]

You expect us black folks to work around this damned old farm like dogs and you won't even feed us!

[*He turns to face the audience again, and as he speaks the stage is being changed to suggest the interior of a church.*]

It was bad: if we slaves hadn't learned to *steal* in order to feed and to clothe ourselves, we might have died from hunger and exposure.

[*The* COMPANY *has assembled on stage as if they were in church.* WHITE BOY, *dressed as a minister, Cookman, holds a Bible in his hand.* WHITE MAN *and* WHITE WOMAN *are his white audience, standing in the front row. Behind them are the slaves:* BLACK MAN, BLACK WOMAN, *and* BLACK BOY, *who are looking on with interest. They are humming "Give Me That Old-Time Religion."*]

FRED   But one night my master and his wife went to a revival meeting. And something totally unexpected happened.

[FRED *moves to join the slaves in the back row as the song begins.*]

COMPANY

Give me that old-time religion
Give me that old-time religion
Give me that old-time religion
It's good enough for me

Give me that old-time religion
Give me that old-time religion
Give me that old-time religion
It's good enough for me

BLACK WOMAN

It was good for my old mother
It was good for my old mother
It was good for my old mother
It's good enough for me

COMPANY

Give me that old-time religion
Give me that old-time religion
Give me that old-time religion
It's good enough for me

BLACK WOMAN

It was good enough for master
It was good enough for master
It was good enough for master
It's good enough for me

[*During the song* WHITE MAN *has been trembling;
now he jumps as if suddenly struck by lightning. He
dances, shouts, groans, and falls writhing to the floor
in the complete ecstasy of religious conversion.*]

WHITE MAN   Oh Lord, I'm saved!

WHITE BOY   Hallelujah!

WHITE MAN   I've been redeemed!

WHITE BOY   Oh, glory!

WHITE MAN   I love everybody!

[WHITE BOY *and the rest respond with fervor:* "*Amen!*" "*Hallelujah!*" "*Oh, give praises!*"]

Everybody is my brother!

[WHITE MAN *runs around the stage in his frenzy, grabbing, hugging, shaking hands with black and white. Even* FRED *responds to this, his hope being— as is that of all the slaves—that the master's conversion will make life better.*]

Everybody is my sister! I love everybody! There is peace in my heart! There is joy in my soul! I love everybody! I love everybody!

[WHITE WOMAN *and* WHITE BOY *help* WHITE MAN *offstage.* FRED *follows them with his eyes, then turns again to the audience, while the* COMPANY *rearranges the set to suggest a Sunday-school classroom.*]

FRED   Could it be true? Could it be that my master had really changed? Had he really come to believe that everybody—including black slaves like me—were really his brothers and sisters?

[*To* WHITE BOY, *who has entered with an armload of books and papers*] Do you believe it, Mr. Cookman?

46

Do you believe Master Thomas has really changed?

WHITE BOY   God moves in mysterious ways—his wonders to perform. Here, help me with these.

[FRED *takes some of the books and papers from his arms and helps distribute them to the slaves, who are sitting on the benches waiting for the lesson to begin.*]

FRED   You really think Master Thomas is going to allow us to hold Sunday school for the rest of the slaves?

WHITE BOY   Frederick—where is your faith?

FRED   [*To audience*] Mr. Cookman was a fine man, a member of our church who hated slavery as much as I did, and he and I had decided to set up a Sunday school in a house nearby.

[FRED *crosses in to scene.*]

WHITE BOY   [*To the class*] Though you are slaves and I am not, in God's sight all men are equal, all men are brothers.

[BLACK WOMAN *stands to ask a question.*]

BLACK WOMAN   Is Master Thomas equal too?

WHITE BOY   Master Thomas is a Christian; he has accepted Christ, and that means—

[BLACK MAN *rises.*]

BLACK MAN   That means all mens, and all womens, are Master Thomas's brothers and sisters—no matter they black or white—ain't that right, Fred?

47

FRED   [*Skeptical*] We'll see. We'll see. Now, the purpose of this Sunday school is to teach you—all of you—to read and write.

[BLACK WOMAN *rises.*]

BLACK WOMAN   Do reading and writing make people free?

[FRED *and* WHITE BOY *look at each other.*]

WHITE BOY   No, I'm afraid not, but—

FRED   —but it can help. For instance, there was a slave in Baltimore who learned to read and write, and the first thing he did was to write himself a pass—

BLACK WOMAN   A pass?

FRED   A pass is a piece of paper, like this—

[*Shows slave's pass.*]

—with writing on it—like this—that says: this black man, or this black woman, is free.

[*He looks at each of them intently.*]

BLACK MAN   You mean—if I had a paper like that—I'd be free?

FRED   Well, down here in Maryland where everybody knows that you and me belong to Master Thomas, no. But if you were to run away and go up north to Pennsylvania or to New York—

BLACK WOMAN   You can read, Fred, and you can write?

FRED   Yes, I can.

48

BLACK WOMAN   Well, in that case, why ain't *you* run away? Why ain't *you* free?

[FRED *and* WHITE BOY *look at each other.*]

WHITE BOY   [*Quickly*] Let us bow our heads in prayer. Oh, Lord, we ask thy blessings on this our Sunday school and on all of us thy children and equal in thy sight, and on our newly converted brother Master Thomas Auld. Help him to see, oh, Lord, that in thy sight that none are slaves, that all, indeed, are free, that all of us regardless of the color of our skin are indeed sisters and brothers—

[WHITE MAN, *carrying a whip, and* WHITE WOMAN, *brandishing a broom, come running in, shouting.*]

WHITE MAN *and* WHITE WOMAN   Caught you, caught you, caught you!

[WHITE MAN *starts beating the slaves with his whip.* WHITE WOMAN *takes after* FRED *with her broom.*]

WHITE MAN   Teach slaves to read and write, will you? Over my dead body!

[FRED *and the other slaves are driven off.* WHITE MAN *picks up a fallen book and waves it in the face of* WHITE BOY.]

WHITE BOY   But you're converted, Master Thomas, you're a Christian!

WHITE MAN   Get off my property! Before I take my gun and blow you off! And take your filthy junk with you!

[WHITE BOY *quickly gathers up whatever books and papers have fallen, and exits.*]

Dirty abolitionist—

WHITE WOMAN   You *know* who's behind all this, don't you? You know who started it?

WHITE MAN   Frederick?

WHITE WOMAN   Frederick! Reading, writing, all them books —I warned you.

WHITE MAN   But I took his books. I threw them away.

WHITE WOMAN   Don't do no good, taking 'em—he always seems to find some more somewhere—

WHITE MAN   And now he's teaching the *others* to read and write—that's what makes him so dangerous. What are we to do with that boy, Rowena?

[*They both ponder a moment; then* WHITE WOMAN *has an idea.*]

WHITE WOMAN   Well, there is one thing we can do: we can send him to Covey's.

WHITE MAN   Send him to Covey's—why didn't I think of that?

WHITE WOMAN   Covey will break him—

WHITE MAN   Of course—we'll send that arrogant, bullheaded boy to Covey's!

[*They exit smiling.*]

Scene Four

[*During the song the* COMPANY *changes the set to Covey's slave-breaking plantation as they sing.*]

COMPANY

>Look a-yonder (huh)
>Hot boiling sun coming over (huh)
>Look a-yonder
>Hot boiling sun coming over (huh)
>And it ain't going down
>And it ain't going down
>
>Thought you wasn't coming (huh)
>Thought you wasn't coming this morning (huh)
>Thought you wasn't coming
>Thought you wasn't coming this morning (huh)
>But you're here on time
>But you're here on time

[FRED *is standing waiting.* WHITE MAN, *as Covey, stands reading a letter which* FRED *has given him.*]

FRED   [*To audience*] Covey was a slave breaker—if a slave was rebellious and stubborn and did not obey orders quickly enough, he was sent to Covey's for a period of one year to be tamed.

[WHITE MAN *folds the note, puts it into his pocket, and crosses to look* FRED *over.*]

WHITE MAN   So—they tell me you can read and write like a white man.

FRED   Yessir—

WHITE MAN   Well, first time I catch you with a book or a pencil and paper, I'll break your neck, is that clear?

FRED   Yessir—

WHITE MAN   Speak up, boy, I can't hear you!

FRED   [*Louder*] Yessir.

WHITE MAN   And don't look at me—look down on the ground like you're supposed to.

[*He slaps the ground with his whip.* FRED *does not answer, but lowers his eyes as ordered.*]

Now, the first thing I want you to do is to go yonder where them two oxen is and hitch them up.

[FRED *looks off.*]

Go, boy, and bring them here and be quick about it.

[WHITE MAN *stands and watches as* FRED *returns with* WHITE BOY *and* BLACK BOY, *who are costumed in a manner suggesting that they are the two oxen.*]

FRED [*Totally at sea*] What do I do now, sir?

WHITE MAN Listen carefully—I don't intend to tell you this more than once. This is the in-hand ox. His name is Buck. And this is the off-hand ox. Call him Darby. You understand?

FRED [*Trying to get it straight.*] In-hand ox, Buck—off-hand ox, Darby—yessir—

WHITE MAN Want them to start, say Giddap.

FRED Giddap!

WHITE MAN Want them to stop, say Whoa!

FRED Say Whoa, yessir.

WHITE MAN For turning to the right it's Gee! For turning to the left it's Haw! Got that?

FRED To the right is Gee, to the left is Haw. Whoa!

[*The oxen turn to the right, to the left, and stop.*]

WHITE MAN Now get on down to the thicket and bring me back a cartload of firewood.

FRED [*Anxious to please*] A cartload of firewood—

WHITE MAN And if you're not back in an hour I'm coming after you with my whip. Now get going!

FRED Get going, yessir.

[FRED *fiddles with the reins as he gives himself a quick refresher.*]

In-ox—off-ox—Gee is for right—Haw is for left—Giddap, oxen!

[*The oxen start off.*]

Go right, oxen, go right—I mean Gee! Gee!

[*The oxen go right.*]

Haw, oxen, Haw!

[FRED *has to pull hard on the reins, but the oxen finally go left.*]

Straighten up now, oxen, I mean—go forward—I mean Giddap. No, not Giddap, I mean Whoa, oxen, Whoa!

[*But the oxen pay no attention as they pull the protesting* FRED *along.* WHITE MAN *stands and watches him with a wicked smile. The oxen move across the stage, gathering speed as they travel, until finally they drag the cart through a gate and knock it down.* FRED *falls to the ground and, before he can rise,* WHITE MAN *is on him with the whip.*]

WHITE MAN   Break down my gate, will you, you lazy, trifling thing—tear up my property—I'll fix you!

[FRED *staggers to his feet, but the blows are coming so fast and furious he can barely manage to keep on his feet as he stumbles offstage,* WHITE MAN *right behind him, still laying it on.*]

SCENE FOUR

[BLACK MAN, BLACK WOMAN, BLACK BOY, and FRED *enter, humming a low noise, and all lie in a heap at center, as if asleep. From offstage we hear a blast from the driver's horn, jolting them awake.* WHITE MAN *leaps onstage yelling, stomping, and cracking his whip—a new workday has begun.*]

WHITE MAN   [*At the top of his voice*] Rise up—rise up, I tell you, rise up! Let's everybody rise up and hit that cornfield! Rise up, I say!

[*The* SLAVES *rise up, stiff and stumbling, moving slowly at first, bumping into each other. Not yet fully awake, trying, as they grope about, to escape the ever-present lash.* WHITE BOY *stands by, with rifle, to make sure they do as they are told. The* SLAVES *sing:*]

SLAVES

> *Look a-yonder (huh)*
> *Hot boiling sun coming over (huh)*
> *Look a-yonder*
> *Hot boiling sun coming over (huh)*
> *And it ain't going down*
> *And it ain't going down*

[*A trough of porridge is pulled in from offstage by* WHITE WOMAN, *as Covey's wife, and the* SLAVES *dip their hands into the porridge and stuff their mouths as quickly as they can, before she drags it off. As ever,* WHITE MAN *circles around and among them, pushing, shouting, making sure that everybody keeps moving.*]

> *No I don't*
> *No I don't*

> No I don't, don't, don't
> No I don't
> I don't like no redneck boss man
> No I don't

> Had to get up this morning too soon
> Had to get up this morning too soon
> Had to get up this morning too soon, soon
> Had to get up this morning too soon

[*Quickly the slaves fall in line and start running in place, pantomiming running to the cornfield.* WHITE MAN *cracks his whip as he pantomimes riding a horse alongside them.*]

> You better run, run, run, run, run, run
> You better run, run, run, run, run, run
> You better run to the city of refuge

[*The song speeds up as the* SLAVES *run faster and faster. All the time,* WHITE MAN *ad-libs "Move it!" etc.*]

> You better run, run, run, run, run, run
> You better run, run, run, run, run, run
> You better run, run, run, run, run, run
> You better run to the city of refuge

WHITE MAN   All right, hit that cornfield!

[*The* SLAVES *slow down and finally stop, already exhausted. They mime picking corn as they sing:*]

SLAVES

> No I don't
> No I don't

> *No I don't, don't, don't*
> *No I don't*
> *I don't like no redneck boss man*
> *No I don't*
>
> *Had to get up this morning in such a haste*
> *Didn't have time to wash my face*
> *Had to get up this morning too soon*
> *Had to get up this morning too soon*
> *Had to get up this morning too soon, soon*
> *Had to get up this morning too soon*
>
> *No I don't*
> *No I don't*
> *No I don't, don't, don't*
> *No I don't*
> *I don't like no redneck boss man*
> *No I don't*

WHITE MAN   Quitting time!

[*The* SLAVES *fall down, exhausted.* FRED *spills a sack of corn.* WHITE MAN *is infuriated.*]

WHITE MAN   You lazy thing! Spill my corn, will you!

[FRED *falls to the ground;* WHITE MAN *exits.*]

[*From offstage we hear* WHITE BOY *and* WHITE WOMAN *singing "Go Tell It on the Mountain." The song continues under the dialogue.*]

WHITE BOY *and* WHITE WOMAN
> *Go tell it on the mountain*
> *Over the hills and everywhere*

> *Go tell it on the mountain*
> *That Jesus Christ is born*
>
> *Go tell it on the mountain*
> *Over the hills and everywhere*
> *Go tell it on the mountain*
> *That Jesus Christ is born*

WHITE BOY

> *He made me a watchman*
> *Upon the city wall*
> *And if I am a Christian*
> *I am the least of all*

WHITE BOY *and* **WHITE WOMAN**

> *Go tell it on the mountain*
> *Over the hills and everywhere*
> *Go tell it on the mountain*
> *That Jesus Christ is born*

WHITE MAN

All right, all right, all right, all right, all of you come on out here!

[BLACK MAN, BLACK WOMAN, BLACK BOY, *and* FRED *all drag themselves in and stand, bone weary, before* WHITE MAN. WHITE BOY *and* WHITE WOMAN *enter with presents for the* SLAVES.]

WHITE MAN

Today is Christmas, birthday of our Lord and Savior, Jesus Christ. It's a holiday—for everybody—and that means no more work until tomorrow.

[*The* SLAVES *begin to perk up at the news.* WHITE BOY

and WHITE WOMAN *distribute presents to the* SLAVES.]

Remember—Christ our Savior was born on this day, and that's good news not only to us white folks, but also to you niggers. And I can swear to you that if you all work hard, behave yourselves, and don't give me and your masters no trouble, there's gonna be a place for you—a special place for all good niggers— right up there in Heaven!

[*He picks up a gallon brown jug.*]

So eat, sing, dance—all you want—and here's a jug of corn spirits for all of you. Drink up, everybody! Drink up, I say!

[*He hands the jug to* BLACK MAN, *who drinks from it and passes it on to the other* SLAVES.]

Let's liven this thing up for Heaven's sake. I want to hear me some singing and I want to see me some dancing—and I mean right now!

[WHITE MAN *begins to pat his foot and clap his hands, singing "Blue-Tail Fly" as he does so. The* SLAVES *join in as they continue drinking, singing, strutting, giggling, laughing, staggering, playfully tussling among themselves for another drink from the brown jug, much to the delight of the whites, who laugh and are highly amused.* FRED *stands on watching in undisguised disgust.*]

SLAVES

> *Jimmy crack corn and I don't care*
> *Jimmy crack corn and I don't care*

> *Jimmy crack corn and I don't care*
> *The master's gone away*
>
> *When I was young I used to wait*
> *Upon old master and pass the plate*
> *And fetch the bottle when he got dry*
> *And brush away the blue-tail fly*
>
> *Jimmy crack corn and I don't care*
> *Jimmy crack corn and I don't care*
> *Jimmy crack corn and I don't care*
> *The master's gone away*

WHITE WOMAN   [*Moving in to break it up*] All right, all right, it's time. Come on, everybody, let's go up to the big house. I got some friends up there who are just dying to see you darkies sing and dance. Come on, come on!

[*Everyone except* FRED *exits, singing another chorus of "Blue-Tail Fly."* FRED *turns to the audience.*]

FRED   Dancing, singing—and drinking whiskey. The slave masters knew that if they could just make us drunk, we would forget our misery; if they could keep us singing and dancing and cuttin' the fool like a bunch of idiots we wouldn't be angry any more—would lose our desire to fight back—to escape. "Merry Christmas" and "Happy New Year"! And for a lot of us—tired, ignorant, not knowing any better—that's exactly what it was. But not for me. Holidays on a slave plantation only made me madder, and sadder, and more miserable than I had ever been before.

[BLACK MAN, BLACK WOMAN, BLACK BOY, *and* WHITE MAN *enter. The* SLAVES *mime a wheat-threshing operation. They sing one line of "Death's Gonna Lay His Cold Icy Hands on Me" as they get into place, and then freeze.*]

SLAVES

> *Oh Death*
> *Death's gonna lay his cold icy hands on me*

[WHITE MAN *walks over to* FRED.]

WHITE MAN   Now, you ain't no good at all in the cornfield, so I'm gonna try you out at another job. I'm leaving you here to fan wheat—and if you don't do no better at fanning wheat than you did at picking corn, God help you!

[WHITE MAN *exits.*]

FRED   [*To audience*] In a short while Covey succeeded in breaking me—in body, soul, and spirit. My mind was a blank. All interest I had ever had in reading and writing, in any books at all, I completely lost. Covey had finally made me what I swore I would never become: a nigger and a slave. I would have been better off if I were dead.

[FRED *turns and crosses up to partake in the work of fanning wheat. As he moves into the routine, we hear a song from the* SLAVES: *"Death's Gonna Lay His Cold Icy Hands on Me." As the song proceeds, we begin to see that* FRED *is having an even tougher time trying to fan wheat than he did picking corn. The stage ac-*

tion here must suggest some operation by which a bundle of wheat is fed into a machine which threshes it, separating the wheat from the chaff. FRED is engaged in carrying huge bundles to the machine and placing them properly, then bending down, picking up the chaff, and carrying it away. He then picks up another bundle, moves to the machine where the whole operation is repeated. FRED always winds up just a little behind.]

SLAVES

Oh Death
Death's gonna lay his cold icy hands on me
Oh Death
Death's gonna lay his cold icy hands on me

Master holler hurry
Death's gonna lay his cold icy hands on me
   But I'm gonna take my time
Death's gonna lay his cold icy hands on me

Oh Death
Death's gonna lay his cold icy hands on me
Oh Death
Death's gonna lay his cold icy hands on me

He say he's making money
Death's gonna lay his cold icy hands on me
But I'm making time
Death's gonna lay his cold icy hands on me

Oh Death
Death's gonna lay his cold icy hands on me

> *Oh Death*
> *Death's gonna lay his cold icy hands on me*
>
> *Oh Death*
> *Death's gonna lay his cold icy hands on me*
> *Oh Death . . .*

[FRED *has become so exhausted that he begins to stagger.* BLACK MAN *and* BLACK WOMAN *look at him with growing concern. They know he will soon collapse, but dare not stop to help him. Finally* FRED *falls under the weight of the huge bundle of wheat he is carrying. He tries to rise, gets as far as his knees, then tumbles over again—this time he just lies there.*]

BLACK MAN   Fred! Fred!

BLACK WOMAN   Oh, my Lord, Fred!

[*They run over to the prostrate boy and try to lift him.* WHITE MAN *suddenly appears.*]

WHITE MAN   [*To the slaves*] Back to your work!

BLACK WOMAN   But Freddie's sick, Mr. Covey!

WHITE MAN   Back to your work, I say, all of you!

[*The* SLAVES *go back to work, slowly.* WHITE MAN *stands over* FRED *and kicks him.*]

All right, boy, up on your feet.

[FRED *groans and tries to rise. In background* BLACK MAN, BLACK WOMAN, *and* BLACK BOY *try to operate the machine, though shorthanded, and to keep an eye on what* WHITE MAN *is doing to* FRED.]

Up on your feet, I tell you!

[WHITE MAN *reaches down and snatches* FRED *to his feet.* FRED *wobbles unsteadily, but finally is able—just barely—to stand.*]

Now get on back to work!

[FRED *wants to move but dares not, afraid that he might fall.*]

FRED I can't, Mr. Covey—

WHITE MAN Damn you, boy, I said get back to work!

FRED [*Still wobbling*] I can't, Mr. Covey, I just can't! I—

WHITE MAN [*Shouting*] This is the last time that I am going to tell you, boy—get on back to work!

[FRED *tries to move, but his trembling legs refuse to obey.*]

FRED I can't, Mr. Covey—I can't!

[WHITE MAN *grabs up a hefty barrel stave.*]

WHITE MAN Oh, yes, you can—I'll help you!

[*He raises the stave and advances on* FRED.]

BLACK MAN Don't hit him, Mr. Covey, please, sir!

BLACK WOMAN We'll make it up for him, Mr. Covey!

WHITE MAN Shut up and get back to work, the both of you!

[BLACK MAN *and* BLACK WOMAN *return to their operation.* WHITE MAN *turns to* FRED.]

I knowed the minute I set eyes on you that one day I would have to teach you who was the boss on this here plantation!

[*He hits* FRED *across the shoulders with the stave and knocks him down.*]

Tell me, boy—what do your books have to say to you now?

[FRED *staggers to his feet, and* WHITE MAN *knocks him down again.*]

What good is your reading now, eh, boy?

[FRED *staggers to his feet.* WHITE MAN *swings again, but this time* FRED *somehow manages to duck and avoid the blow.* WHITE MAN *is angered.*]

So that's your game, is it? I'll show you!

[*He swings again.* FRED *wobbles but manages to get out of the way again.* WHITE MAN, *toppled by the force of his own blow, falls heavily to the floor. Immediately he springs to his feet, drawing his pistol from his belt at the same time, but before he can shoot,* FRED *snatches the pistol and flings it offstage.* WHITE MAN *is now not so sure of himself, for all of a sudden the nature of the battle has changed.* FRED *is still on his feet, wobbling, but not cringing any more.* WHITE MAN *rushes, but this time* FRED *steps aside, grabs* WHITE MAN'*s arm and twists it until the stave drops.* WHITE MAN *leaps free and turns to face* FRED, *who kicks the stave clear. He then moves forward, crouched, to confront his attacker. From background the* SLAVES *watch with keen interest this change in circumstances.*]

WHITE MAN   [*Trying to finesse it*] All right, boy, I'm ordering you—you go on back to work.

FRED   [*Moving forward*] Make me, Mr. Covey—you make me go back to work—

WHITE MAN   [*Beginning to circle away*] I'm warning you one more time, get back to work or I'll kill you!

FRED   [*Still moving in*] That may well be, Mr. Covey, maybe you will kill me—but if you don't, I sure intend to kill you!

WHITE MAN   [*Appealing to the* SLAVES] Hey, some of you all better talk to this nigger boy—I think he's gone crazy!

FRED   I ain't crazy, Mr. Covey, and I ain't a nigger boy—not any more. I am a man—a *man*, Covey—as much of a man as you are—or more!

[*Suddenly* WHITE MAN *ducks and picks up the stave, toward which he had been inching all along. He swings it at* FRED's *head.* FRED *ducks, moves in, grabs him in a bear hug and squeezes with all his might. In the frantic struggle to free himself,* WHITE MAN *drops the stave, then* FRED *wrestles him to the ground. They twist and turn as* WHITE MAN *struggles to free himself from* FRED's *grasp. They roll around and thrash about until* FRED *finally winds up on top, his hands clutched around* WHITE MAN's *throat, squeezing.*]

WHITE MAN [*His voice hoarse*] Sarah! Toby! Pull him off of me, pull him off!

BLACK MAN We can't stop to pull nobody off of you, Mr. Covey!

BLACK WOMAN You told us to keep on working, Mr. Covey, and that's just what we gonna do!

[*They keep on working, furiously. The struggle continues until* WHITE MAN *breaks* FRED's *grip and scrambles to his feet.* FRED *scrambles up, too, ready to resume the battle.* WHITE MAN *backs away.*]

WHITE MAN [*In fake reconciliation to* FRED] All right!—All right!—All right! Don't make me hurt you!

[FRED *recognizes this as a surrender and finally stops.*]

All right—since you say you're sick, I'm letting you off light this time—but from now on, boy, you'd better watch your step around me—you hear?

[*He looks around at the* SLAVES, *who are still working as if nothing had happened.*]

Now—get on back to work.

[*He looks around, not knowing what else to do—or say—and then leaves. As soon as he clears, the* SLAVES *leave the machine and run to* FRED.]

BLACK MAN [*With pride and happiness*] Man, oh, man, that was something!

BLACK WOMAN You whipped ol' Covey to a fare-thee-well!

BLACK MAN I ain't never seen nothing like that in all my life!

BLACK WOMAN [*Seeing* FRED *wobble*] How do you feel?

FRED [*Still winded, but proud, nonetheless, of his accomplishments*] I'm still a little weak, but I'm all right—

BLACK WOMAN Here, sit down and rest yourself.

[*She takes* FRED *by the arm, but suddenly he is not as tired as he thought.*]

FRED [*Freeing himself*] Thank you, but I feel all right—no, I feel more than all right—I feel fine—I feel—

[*He tries to find the right word for it.*]

I feel—*free*—I *am* free!—I'm FREE!

[BLACK MAN *and* BLACK WOMAN *look at each other; perhaps* FRED *is losing his reason.*]

BLACK MAN Fred, son, are you sure you feel all right?

FRED Of course I feel all right—I'm free—I am free!

[BLACK MAN *and* BLACK WOMAN *are as saddened as they are confused.*]

BLACK WOMAN Lord, have mercy—

BLACK MAN Fred, son—

FRED   What I'm trying to explain is: I know I am still in bondage, like everybody else—I got to work and slave and take hard times, like everybody else. But I ain't scared now, and that makes me free! I am just as good, just as worthy, just as free as any other soul that God ever made. It's just a feeling right now, and that's all it's gonna be until I make my escape—nothing but a feeling, but it's the most important feeling in the world! You know what I mean?

FRED *and* **SLAVES**

> *Don't you let nobody turn you round*
> *Turn you round*
> *Turn you round*
> *Don't you let nobody turn you round*
> *Keep the straight and the narrow way*
>
> *Ain't gonna let nobody turn me round*
> *Turn me round*
> *Turn me round*
> *Ain't gonna let nobody turn me round*
> *Keep the straight and the narrow way*

[*They continue to hum melody as the set is changed.*]

Scene Five

[*In one corner of the stage is the representation of the hulk of a wooden ship. There* FRED *is busy at work caulking and painting the hull.* FRED *talks as he works.*]

FRED   [*To audience*] Covey never tried to whip me again, and my master, Thomas Auld, decided that I was incorrigible—that it was dangerous to keep me around the other slaves, and finally sent me back to his brother Hugh, in Baltimore, just where I wanted to be to make my escape—but how?

[WHITE BOY *enters, dressed as a shipfitter. He inspects* FRED'S *work.*]

WHITE BOY   You're a good caulker, Fred; you're fast and

you're thorough, the best I've got. Tell your master
I'm very pleased.

FRED I'll do that, sir.

WHITE BOY   And here's your wages for the week.

[*He counts out some bills and silver into* FRED's
hand.]

FREC Thank you, sir.

[*He exits.* FRED *counts the money, an exercise which
makes him angry.*]

FRED I *was* a good caulker; I worked hard and was paid
good wages—every cent of which I had to turn over
to Master Hugh. He was at home, waiting for me to
come and put these nine dollars into his hands.

[*We hear a harmonica playing offstage.* BLACK MAN,
BLACK WOMAN, *and* BLACK BOY *bring on several chairs.
They are all dressed neatly as becomes free Negroes,
which is what they are.*]

Let him wait! Tonight there was a meeting of the
East Baltimore Improvement Society, an organization
made up of free Negroes who had let me attend their
meetings, although I was, myself, still a slave.

[FRED *steps into the meeting, finds a seat beside
BLACK WOMAN, who looks at him with a warm but
shy smile.*]

COMPANY

I know my name's

> *Been written down*
> *I know my name's*
> *Been written down*
> *Upon the wall*
> *Been written down*
> *Upon the wall of heaven*
> *Been written down*

FRED   We practiced reading and writing and discussed the news sent to us by the abolitionists. I made friends here who became very important to me. Usually the news was good, but sometimes it was bad.

[BLACK MAN, *as president of the society, is addressing the group.*]

BLACK MAN   —So forged passes are no longer safe.

FRED   Why not?

BLACK MAN   The patrollers are too watchful, and it's just too dangerous. But Brother Mentor is to be commended for lending his free papers to a black brother and thus helping him to escape from bondage.

[BLACK BOY, *as Mentor, accepts the congratulations of the group.*]

FRED   Excuse me, Brother Mentor, but just how does that work?

BLACK BOY   My free papers carry a written description of me—my age, weight, height, the color of my eyes, and so forth.

BLACK MAN   Brother Horace looked enough like Brother
Mentor to fit the description, so—

BLACK BOY   So he got on the train here in Baltimore, showed
the conductor my papers, and went on through.

FRED   But suppose they had found out that he wasn't you.

BLACK BOY   Well—they would have brought him back and
put me in jail.

[*Everybody reacts to the ever-present danger that
lies in what they are doing.*]

BLACK MAN   [*Snapping them out of it*] But, thank God, they
didn't find out.

BLACK BOY   Mr. President, I move we adjourn so we can
get to the camp meeting.

BLACK MAN   So be it, Brother Mentor. Sister Anna, will you
join us?

BLACK WOMAN   [*Glancing shyly at* FRED] I'd like to, but—
maybe I better not.

BLACK MAN   Well—Brother Fred, will we see you next week?

FRED   I'll be here, all right.

BLACK MAN   [*Gives them a kindly but knowing look.*]
Well—er—

[*He exits.* BLACK WOMAN *then hesitates and starts off.*
FRED *stops her.*]

FRED   Miss Anna?

73

BLACK WOMAN   [*Shyly*] Yes?

FRED   The society has meant a lot to me—I wouldn't miss a meeting for anything in the world.

BLACK WOMAN   Neither would I—Frederick.

FRED   I've learned so much—the books, the talk, the debates—but, most of all, I come because of you.

[**BLACK WOMAN** *is too shy to make any response, but she is deeply affected.*]

You are not a slave like I am, Anna—

BLACK WOMAN   No, my parents bought their freedom just before I was born.

FRED   If I was free—like you and all the others in the society—would you marry me?

BLACK WOMAN   Oh, yes, Frederick, yes!

[**FRED** *can scarcely conceal his joy.*]

FRED   I *will* be free, Anna, just like Brother Mentor—free, and when I am, Anna, Anna—

BLACK WOMAN   Fred, shouldn't you be getting on home? You told me how your master waits for you each Saturday evening to come and give him your money—

FRED   Let him wait! Come on, Anna, let's catch the wagon before it leaves for the camp meeting.

[*They exit singing.*]

BLACK WOMAN

I know your name

FRED

Been written down

BLACK WOMAN

I'm sure your name

FRED

Been written down
Have you seen my name?

BLACK WOMAN

Been written down

FRED

Upon the wall of heaven

BLACK WOMAN *and* FRED

Been written down

[FRED *and* BLACK WOMAN *rush off.*]

[*From the opposite side a cutout of the Auld house in Baltimore is pushed on.* WHITE MAN, *as Hugh Auld, and* WHITE WOMAN, *as Sophia Auld, enter.*]

WHITE MAN   [*Agitated, pacing*] Where is he—where the hell is he?

WHITE WOMAN   He's never been this late before. Perhaps those white caulkers have hurt him again.

WHITE MAN   Not as much as I am going to hurt him.

WHITE WOMAN   [*Looking off*] Hugh, here he comes!

WHITE MAN [*Following her gaze*] I'll kill him—I'll break his neck—I'll sell him down the river! I'll—

[FRED *enters.*]

Boy, where have you been?

FRED I got your money, Master Hugh, got it right here.

WHITE MAN You're late.

FRED I'm sorry, sir.

[*He hands money over to* WHITE MAN, *who counts it.*]

If you let me off this time I'll give you an extra day's pay next Saturday.

WHITE MAN Extra day's pay—where you gonna get the money from? You ain't stealing, are you?

FRED I found another job—a place where they'll let me work at night. That way I can make extra money— if you'll let me.

WHITE MAN [*Very much interested*] Extra money, eh— Well, now, Fred, I'm pleased, I really am. Extra money for me and your mistress!

WHITE WOMAN Oh, Fred, that is so wonderful! God is surely going to bless you—

WHITE MAN Here's a dime—a ten-cent piece. Now you run along and buy yourself a pretty, you hear?

[WHITE MAN *and* WHITE WOMAN *start off, but* FRED *stops them.*]

FRED   What I had in mind was—well, some masters let their slaves buy themselves free with the extra money they make, and—that's what I'd like to do.

WHITE WOMAN   Why, Fred, whatever's got into you? Haven't we always tried to treat you like a son?

FRED   I'm not your son, I'm your slave, and—

WHITE MAN   The answer is no! You are free to work extra if you want to, and I might even let you keep some of what you earn, but every cent you make belongs to me, every penny—is that clear?

WHITE WOMAN   You are a gift to me, Fred, a personal gift to me from my father!

WHITE MAN   And that's enough of that freedom talk!

[WHITE MAN *and* WHITE WOMAN *exit.*]

FRED   Well, if you won't let me work for my freedom I sure ain't gonna work for you!

[*Hurls dime offstage at them.*]

I'm going!

[*Tambourine indicates passage of time.* FRED *turns and whispers offstage.*]

Anna!

BLACK WOMAN   [*Enters, quickly and surreptitiously.*] Fred—

FRED   Come with me, Anna, you and me, let's make a run for it, you and me.

BLACK WOMAN   Fred, you could be killed if—

FRED   Let them kill me, kill me, kill me! And get it over with!

BLACK WOMAN   Fred, love, I know how you feel, but—does your Master know you are gone?

FRED   No—he still thinks I'm out working on a ship making money for him.

BLACK WOMAN   Go back, Fred—

FRED   What!

BLACK WOMAN   Go back before he finds out you're missing and puts the Sheriff on you—

FRED   No, Anna, I'm leaving—one way or the other—

BLACK WOMAN   How can you leave? You have no money, no free papers to show the conductor—they'll catch you, Fred, and kill you, or sell you down the river.

FRED   Let them catch me, let them kill me—I don't care any more.

BLACK WOMAN   But I do, Fred, I care—

[FRED *looks into her face, loving her, and more miserable in his love now than ever before.*]

FRED   Oh, Anna—Anna—Anna!

[*She holds him close in her arms.*]

BLACK WOMAN   I know, I know, I know—Fred, I have some money—

FRED   What?

BLACK WOMAN   I have some money I've been saving—I want you to take it.

FRED   [*Groaning*] Anna—

BLACK WOMAN   Listen to me: take nine dollars and give it to your master. Beg him to forgive you—do anything, say anything, so that he won't be suspicious.

[*She pulls a knotted handkerchief from her bosom and forces it into his hands.*]

The rest of it will be for your escape. It's not much—but it's all I got, and, Fred—

[WHITE WOMAN's *voice—as* ANNA's *mistress calls to her from offstage*]

WHITE WOMAN   Anna! Anna, what's keeping you out there so long?

BLACK WOMAN   [*Calling off*] Coming, Miss Sarah—

[*Back to* FRED] Mentor, the sailor, is back in town. He wants to see us. Tonight.

WHITE WOMAN   [*Offstage*] Anna!

BLACK WOMAN   Coming, Miss Sarah!

[*To* FRED] I'll be there—

[*She exits.* FRED *looks off after her. He then opens the knotted handkerchief and takes out a small clump of bills. He straightens them out, then looks off after*

BLACK WOMAN *for a beat, then runs off.* WHITE MAN, *as Hugh Auld, enters, talking to* WHITE BOY, *as the Sheriff.* WHITE WOMAN, *as Sophia Auld, follows the two in a state of agitation.*]

WHITE MAN   —He answers to the name of Fred. He's twenty, twenty-one years old, tall and well-built. Woulda been a good slave except that my wife, Sophia, helped him to learn to read.

WHITE BOY   Yeah, that'll ruin 'em every time.

WHITE WOMAN   Sheriff, if only I had known—

WHITE MAN   But ruined or not, he's still my property, and I want him back—I'll even offer a reward.

WHITE BOY   When did you miss him—I mean, when did you see him last?

WHITE MAN   Well, the other night he—

WHITE WOMAN   [*Looking off*] Hugh, Hugh, here he comes now!

[FRED *enters. She crosses to meet him.*]

Fred—Fred, where have you been?

FRED   I'm sorry, Miz Sophia.

WHITE BOY   Is this the nigger you talking about?

WHITE MAN   It's him, all right. Where in tarnation have you been, boy?

FRED   I been working, Master Hugh.

WHITE MAN   Working? I didn't arrange with anybody to hire you out.

FRED   I did it myself. Went to Old Man Carter and told him you sent me, so he took me on. Here's the money—

[FRED *offers the money.* WHITE MAN *greedily snatches it out of his hand and starts counting.*]

WHITE BOY   Well, seems like everything's gonna be all right.

WHITE WOMAN   Oh, yes, Sheriff, our Fred didn't run away after all—but thank you ever so much for coming over.

WHITE BOY   Consider it a privilege, ma'am. Good-by, Mr. Auld.

[*But* WHITE MAN, *counting the money a second time in miserly glee, has already hurried off.*]

WHITE BOY   Good day, ma'am.

[*To* FRED] You got a good master and mistress here, boy—I hope you appreciate that fact.

FRED   Oh, I do, Mr. Sheriff; Master Hugh and Mistress Sophia are the best white folks in all this world, and I love 'em.

WHITE BOY   Make sure you do.

[*He exits.* WHITE WOMAN *turns to Fred and leads him off.*]

WHITE WOMAN   I just knowed that you were too fine, too decent, too intelligent to run off from your master.

FRED   Run off from you, Miz Sophia, and from Mr. Hugh—never!

[*They exit.*]

[BLACK WOMAN, *as Anna, and* FRED *enter. They are met by* BLACK BOY, *as Mentor, the sailor, who is carrying a package.*]

FRED   [*To* BLACK BOY] What's that?

BLACK BOY   For you to wear.

[*He opens the carton.* FRED *takes out a sailor suit and begins hurriedly to get into it.*]

But don't buy your ticket until you get on the train.

FRED   Why not?

BLACK BOY   The ticket seller might recognize you. But on the train there's usually a crowd, the conductor will be busy, and maybe he won't notice.

BLACK WOMAN   Maybe won't notice what?

BLACK BOY   The description on my seaman's papers don't resemble Fred at all.

[FRED *takes the papers and looks at them. His face becomes worried, but he makes a decision.*]

FRED   They'll do—they'll have to do.

[*He puts on his sailor hat, turns and shakes hands with* BLACK BOY.]

You've been a brother—a true brother. I'll send these papers back to you the usual way.

BLACK BOY   [*Nods his head.*] Good luck.

[*He exits.* FRED *turns to* BLACK WOMAN.]

FRED   Anna.

BLACK WOMAN   Fred.

[*They embrace.* BLACK WOMAN *pulls away.*]

You'd better go.

FRED   I'll write you as soon as I can, but I'm taking a new name for myself, just in case someone else reads my letters to you. I think I'll make it Douglass—Frederick Douglass.

BLACK WOMAN   [*Memorizing*] Frederick Douglass.

FRED   I'll send for you as soon as I get settled, and then we'll be married.

BLACK WOMAN   I'll wait—but hurry.

[FRED *kisses her again and leaves. She stands and watches him.*]

[*The set is rearranged to suggest seats on a train.*

WHITE WOMAN, BLACK MAN, *and* BLACK BOY *are passengers seated on the train. The voice of* WHITE MAN, *the conductor, is heard.*]

WHITE MAN   All aboard!

[*Sound effects of train whistle, etc., suggest that the train has begun to move.* FRED, *dressed as a sailor, enters at the last minute and sits near the other blacks. No sooner has he settled than* WHITE BOY, *dressed as a Baltimore businessman, enters from the opposite direction. He starts toward a seat near* WHITE WOMAN, *but stops when he sees* FRED. *He stands for a long moment, as if trying to place him.*]

WHITE BOY   Hey, sailor boy—don't I know you?

[FRED *does not answer.* WHITE BOY *finally passes on to sit beside* WHITE WOMAN, *still looking at* FRED. *He speaks to* WHITE WOMAN.]

You know, I could swear I know that boy.

WHITE WOMAN   If you do, you beat me—all the darkies look alike to me.

WHITE BOY   That's true, but—

[*Suddenly, to* FRED] Hey, boy, did you ever live up near St. Michael's?

[FRED *begins to sweat, but does not answer.* WHITE MAN *enters and starts down the aisle.*]

WHITE MAN   All tickets, please.

[*He comes to the place where the blacks are clustered.*]

Let me see your papers—your free papers.

[*The blacks all show their papers.* WHITE MAN *comes to* FRED *and first takes his money.* WHITE BOY *rises from his seat, saunters over, and stands above* FRED.]

WHITE BOY   [*As if he suddenly recognized him*] Yeah—I

know this boy, conductor—I know him.

FRED [*Wiping his face*] Of course you know me, sir, I sailed on a packet out of Philadelphia.

WHITE BOY Out of Philadelphia?

FRED Well, not only Philadelphia—I've shipped out of every port on the eastern seaboard—Savannah, Charleston. New York—I'm sure we met on one of my ships, sir.

WHITE BOY Well, if that's the case, why didn't you answer when I spoke to you? What are you hiding for?

FRED [*Suddenly friendly and jovial*] Oh, I'm not hiding. It's just that—

WHITE MAN You have your seaman's papers?

FRED Yes, sir. Here they are right here.

[*He reaches inside his pocket for papers, but meanwhile continues his bluff.*]

You see, sir, although I'm a sailor—a darn good sailor —I still get seasick. And one time—[*He is still stalling.*] one time, I'm ashamed to admit it, sir, one time I ran to the rail to settle my stomach and fell overboard! All the people had a right good laugh at my expense.

WHITE BOY [*Trying hard to figure it*] And where'd you say all this happened?

FRED Charleston Harbor, don't you remember? It whistled up rough with a high wind to starboard, and breakers coming in fast and white o'er the gunnels. I grabbed at the bosun and missed—couldn't swim, either, so there I was, if you remember, sir, damn near drowned.

[FRED *is laughing uncontrollably as he puts the false seaman's papers into* WHITE MAN's *hand. Before* WHITE MAN *can examine the papers,* FRED *pulls him into the story.*]

You should have seen this black sailorman, conductor, flapping around like a catfish in a hot skillet.

[WHITE MAN *laughs, then has another go at the papers.* FRED *grabs his elbow as he continues the recital.*]

I swear—first time ever in my life—I seen somebody black as me—turn blue!

[*This is a joke that both* WHITE MAN *and* WHITE BOY *can appreciate. They double over in laughter, and while they are howling,* FRED *deftly lifts his papers from* WHITE MAN's *hands, and puts them back into his pocket.* WHITE MAN *and* WHITE BOY *keep laughing as they leave* FRED *and move on up the aisle.* WHITE MAN *has a funny story of his own.*]

WHITE MAN   That reminds me of this ol' nigger man, Uncle Somby, who used to take us boys fishing. Now, Uncle Somby was as fine a darky as you ever wanted to see, but he was blind in one eye and couldn't see much out of the other—but too proud to admit it. So one night ol' Somby—

[*The* COMPANY *freezes.* FRED *rises and steps out of scene to address audience.*]

FRED   On the third day of September, 1838, I left my chains behind and succeeded in reaching New York without any further interruptions.

[*The cast begins to hum the melody to "Freedom Land" as* FRED *continues.*]

The first thing I did was to send for Anna.

[BLACK WOMAN *runs in, carrying bag, dressed in traveling clothes. She and* FRED *embrace warmly.*]

Come on.

BLACK WOMAN   But, Fred, where are we going?

FRED   To find Reverend Pennington, so you and I—two free people—can get married!

[*The cast rearrange themselves to suggest a parlor.* FRED *and* BLACK WOMAN *stand before* BLACK MAN, *the minister.* BLACK BOY, WHITE MAN, WHITE BOY, *and* WHITE WOMAN *are also present as abolitionist friends.*]

BLACK MAN   I now pronounce you man and wife.

[BLACK WOMAN *comes down front.*]

BLACK WOMAN   [*To audience*] Frederick Douglass went on to become one of the greatest orators America has ever produced.

[WHITE WOMAN *joins her.*]

WHITE WOMAN   [*To audience*] Later, in order to reach more people, he published an abolitionist newspaper in Rochester, New York—*The North Star.*

Escape to Freedom

[BLACK MAN *comes down.*]

BLACK MAN [*To audience*] He wrote several books about his life, and many books were written about him.

[*The others come down.*]

WHITE MAN He was an adviser to President Abraham Lincoln.

BLACK BOY He persuaded Lincoln to let the black man fight in the Civil War for his own freedom.

WHITE BOY He became U.S. Ambassador to Haiti, the first black man to hold a diplomatic post—

BLACK WOMAN —and one of the first to speak for women's rights.

FRED Frederick Douglass—an extraordinary American.

COMPANY

> *I'm on my way, great God*
> *I'm on my way*
>
> *I'm on my way*
> *To the freedom land*
> *I'm on my way*
> *To the freedom land*
> *I'm on my way*
> *To the freedom land*
> *I'm on my way, great God*
> *I'm on my way*

CURTAIN

Selected Bibliography

Brackett, Jeffrey. *The Negro in Maryland: The Study of the Institution Slavery.* Freeport, N.Y.: Books for Libraries Press, 1969.

Douglass, Frederick. *Life and Times of Frederick Douglass.* New York: Collier Books, 1892, reprinted, 1962.

Graham, Shirley. *There Once Was a Slave, The Heroic Story of Frederick Douglass.* New York: Julian Messner, Inc., 1947.

Holland, Frederick May. *Frederick Douglass: The Colored Orator.* New York: Funk and Wagnalls Co., 1895.

Williams, Eric. *Capitalism and Slavery.* Chapel Hill, N.C.: University of North Carolina Press, 1944.

About the author

OSSIE DAVIS is the well-known actor and playwright. He wrote and performed in the comedy *Purlie Victorious* and directed the movie *Cotton Comes to Harlem*. He has made many television appearances, has starred in numerous films and plays, and has long been an activist in the cause of human rights.

PENGUIN BOOKS

MURDER IN MONTPARNASSE

Howard Engel was born in Toronto and raised in St. Catharines, Ontario. He later lived in Nicosia, London and Paris, where he worked as a journalist and broadcaster. Back in Canada he was for many years a distinguished producer for the CBC.

His engaging private eye, Benny Cooperman, has been described as a cherished national institution, and is featured in seven previous mystery novels: *The Suicide Murders*, *The Ransom Game*, *Murder on Location*, *Murder Sees the Light*, *A City Called July*, *A Victim Must be Found* and *Dead and Buried*. Both *The Suicide Murders* and *Murder Sees the Light* were made into TV films, and many of his novels have been translated into other languages.

Howard Engel is a member of the Mystery Writers of America and the British Crime Writers' Association, and is a founding member of the Crime Writers' Association of Canada. He was the 1990 winner of the Harbourfront Festival Prize for Canadian literature and the 1984 winner of the Arthur Ellis Award for crime fiction. He lives in Toronto with his wife, Janet Hamilton, their son Jacob, and their two cats.

Murder in Montparnasse is his first departure from the Cooperman series.

Murder in
Montparnasse

HOWARD ENGEL

Penguin Books

PENGUIN BOOKS
Published by the Penguin Group
Penguin Books Canada Ltd, 10 Alcorn Avenue,
Toronto, Ontario, Canada M4V 3B2
Penguin Books Ltd, 27 Wrights Lane, London W8 5TZ, England
Penguin Books USA Inc., 375 Hudson Street,
New York, New York 10014, U.S.A.
Penguin Books Australia Ltd, Ringwood, Victoria, Australia
Penguin Books (NZ) Ltd, 182-190 Wairau Road,
Auckland 10, New Zealand

Penguin Books Ltd, Registered Offices: Harmondsworth,
Middlesex, England

First published in Viking by Penguin Books Canada Limited, 1992

Published in Penguin Books, 1993

10 9 8 7 6 5 4 3 2 1

*Publisher's note: This book is a work of fiction. Names, characters,
places and incidents either are the product of the author's imagination
or are used fictitiously, and any resemblance to actual persons living
or dead, events, or locales is entirely coincidental.*

Manufactured in Canada

Canadian Cataloguing in Publication Data

Engel, Howard, 1931–
  Murder in Montparnasse

ISBN 0-14-015728-X

I. Title.

PS8559.N44M87 1993   C813'.54   C92-093793-4
PR9199.3.E54M87 1993

*This book is dedicated
to the memory of
Morley Callaghan
and John Glassco,
as well as to the
generations of expatriates
who found heaven if not fame
in Montparnasse*

Writers of fiction are always playing around with the facts in order to find the truth that lies behind them. Even in a crime novel, where part of the game is the blurring of the facts, it is the truth we want in the end. In this book, my fiction rubs very close to the facts of what happened in Paris to a small group of expatriates in 1925. Some of these people are inventions, others are based on people who were kidnapped earlier into another book, and others appear here under their real names. The places mentioned are as close to the places that existed in the middle twenties as I could make them.

In trying to recapture the flavour of that time, I have made use of expressions and sentiments that are no longer acceptable. I did this for reasons of verisimilitude and ask for the reader's pardon in advance.

My literary debts are enormous; a true accounting would add another dozen pages to this already name-studded volume. But I would like to thank by name individuals who have helped me bring the book to this final stage: Kildare Dobbs, Linda Kooluris Dobbs, Charles Oberdorf, Nancy Vichert, Sheila Kieran, Véronique Gaspard Le Drew, Frédéric Larsen, Dominique Roydor, Michelle Lapautre, Beverley Slopen, Donald Summerhayes and my wife, Janet Hamilton. I would also like to thank Mme. Jacqueline Milan, the proprietor of the celebrated Closerie des Lilas, for her kindness and help.

Also by Howard Engel

Murder in
Montparnasse

PARIS
Autumn
1925

"... Paris in the early twenties was my university. Here, in the streets of Montparnasse, I met my peers. What I learned about the craft of writing, I learned here. I will not say I learned it from them, although I learned much from the smoke in the air we breathed together and the talk that rose from the terrasses along the boulevard. To outsiders we seemed to be time-wasters and drunks. Some of us were. But even for those who had no purpose in exploring the tables of the Café du Dôme or the Select beyond the possibility of finding a free drink, it was a golden time, a time of high excitement and joy in the chill early morning, a time we will always remember..."

Jason Waddington
from *New Wine*

Parisians shut their doors tightly that autumn. Women carried their keys and arranged to be escorted through the dark streets leading to their homes. Even on the boulevards, especially in the Quarter, people kept to the brightly lit cafés and perhaps laughed more metallically because of Jack, who was out there, somewhere, waiting.

Jack's blade had already claimed five victims in the streets, passages and alleys near the studios used by painters around Montparnasse. He usually picked models; once he chose a young painter on her way home from a brasserie. The police were working on the case. The public had been cautioned to remain calm. Nevertheless, the concierge made very sure that it was a tenant for whom she opened the door at night. The police sifted the crowds sitting on the terraces of the Dôme and the other cafés in the early morning, checking papers, especially those of the foreigners who had made Montparnasse their headquarters in France. The gay conversation never flagged, even as passports were examined and returned to their owners, while another round of drinks was ordered and the moment of parting from the crowded tables under the electric lights was postponed. Still, for one and all of the celebrants, celebrating perhaps the fact that they had survived the war, there remained the moment when they would have to begin the long walk back through the cobblestone streets to dark courtyards and unlighted stairs.

CHAPTER 1

I first ran across him walking along the quays. We were both looking over the books in the stalls along the embankment and both of us reached for the same copy of *The Green Hat* by Michael Arlen. When he realized that we weren't going to get anywhere tugging, he shot me that wonderful grin of his, with the right side of his mouth pulled up so high his moustache hung lopsided under his nose.

"You take it," he said, suddenly letting go. "Arlen's not my meat anyway."

"I was just going to check the price," I said, opening the cover. "Sixty francs."

"It's only been out a year, but it's still too much."

"I thought this was where you could pick up bargains."

"Oh, you can, but you have to know which stall to deal at. You have to study out the land, get to know your man. This fellow speaks a little English, so you can't fool him. You're not English, are you? I can tell you're not American."

"Canadian," I admitted, "and newly arrived."

"Well! I used to live in Toronto. Canada's a second home for me. Used to box at the Mutual Arena."

"So, you're a fighter who reads Michael Arlen?"

"Retired professional. I nearly lost the sight in this eye from a middleweight's thumb. The thumb was heavyweight." He indicated his left eye with his own thumb. "What's your name?"

"Michael Ward, but people call me Mike. I come from Toronto too, as a matter of fact."

"Wonderful! This calls for a drink! Have you any objections to a *demi-blonde* before the sun hits the yard-arm?"

"None whatever. The morning's growing hot. What's your name? I'm guessing that you're an American. Canadians are generally more stand-offish, as you no doubt discovered in the Queen City."

"*Je m'appelle* Jason Waddington," he said, giving the names a twist of his deep voice as though he thought of himself in italics or quotation marks. "You may call me Wad, if you like. I get called all kinds of things but never Jason. I will tell you only once."

I replaced the Michael Arlen on the pile where I'd found it and tried not to look at the vendor's face as the two of us moved off to the left, with the east end of Notre Dame looming up over the chestnut trees. I followed him across the cobblestones to a small café that looked out on the river. He ordered the beers and we watched a group of *bouquinistes*, second-hand booksellers, talking together, no doubt cursing the slack season. When the beer came, Wad looked at the beads of moisture as they formed around both glasses, clouding the amber beer within. There was an intensity about the way he watched things. When he was doing one thing, you couldn't mistake him for doing another, although he surprised me sometimes. I can remember him carrying on an argument with a friend about bullfighting, I think — he was often talking about bullfighting — and then giving me hell for saying something in a conversation I was having with somebody at my end of the table. That was when I knew him better.

Anyway, this first meeting went off without a shadow of all that. He told me about a couple of his Toronto fights, and I told him that I had just started work at one of the news service agencies.

"Oh," he said, "so you're a writer?" His forehead furrowed unexpectedly. I felt as though I'd just admitted to having a social disease. A mild case.

"What I do isn't writing," I said. "I translate stories clipped from the French papers."

"You'll have to do more than translate. French news style buries the lead in the last paragraph. You have to rebuild every story from the ground up. You'll take a while to get onto it."

"For a retired professional fighter, you know quite a lot about writing cables."

"Hell, I've got a family to support! I can't get a fight over here, except some club dates at the American Club. I've been sending stuff to the Toronto *Star*."

"Of course! You're *that* J. Miller Waddington! Greg Clark told me to watch out for you. He said you'd gone off to Paris to write the Great American Novel!"

"How is Greg? We used to go fishing for trout up on the Mad River. He's a great little bantam rooster. You worked at the *Star* too, did you?"

"I put in a few months until I had a run-in with the editor."

"Harry Comfort Hindmarsh!" Waddington grabbed my hand and shook it. "I'm glad I ran into you, Mike Ward. How's Jimmy Frise? He and Clark — Mutt and Jeff. What a pair!" Wad finished his beer and sat back in his chair so that it balanced on its hind legs. In a minute he had pulled over a chair for each of his large feet. He began telling me about growing up on the North Side of Chicago on the wrong side of the tracks and getting into the fight game in Waukegan, a tough town where the local boy doesn't like to lose. "That's where my left eye met its Waterloo," he said.

By the time the waiter brought another two glasses, Wad had commandeered a chair for each of his arms.

"*Monsieur,*" the waiter said somewhat sharply. "*Vous n'êtes pas tout seul ici, monsieur. Il y a des autres.*" Wad sat up and the waiter restored the chairs to their original tables. An angry look followed the waiter out of sight.

"When I was in Turkey, everybody sat that way. The French, I think, are at least 50 percent Presbyterian. They are so worried about good form. Really, they only care about money. Money and British royalty."

Jason Waddington was a big man, at least a six-footer, with a ready grin and intense brown eyes. When he smiled, he looked like a boy dressed up in a man's suit. I thought he was in his twenties, as I was — although I was sure he was a few years older than me, and he was thickening out. Maybe it was the beer and maybe it was muscle, if what he said about being a boxer was true. He didn't move like a boxer, though. In fact, with his big feet, he was a bit of a stumbler, missing the curb up to the sidewalk, and — as I discovered later — always showing a cut or a bruise on his head from some low doorway. Looking like a lazy panther, he drained his second glass.

"Well?" he said.

"Well, what?"

"You want to put the gloves on?"

"Of course not. You're a professional. I've never done any real fighting. Not since school. Three fights, lost all of them. How's your tennis?"

"I play a little."

"Ah!" I said, finishing my own beer, which left a bitter after-taste in my mouth.

"Ah, what?"

"Whenever someone says he plays a little, I get ready to lose a few sets. Where do you play in this town?" I was beginning to relax and take my surroundings for granted. It felt good.

"There's a gym in the basement of the American Club. There are a couple of good outdoor courts too. If the weather holds, we can have a few weeks of playing outside. I haven't delivered my quota of newly arrived Canadians this month."

"I'll leave a letter with my bank about where I'm going. I've heard about your sort." He laughed and we got up. I paid for the drinks, while Wad protested that he would get them next time. From the look of his shoes and the worn elbows of his tweed jacket, I had my doubts.

Together we walked along the quays, keeping the river on our right, letting the big church slide by. There were a few drifts of fallen leaves caught against the embankment. It would be pretty to say that the river caught the blue of the autumn sky and reflected it, but the fact is the river ignored the sky and gave us something brown does to green even in summer. Wad led the way across St-Michel and down a narrow street of shops leading away from the river. There were small antique shops and dusty places selling tassels and flounces for decorators. We looked into the windows of the antique dealers, filled with armoires, sconces, candelabra, corner cupboards and weather vanes. I fancied a fine copper *coq, a giroutte* that had turned green in the wind at the top of some weathered country church or château.

"I wouldn't mind taking that back to Toronto with me," I said. "How old do you think it is? Twelfth century? Thirteenth?"

"I know the painter who made it," Wad said. "You can ask him yourself when you meet him."

"You seem to know your way around, Wad."

"I know the Quarter. I've been here since the war."

"Except for your time in Toronto," I added, wanting to believe him.

"Sure," he said. "Except for Toronto." He clipped me on the shoulder playfully. "And listen, kid, I don't think you should start thinking of collecting stuff to take home with you. You'll sour your time here that way. Toronto's a long way from the rue St-André-des-Arts."

We continued up the street, with Wad jumping up and trying to hit overhead shop signs, until we wandered into the Marché du Buci. Here Wad bought some small grey shrimp and a dozen "*portugueses*," which turned out to be oysters. When I left him, he had given me his address on the Notre-Dame-des-Champs and an invitation to dinner at eight o'clock that night. I took the Métro back to my hotel, where I looked up the street on my folding map. My brand new Baedeker on the bedside table was already beginning to look like a leftover from my early days in Paris. It felt good. I grinned at the familiar jug-eared face in the mirror. At last I was getting to meet people. At last I was finding my way around and feeling as though I had finally arrived. I hoped, as I began to run the water for a bath, that it wasn't because I had spent nearly an hour and a half speaking my own language in this foreign place.

CHAPTER 2

It took me a few weeks to get used to the fan-shaped patterns of the cobblestones I could see from the third-storey windows of Agence-Européene-Presse on rue Jean Goujon. But the office surroundings (dirty walls, noticeboards and broken-down typewriters) and routine were easier to manage. Everybody was always on the edge of a holiday mood, and, except for the hour or two before deadlines, we always had time for talk and trips downstairs to the brasserie for a drink. The agency was next door to the Anglo-American Press Association, so one was always bumping into friends and colleagues. Without knowing it, I slipped easily into the habit of working hard in short bursts, running with dispatches to catch the boat-train and getting away from the Right Bank as fast as I could without losing my job.

I usually walked home. I had a choice of seven bridges and the best scenery in the world to walk through. By now I had a room at the top of a building on rue Bonaparte. It had a slanted ceiling facing east, a floor of large terracotta tiles, some of them loose and used for covering valuables, and a few simple sticks of furniture. For use of the splendid bathroom, I had to apply to the concierge, who was understanding and sympathetic as long as bathing did not become excessive. The toilet was hidden behind a wall panel on the landing below, directly off the stairs. From my single window, if I leaned out far enough, I could see both St-

Germain-des-Prés and St-Sulpice: three steeples for one hundred and forty francs a week.

Waddington and his wife Priscilla helped me find it. "Hash," as Wad called her, was sometimes called "Cilla." I usually called her Hash and she didn't seem to mind. They both started calling me "Michaeleen" and "Wardo." They had nicknames for everybody. Hash was a few years older than Wad, a grand pianist and an endlessly tolerant help-meet for Wad, who never knew when he was coming home for dinner and never thought of sending word ahead when he was bringing a friend. That was how I met her, with her red hair hanging undressed about her shoulders and surprise written all over her smiling, broad face, and nothing in the larder or cooling on the windowsill. I got the feeling that anything her "Tatie" did was fine with her. You could see by the way she looked at him.

The baby, whom they addressed as "Snick-a-Fritz-Piddler," "the Pid," or "Snick" for short, was a stocky, bright, blond imp of twenty-three months, who could stand up and take a Firpo-like pose with both his dukes up and spoiling for action, calling "'Fraid o' nothin'" at the sound of the bell. I often took him walking in the Luxembourg Gardens to watch French children with their hoops and sailboats near the octagonal pool while Hash went for a French lesson and Wad was working. Snick and I got along well.

Wad worked on a back table at the Closerie des Lilas, a café at the edge of Montparnasse, a little fancier than the cafés that had been pointed out to me. As he told me this, Wad also made it clear that when he was working, he didn't want to be interrupted. He took his work seriously and made sure that I understood that the Closerie des Lilas was forbidden to me while he was busy. After a good deal of questioning, I discovered that his writing was not journalism but stories. He wasn't able to sustain the fiction that he was a boxer beyond that first meeting. Although he didn't tell me where I could buy any of his stories, he did say that two of his books had been printed by Paris publishers.

While I was excited by his publishing success, I was a little disappointed to discover that Wad was just another hopeful writer like myself. I wished he had held on to his stories about being a prizefighter. I quite liked to think of him working out with the pugs at Leida's. He talked about the best-known local fighters all the time, fibbing about keeping well out of the reach of Mascart's murderous left or Ledoux's upper-cut. He enjoyed talking about bullfighting, too, but never said he'd actually fought in the bullring. There was some talk about running with the bulls in the Basque country of Spain, but that failed to catch all of my attention. When I changed the subject from sports to his writing, I got the furrowed brow again and monosyllables. He was free with advice about the journalism I was doing, but he kept mum about his own work and got mad if I pestered him about it.

He was a fair tennis hand, but one of his legs was dependably weaker than the other and his bad eye proved to be no lie: I could do what I wanted on his left side when I was in control of my game. We were evenly enough matched so that whichever of us won, we both got a good game. In the beginning, I saw Wad for dinner at Notre-Dame-des-Champs a few times, as well as our regular meetings for tennis. Gradually, I saw him for tennis and a beer afterwards if I didn't have to run across the river to do some work.

During those weeks, I made myself comfortable under the roof tiles on rue Bonaparte and did a lot of walking in the Quarter. The little writing I did was on the backs of postcards with sepia views of the Arc de Triomphe and the

Tour Eiffel. I took a certain pleasure in writing:

> 56, rue Bonaparte
> Paris, VIe
> FRANCE

Having an address that wasn't a hotel gave me a stake in all that was happening around me. In the course of my job, I went through all the French newspapers. I studied the police reports and read the back files on the latest Paris sensation: "Jack de Paris." On my own time, I heard a concert given by Paderewski in the Salle Pleyel, visited the public and private galleries and haunted several bookstores. In order to appear less of a tourist and to erase the earnest Canadian features that looked out from my passport, I bought a *béret basque* and began wearing a grey scarf. I was still too much the over-clean, washed and pressed, serious young man with a look of innocence stamped on his face. I tried brushing my hair in a new way, but the errant brown forelock always found its way back over my eyes. The scarf removed the sharp Adam's apple from the picture, but only time would grow my hair long enough to reduce the impact of those jug-ears. I watched the way Frenchmen dressed and tried to model myself after them.

Meanwhile, I pursued another course of discovery as I sought out the narrow, twisting, older streets of the Quarter. Exploration did not wait upon a return to my room to change out of my office suit: I explored all the time, especially while returning to the Quarter and while looking for new places to eat. This was how I discovered the delightful Place Furstemberg, the Cour de Rohan and the perfect *tourelle* on the rue Hautefeuille. These were private discoveries that helped make me feel at home in the city. The streets of the Quarter were friendlier than the great boulevards that Baron Haussmann had pushed through the remains of mediaeval Paris.

Living alone in a strange city requires a certain discipline in order to survive. For instance, there's the question of dining alone. The selection of the right restaurant is important. A mistake can be tragic, like the time I went by myself to one of the famous after-hours restaurants near Les Halles for a bowl of soup. It was bright, gay and noisy. It came well recommended in my guidebook. I sat there thinking of home. Bright, noisy places that are recommended in guidebooks are to be avoided by those who return to a room under the roof by themselves.

On my way back to the rue Bonaparte one night after one of these disastrous experiments, deep in thought, I saw a young woman in a bright cloak making her way along the narrow street ahead of me. For awhile, I followed her retreating shadow and the echo of her heels on the cobblestones. The sound acted as a sullen metronome to my thoughts. Suddenly, she turned and, seeing me, gathered up her skirts and fled down the street towards the light of the *carrefour*. I stopped where I was, trying to imagine the fears my own footsteps had awakened in her. Did she take me for Jack, the murderer? Was that how Jack found his victims: searching out the stragglers from life's march, stabbing the women who had strayed from the main group? I took that thought to bed with me.

One early October night, while having a late supper at the Nègre de Toulouse on Montparnasse, I saw a party of well-dressed British and American revellers come in rather noisily out of the rain. The owner took their umbrellas from them and directed them to the only large table that was still unoccupied. They were speaking English in an aggressively loud manner that made me wonder why such people come abroad at all. I was chewing on these ungenerous thoughts when into the restaurant came Waddington and his wife, laughing and wet. Wad had covered both of them in a large military-looking cape. He shook it off and was welcomed into the chic gathering with shouts and cries. I put my head down and continued eating my bouillabaisse and reading my newspaper.

It was Hash who saw me. Then Wad jumped up and asked me to join them for coffee when I finished, if I cared to. For Wad, it sounded elaborately polite, and I felt I should decline. It was plain that they were well ahead of me in their evening. But as soon as I began to back away from the invitation, which, as I say, had been no more than good form, Wad seized me by the arm and pulled me over to his table. My protests were disregarded, and soon my bouillabaisse had been moved to the large table, where I found myself drowning in a sea of new faces.

"Mike Ward, better known as Michaeleen McWardo, these are my friends," Wad called over the wine glasses. "Friends, this is Michaeleen McWardo from Canada." The woman next to me frowned at the scant formality and quickly introduced herself and her husband as Stella and Cyril Burdock. Wad had seated himself again and showed no further interest in helping me find my way with a tableful of strangers. In fact, he seemed a little put out, but whether it was because I hadn't fought off his invitation more successfully or whether it was the sallow fellow in the spectacles he kept glaring at, I couldn't tell.

Cyril Burdock had washed-out blue eyes and a walrus moustache. He was a portly English gentleman who seemed to assume that he was the father of this feast. I learned later that he was a former collaborator of Joseph Conrad's, and that he edited a small literary magazine that Wad sometimes worked for without pay. Stella, his wife, looked like an aging ballerina, with a round face and dark hair pulled back from her high forehead. She plied me with questions about my origins. She wanted to know whether I was in any way related to the Canadian Wards that she knew. I was always being asked that and I gave her my usual answer.

"Yes, but I'm a distant relation. I've never seen their Vancouver house and have spent little time in the family castle overlooking a Toronto ravine."

"I met the Vancouver Wards in Fontainebleau last year," she said. I said nothing to encourage further conversation in this direction. Wad was looking at me as though I'd been lying about my prowess in the ring. He gave me a touch of that slow, Midwestern grin of his.

To Wad's left sat Hal Leopold, who was the sometime object of Waddington's scowl. He was a pale, heavy-set man wearing spectacles that failed to hide a broken nose. I learned later from Wad that he had been middleweight boxing champion of Princeton and was rather proud of the fact. Wad also told me that Hal came from one of the richest Jewish families in New York. Leopold didn't seem to notice Wad's scowl; his interest was focused on the woman seated to my left.

Next to Leopold sat two sisters, Julia and Victoria Lowry, from somewhere in the American South. I learned that Julia was working for the Paris edition of *Vogue* magazine. Her beautiful yellow coat was draped over the back of her chair. Across from her sat the woman that Hal Leopold couldn't keep his eyes away from. She was every bit as chic as Julia Lowry, but it appeared that she did it more with her eye than her pocketbook. She was wearing a man's felt hat and a jersey top over a tweed skirt. The effect was more than the sum of its parts. Whenever I saw Lady Biz Leighton, she seemed to embody the times we were living in. She seemed to do it naturally, without any fuss. Even when I got to know her better, I couldn't imagine her worrying about her clothes. In fact, I often saw her leave clothes discarded in a heap on the floor of her studio and sail out without a glance at the looking glass. "Biz" was short for Elizabeth. She was British and had been married to a man whose family filled a page in *Burke's Peerage*. Hardly anybody called Biz "Lady Biz." She didn't seem to mind. Wad told me later that she'd had a hell of a time during the war. I knew a few people who claimed to have had a good war, but I didn't believe them. Biz looked as if she'd been hurt, and, like all of the men in her life, I wanted to protect her from further injury.

The other woman at the table was Arlette La Motte, a stunning, assured French woman in a fashionable frock. She looked sleepy and not at all interested in the two noisy Americans who appeared to be her escorts. Occasionally, she looked at one or the other of them and stared, as though to say, "Where did I offend the gods enough to deserve you?" She exchanged a smile from time to time with Burdock, who pretended not to notice, though his wife did, letting go an arpeggio of annoyance by suddenly moving her bangled right arm. Arlette was wearing heavy make-up on her mouth and cheeks, after the French fashion. Lady Biz wore no make-up at all; her face was like a cameo cut in rose jasper. I kept looking back at her.

"I've seen you playing tennis with Waddington," Leopold told me across his plate of roast duck. "Has he got you boxing yet?"

"We discuss it from time to time," I said. "When he's beating me on the courts, boxing doesn't seem such a bad idea."

"You learned boxing, of course, in Vancouver?" Burdock asked and stated at the same time.

"The Wards have been a bastion of support for the fine

arts in Vancouver," added Mrs. Burdock to the rest of the company. I said again that I lived in Toronto.

"Leopold will appreciate this," said Burdock, leaning languidly across the table in my direction. "I don't suppose you know it, but the first great English boxer whose name has come down to us was a fellow named Mendoza." Burdock wiped his stained moustache on his napkin and caught his breath. "Spanish Jew, you know, from the East End of London, if I remember aright."

"Really?" said Leopold with a fixed smile. Wad shot me a conspiratorial glance. Other conversations died at once. "Is this the same Mendoza who fought Lord Byron?" Leopold asked.

"Why, that's right," Burdock said. "No gloves in those days, you know!" He was looking up the table at Waddington.

"Indeed," observed Leopold, his smile still hunting for a hidden meaning.

"Bare hands!"

"Why are you telling me this, Mr. Burdock? I know that Daniel Mendoza is the supposed father of scientific boxing. What more needs to be said?"

"Well, I . . . I just . . ." Burdock caught up his napkin again and coughed into it. When he came up for air, Leopold was still looking at him, not letting the awkward moment pass. Wad was shaking his head at Leopold, at the way he insisted on calling Burdock out.

"I don't suppose you were in Mendoza's league at Princeton, Hal?" Wad said with just a touch of a sneer.

"I don't recall boasting that I was, Wad. Why don't you tell us whom you've knocked down lately."

Waddington dodged the question by calling the restaurant owner over to the table. "Monsieur Lavigne," he said, "would you bring us another litre of the *vin de Cahors*, please?" When the wine came, Wad did the honours, getting up from his place and walking around the table.

Julia Lowry turned in her chair prettily and held out her glass. It was a thin, rather bird-like arm that went well with her boyish Dutch bob.

"I was talking to somebody about you today," she said, suggesting that she had volumes to say.

Wad grinned at her as he filled her glass. He looked interested.

"Oh?"

"Somebody who could do you a lot of good."

"Tell me all about it," he said, pulling up a chair near her. Arlette caught the amused smile on the face of Lady Biz.

"I would, but I don't want to raise the already high opinion you have of yourself. Some other time," she said, "when there aren't so many people around."

Checked, Wad looked petulant for a moment and then put his big arm around her shoulder. "I'm sure you would make a wonderful agent, Julie."

We all laughed at that, including Hash, who had been watching how Julia was flirting with her husband. Julia's sister, Victoria, was watching what was going on over the rim of her glass. She was prettier than Julia, but quieter, less assured, always thinking and watching. Biz was sitting straight in her chair, with her neck slightly arched, finishing her wine, smiling at some private recollection. When Burdock, returning from the WC, leaned past her to tell me something, he nearly brushed her cheek with his own. I felt myself getting warm. I decided I didn't like him.

"I haven't seen Mr. Joyce tonight," Burdock said when he had regained his chair. "He sometimes comes in here when he's dining modestly. I'd frankly like to miss him," he said, putting his chubby hand, judging by her expression, on Victoria's knee. "He's been on a borrowing streak again. One can't deny him a few francs without being branded a Philistine or Boeotian." He talked in short, breathy bursts, giving the impression that he had just run up a flight of stairs. "People seem to think I'm his guardian. I am only to the extent that I don't send every tourist around to see him and collect his autograph."

"They want to show off about meeting the great pornographer when they get back to Oak Park," Wad said with a sneer.

"I say, Mr. Ward," Burdock said brightly, "Waddington tells me that you've written a few things. Would you mind awfully if I asked to see some of them? I'm on the watch for glimpses of the new, you know. Trying to find a few people who aren't trying to sound like Trollope or Thackeray, don't you know? I dare say that if you're a friend of Waddington's, and you've come to Paris from Vancouver to write, you must be doing the right sort of thing."

"It's Toronto, really."

"You might care to drop around to our rooms on the Île St-Louis. Do you know where that is? Paris must be very confusing after the Canadian West."

"I'd like to drop in very much."

"Splendid! Say around tea time tomorrow, unless tonight degenerates into one of those evenings that go on and on."

"You're getting old, Cyril!" challenged Arlette from across the table. There was a proprietary note in her husky voice.

"Not a bit of it. One likes to keep one's head clear when talking to writers about their work. It's only polite."

"I don't think I'd care to be a fly on the wall when you geniuses put your heads together," Lady Biz said, mostly to Stella Burdock.

"Afraid we may talk about you, Biz?" Hal Leopold asked with a lazy smile.

"Of course not. I'm sure you wouldn't talk about me. That's the trouble. You'd be so busy shredding literary reputations that a mere woman wouldn't have a chance."

"They won't be talking about me, either," Leopold said. "The New York papers made confetti of my book. My ears are still ringing."

"Biz," Wad said, "we boast about being in print but forget to mention that the Paris publishers don't export and that the print run amounted to three hundred copies."

"You've got post-publication depression symptoms. A mild case. Wait until you have a book come out in the States. Then you can get a serious case and take to your bed." Hal was delighted when the whole table responded to his joke. Wad smiled too, but there was no illumination behind it. When the table moved to talk of other things, Wad was still looking at Hal, as though the latter were standing on his prayer rug. Later, Wad told me that Hal's book, *Gadget*, had been not so much chopped up by the press as ignored. He made it seem important to set the matter straight.

"Shall we have something more to drink, you chaps?" Biz asked. "This *vin de Cahors* makes a strong case." Another bottle was ordered and poured.

Burdock continued to talk about writers, his wife joining in with sly comments about the women they were living with. While Stella Burdock was talking, her eyes followed Wad's every movement as he sat next to Julia, drinking in her latest flatteries. As soon as she caught me watching too, she caught my sleeve and said:

"Hash must have a terrible time with Waddington. Wad and his harem. I don't see why she allows it, do you?"

"I'm afraid I'm rather new on the scene."

"He's been like this ever since she lost his manu-scripts."

"Who? Hash? God, how terrible!"

"He walked around with a hangdog expression for months afterwards."

"That's my own nightmare, losing everything like that. It's terrible!"

"What's terrible?" It was Wad, back with more wine and now looking ruddy in his cheeks.

"Your manuscripts, Waddington," Mrs. Burdock said. "I just told your friend, Mr. Ward."

Wad's smile became a frown. I felt I should say some-thing.

"What a horrible thing, Wad."

He shook his head. "It makes no sense to talk about it. Have some more wine?" He filled Mrs. Burdock's glass steadily.

"You're damned cold-blooded about it," I said.

"Over and done with, dead and buried. There are a lot of expressions like that. I think I know them all. Hold out your glass, Michaeleen."

I watched the wine fill my stained glass. As Stella Burdock lifted hers, it was shaking, so that her bangles made a noise that caught Lady Biz's attention. She turned her head to discover its origin. This was a head for Jo Davidson or Brancusi. Modigliani should have been spared to paint Biz Leighton.

From across the table, Hash was getting an earful from Julia Lowry, while her sister, Victoria, looked on. Julia had moved to Wad's chair, while Wad foraged for a box of matches.

"I think it's wonderful the way you cope with Wad and the baby. I really do. I mean, is there anything you can't do? Are you really Peter Pan?"

"Oh, Julia. You exaggerate! My Tatie and I manage just fine."

"And how you manage in that squalid little flat is a miracle, nothing short of a miracle!" Hash was looking trapped. Julia had no intention of being brief. "But, of course, you are his wife. You get to read everything he writes first. Before everybody. What a marvellous opportunity! I mean, just imagine being the first person to have read Shakespeare or Milton or Walt Whitman!"

"I don't think there was a Mrs. Walt Whitman."

"Well, you know what I mean, Hash. I'm just so envious. I mean, you are right there next to him when he is writing his poems and stories. You watch the characters come out of the chaos, like Michelangelo chipping away the marble that isn't David. I can't put it better than that. And we all know how far he's going to go. People are talking about him. And, Hash, you and the baby will be there. You'll be able to look back at the years you spent in your Paris garret."

"You make it sound like Puccini, Julia. At least my cough has gone away."

"You know what I mean, Hash. This is just the beginning." Julia's eyes were shining.

"In the meantime, he still has to carry our trash down all those stairs. His shoes need half-soling and he spends far too much on cigarettes." Hash's attempt to bring Julia down to earth did not begin to stop her. I reached for my wine and emptied the glass. Burdock cocked an ear at what Julia was saying and began pulling at the hair on his knuckles in an orderly fashion, one finger after the other. We finished the rest of the bottle while Wad, who had now returned and was dealing with an impatient Monsieur Lavigne, was being praised all around the table. In the midst of this, Arlette and her ardent friends bade us good night, and we watched as they prepared to go off into the rain again. Arlette had hardly said a word to me, but I wondered how much she had taken in. She gave me the feeling that little escaped her half-closed eyes.

When the door closed behind them, Julia returned to her theme. She linked Wad's name with all my literary gods. She invoked Joyce, Eliot, Lawrence, Wells, Bennett, Anderson and Conrad. Wad tried to get her to stop, but it was a transparent feint.

"In the States," he said, "only writers with three names get ahead. I'll have to sign my stuff Jason Miller Waddington or nobody will take me seriously. Look at all the three-name people: Henry Seidel Canby, James Branch Cabell, John Peale Bishop and —"

"Be serious, Wad!" Julia said. "We're talking about your future!"

"I can't think of a better way to spoil it than by talking about it, Julie. Sorry, but it's like walking under ladders. You can do it in perfect safety until a hod of bricks lands on your head. I'd just as soon we talked about Mike's tennis game. Or Hal's. What kills writing is talk!"

The Burdocks were the next to make a move to leave. I was again reminded about tea the following afternoon and given the address. We groped for our damp outer clothing and went out into the night. The rain had become a fine drizzle, with enough mist to put an aura around the arc lamps up and down Montparnasse. Wad and Biz shook hands formally, while Hal Leopold stood watching. Then the Waddingtons went off in the direction of Port-Royal, a direction I had walked several times during the last few weeks, accompanying the Waddingtons first up to the square with the statue of Marshal Ney under the chestnut trees, and then around the front of the Closerie des Lilas and into the narrow street with apartment buildings on one side and the backs of the stores on Montparnasse on the other.

Cyril Burdock hailed a taxi for the Lowry sisters. He had taken it upon himself to see that all of the women in the group were either chauffeured or escorted out of the Quarter. One couldn't be too careful, he said, with Jack de Paris on the prowl. Julia's eyes still bore the afterglow of her evening at the feet of her favourite genius as she waved at us from the taxi. The Burdocks, Hal and Lady Biz walked along Montparnasse with me. As we walked, the Burdocks in the vanguard, Hal Leopold told me that he had a new book coming out next month with Boni and Liveright. He told me in a shy, almost matter-of-fact manner, such as one might use for giving street directions. I tried to sound impressed, but it was far too late in the evening to correct the balance. Wad had won the evening hands down. Perhaps that is why Hal seemed to stew in Wad's company. I began to wonder why he sought it out, if that was the case.

On the corner of Raspail, where I left them, Lady Biz took my hand and asked me to call her "Biz" without the title. She held on to my fingers perhaps a moment longer than necessary, or so it seemed to me. I wished Biz and the others a safe return to their homes and turned down boulevard Raspail, hoping that I would not frighten any unaccompanied young women as I made my way down the rue Vavin in the direction of St-Sulpice and the rue Bonaparte.

CHAPTER 3

Andrée Chastel was found huddled in the gutter in the rue des Ciseaux, just off St-Germain, at four in the morning by two welders returning late from a wedding in Sceaux. They had missed the last train and had walked back into the city. Quite appropriately, Mlle. Chastel had been stabbed with a pair of scissors. At first, they told the police, they thought she was a heap of old clothes, then, on closer inspection, agreed she was a *clocharde* who had lost her tenure of the nearby Métro gratings. The blood making steady progress along the gutter had pooled next to a roll of burlap by the sewer opening. This sobered them from the wedding wine and their long walk. The *flics* were on the scene with portable arc lights within twenty minutes.

Le Matin was on the street too early to carry an account of the killing, but the afternoon and evening papers made up for it. As the sixth murder of an unaccompanied young woman in ten weeks, it was something for the popular papers to jump at. Andrée Chastel had been selling flowers up on Montparnasse when last seen. She was known as a drunk and sometime model. The papers stated quite firmly that none of the women murdered in the area frequented by artists and foreigners was a known prostitute. She had no enemies. She had last posed for Moïse Kisling seven months previously and was the subject of a sketch by Modigliani, according to a police statement released by the commissioner of police, Léon Zamaron. I was amused by

these irrelevant artistic notes from the policeman. They fed
my habit of sentimentalizing the French. What did her work
with Modigliani or Kisling have to do with her sudden,
violent and untimely death?

Paris Soir had taken to calling the killer of these
women "Jack" after the English murderer of prostitutes.
The paper recited the history of "Jack's" career to date.
Here, I read about Brigitte Lefèvre, an art student and the
mistress of a Polish sculptor. She'd come to Paris from
Nancy when her father deserted the family. Solange
Chatelaine was a painter herself as well as a frequent model
for several of the painters of the Quarter. She left a young
child, who is now having his fate settled in the law courts
on the Île de la Cité. The paper gave the names of the three
others; they were much the same, models and part-time
models, some of them familiar figures in Montparnasse.
The factor that linked them was their physical beauty,
which the papers — all of them — emphasized again and
again. These women for the most part were nobodies. The
best known of them had never had a show of her paintings.
Outside the Quarter, they were unknown. Singly, their
deaths wouldn't have earned space in their hometown
papers, but once they were linked to one another and to the
unknown killer who stalked the streets of Montparnasse, a
monument to death was created, a spectacular interest was
uncovered that eclipsed the state of the unsteady franc, the
League of Nations, German recovery, reparations — everything was swept aside by the headline: "JACK STRIKES
AGAIN!"

The only place in town that was not talking about the
sudden death in the rue des Ciseaux was the office of the
Transatlantic Review on the Île St-Louis. The editor, Cyril
Burdock, was singularly uninterested in the daily news. His
guests consequently avoided the issues of the day, unless

they involved royalty or literary reputations. Stella, his wife, poured tea from a large Sèvres tea service which she said she had rescued from a flea market. The office reminded me of the comfortable and untidy offices of the university newspaper: a mixture of sitting room and work room, with stacks of copy paper and unopened post everywhere. Besides the Burdocks and me, the group consisted of a few unpublished writers, whose names I failed to catch, and Robert McAlmon, an American who edited another literary magazine and who had a glowing literary reputation built upon a very few published works.

"What sort of things have you been doing?" he asked me.

"Not very much, really. These are a few stories I wrote in Toronto." I added my manilla envelope to the stack on the nearest desk. McAlmon snapped it up and was about to open it when Burdock took it from him and placed it on his own desk. McAlmon grinned, shaking his head at Burdock's turned back.

"Toronto is said to have the worst Sunday on the face of the earth," he said. "Is that true?"

"It doesn't go far enough. The city is still ringing from the outcry that nearly prevented streetcars running on the Sabbath."

"I say, Ward," said Cyril Burdock, "have you ever edited a magazine?" I told him about my university experience, which was insufficiently interesting or professional enough for him to pursue that line of questioning. He subtly failed to respond to me; instead he told an anecdote about Waddington, who was doing some editorial work for him.

"I suppose you came to Paris after reading *The Waste Land*?"

I didn't quite like McAlmon's superior air. If he disliked young writers, why did he hang about editorial offices? I forget what I told him.

"Do you like any of the French muck? Fargue, Larbaud and that gang?"

"Ask me when I've read them. I'm still getting the kinks out of my French, living in the present tense."

More tea was poured. McAlmon turned from quizzing me to making comments about Jason Waddington. He was in a sour mood.

"I've tired of Wad's stiff upper lip. I like a writer who tells me a story, not one who demonstrates that he's hurting too much to speak out."

"Oh, I say! That's rather strong, isn't it?" said Burdock. "I thought you were rather keen on him?"

"I'm no longer impressed by his half-stifled whimpers. He is simply lint from the pocket of Sherwood Anderson." Stella laughed at that and then scolded McAlmon.

"Well, old man, history will blame him on you," Burdock said. "You encouraged him. You got him going."

"Don't remind me. I've already joined Sisyphus on the hill."

Stella explained that McAlmon had published Wad's first collection of poems and stories. I recalled the bitterness in Wad's voice when he'd mentioned it at the restaurant the night before.

"What's he working on now? Anyone know?" asked one of the young men, who appeared to be with McAlmon.

"I'm afraid I don't have his confidence as of yore," Burdock confessed.

"I hear that he's trying to make a book out of what went on in Spain this summer," Stella said. "And I have the reputation of being an oracle where Jason Waddington is concerned."

"Ah, Pamplona!" said McAlmon. "I showed him Pamplona the year before last *and* picked up his expenses."

"Don't be petty, McAlmon. Wad's not tried a novel yet."

"It'll be a *roman à clef* floated on *vin ordinaire* if he finishes it."

"I'd write that down, Bob. You might put it in a review."

It was plain to see that the Waddington I had met on the quays was a far more complex figure than I'd taken him for. The jealousy, or whatever it was, in the room was palpable. I sat there for another twenty minutes, listening to McAlmon and the Burdocks talk about other writers of the Quarter and drinking tea.

It was dark when I put my teacup down and made my way across the dim courtyard and through the huge double doors to the Quai d'Anjou. I walked around the island for a few minutes, catching glimpses of the far shores through the cross streets from time to time and hearing some Mozart being played in the church, not far from an old building with gilded fishheaded drainpipes grinning down at me.

I found a restaurant on the island and ate a good meal. Seafood was the specialty and was treated seriously by the family who ran the place. Steaming platters were served all around me on marble-topped tables. I was a little bothered by the fact that almost all of the customers were speaking English. As I ate my hake, I could appreciate how it might feel to be French and hear a foreign tongue making its insidious way into the very heart of the city.

That night, talk of Jack de Paris was all you could hear at the Dôme, where I sat looking out into the boulevard from the *terrasse*. While it was mostly over the heads of the tourists, all of the regulars (and I was now numbering

myself with them) were talking about the last hours of
Andrée Chastel.

"She was standing over there under the streetlights last
night. I tell you, damn it, she was almost pretty. I could see
what Zadkine was always talking about. Good bones." It
was Pascin talking to two of his models. "I was thinking of
painting her. That's the truth. She had the mark of something on her. I didn't know what it was."

"Are we going to eat now?" asked the older of the
girls. "You've told us about that bitch six times and she's
just as dead now as when you began. So what's the use?"

A beautiful redhead walked by with her hand on the
arm of a Japanese wearing a stiff collar and tie. She looked
American. Pascin sang out:

"Foujita!"

The Japanese turned his head, stopped and smiled at
the painter. After a whispered word to the lady, they joined
the artist and his models, which necessitated the shifting of
two tables and several chairs. The models examined the
redhead intently, assessing the possible threat.

"Jules, my dear friend," Foujita said in heavily accent-
ed French. "I hope you will see your lovely companions
home tonight!"

"If we don't go to eat soon," said the model who had
spoken before, "I'll take my chances with Jack. Come on,
Jules! You said we were going an hour ago." Pascin moved
the brim of his derby hat so that it covered one eye. By this
time, the newcomers were seated and had begun to light
their cigarettes. Later, Wad told me that Foujita was a
painter as well. Known as the Japanese Rubens by the critics, he specialized in rendering nudes with lustrous pink
flesh.

I'd just decided to finish my drink and go home for an
early night when I saw Biz getting out of a taxi and holding

up her hand to shelter her eyes from the harsh overhead lights. She saw me sitting behind the painters and models and made her way through the packed *terrasse* towards me.

"Hello there! I'm absolutely dying of thirst! Would you buy a drink for a chap before she drops?"

"Certainly. What would you like?"

"What are you drinking?"

"I was just going to have another beer," I lied. "How does that sound?"

"Bang on. It sounds like the doctor's own medicine. You're Mike Ford, or is it Ward? I'm not very good at names. You'll have to indulge me as a war casualty. I had my memory broken in three places."

"Was it painful?"

"I can't remember."

The waiter came and took our orders and in a short time returned with two lagers in tall glasses. "Here's mud," she said as she smiled at me over her drink. The beer was cold and felt good all the way down. Biz had nearly finished her glass before I had well begun a second sip. "I say, this is good," she said.

"Have you lived in the Quarter long?" I asked.

"Don't let's ask questions, darling Mike, let's just get swizzled. What do you say? I'm all talked out. I just left a man in the Crillon bar who thinks he's my fiancé. Another wants to take me to Scotland. Scotland! From the age of seven I wanted nothing more than to leave Scotland. But this fellow from the Crillon, he couldn't know about that. Give a chap a cigarette, will you? I haven't actually owned a paid-for packet of my own for three days. I'm terrible when I'm like this. Nobody should have anything to do with me."

"Do you want to be spanked and sent home?"

"Oh, I'd hoped you weren't one of *them*." I blushed at

my loose tongue. "There are rather a lot of them in the Quarter just now. Most of them are darling. Do anything for me. Drink *vin ordinaire* from my slipper."

"Sorry," I said. "I never could make it work that way."

"Thank God! The last of a disappearing breed!"

"Would you like another lager?"

"Rather! That's almost a rhyme, isn't it? You're a friend of Wad's, aren't you? He talks about you a good deal. I shouldn't tell you that. Swell your head. I say, does your hair always fall about like that?"

"Afraid that it has always blinded me in one eye or the other."

"Wad says that apart from the two of you, there aren't any serious writers in town. That is a bit thick, isn't it?"

"Waddington's famous imagination. He does work hard, though."

"I know. I hear he's putting our trip to Spain into a book. Can't wait to see it. Of course I never shall. Nobody, not even a Paris printer, would publish rubbish like that. I can't remember half of what happened. It will be an *aide-mémoire* for me if it ever sees the light of day. Do I seem to you to be the sort of chap who might end up in a book?"

"I can see it. I might even try it myself, when I know you better."

"I'll make jolly sure you don't get to know me any better, then. I would rather like sometimes to return to a more formal relationship with myself. Familiarity . . . You know how it goes on."

"Do you think Wad is really writing about you?"

"You never can tell with him, can you? He talks a lot of rot, but then we all do. It's like Wad's boxer friends. They put on those padded gloves. Fibs, lies, stories, exaggerations. These are the paddings I use, and maybe Wad as well."

"You heard about the latest murder?"

"Yes. I don't want to talk about that. That story's been holding up the Crillon bar all afternoon. The bartender says that a story like that saps the alcohol out of his drinks. Leaches it away so that the bar stands still in one place for far too long. I couldn't stand it. I left my fiancé over on the other side of the river. Fiancé and cousin. If we marry, I'll be twice his kinsman, won't I?"

"I thought he only *thought* he was your fiancé. You must have doubts?"

"I owe George a good deal. He got me out of England and brought me here. George may be a drunk, but he has very decent instincts. He's going to be very rich one day, if we all live long enough. He has a mother. Do you know what it is to have a mother who won't let go? He calls her his keeper. He may come looking for me."

"What was it like in Spain?"

"That's one of the things I'd rather not talk about. I was a bitch. The worst kind of bitch. I want to forget all about that. Wad was decent to me, though. He was damned decent. Saw me through the worst of my stupidities and took nothing in return. Of course, Cilla, his wife, was there. She was always there, calming, muting, deadening. Wad's very lucky to have Cilla. She's a brick of the best kind. Makes women like me blush, if we've retained the instinct."

"Do you know anything about the story of Wad losing his manuscripts?"

"Fancy Wad losing anything! Oh, he told me about it. I always thought it was one of his yarns. He tells stories, Wad does. It makes him feel good, like drinking does for most of us chaps. But I never make the mistake of believing him. If you told me you'd leave your wife to live with me, should I believe you? It's just talk and drink."

"I've got no wife to leave," I told her, but she'd

already forgotten the relevance of the statement. I watched the curve of her long neck as she turned her head to follow the waiter through the crowded tables. There was something about the way she held her head. Suddenly, she was smiling at me, and I was caught by surprise, as though I'd skipped a page.

"I say," she said, "this place is looking very dull all of a sudden. Would you walk a chap up the rue Delambre to the Dingo? In case Jack is lurking in a doorway?" It wasn't what I'd hoped she would say, but it meant that the evening was not about to end. I was an optimistic fellow; I lived in hope. I would settle for a walk with Biz to the Dingo.

I waved to the waiter, indicating my pile of saucers, and paid the score. He took his own 15 percent service charge, saving me the effort of figuring it out. I hadn't noticed, but the two painters, Pascin with his derby hat tipped on one side of his head and Foujita with his round eyeglasses and bangs, had vanished with their restless women. I hadn't even noticed them get up.

CHAPTER 4

Biz was well known at the Dingo. As soon as we walked in, she was surrounded by a clutch of young men with their hair slicked back like tango dancers. They minced, they capered, they waved their hands. They spoke in high voices telling Biz everything, *everything* about a scene at a *bal musette* where one of them, Lett Haines, had been bodily evicted by the owner. Lett swore that he would never put a foot in that place again. I believed him the first time; by the time he'd told me for the fifth, I was beginning to think that he might be a part-owner and trying to encourage trade. Biz accepted a warm greeting from the bartender and reserved a place for me next to her. I was on the point of leaving, not wishing to add another stem to this particular bouquet, when Waddington and Julia Lowry came into the room with some other people. Wad saw us at the bar. He saw, and smiled a superior smile. I went over to the table they'd settled at.

"Hello, Wad. How are you, Julia?" I said. "Would you like to have a drink?"

"And join the daisy-chain? No thanks."

I decided not to bother trying to explain anything to Wad. I could see myself digging a deep grave with excuses. And what the hell? They're people. As long as I know who I am, I don't have to worry about Waddington. Julia was looking friendly. She grabbed my arm and insisted that I have a drink with them. I was curious enough to see what was bothering Wad to allow Julia to find a place for me. Wad kept looking at Biz's straight back at the bar. He added a beer for me to the order of drinks that the white-coated waiter was collecting. When he'd gone, I was introduced to the others: Dr. Anson Tyler, an American with rabbit-like teeth, his friend Arlette La Motte, whom I'd already met, and someone they called Tolstoi, who looked more English than Russian.

"Tolstoi, the Doctor and I have just come from a bridge game where Arlette beat the hell out of us," Wad said. Arlette, her superior smile fixed, looked around the room, encouraging Wad to elaborate. Instead, he put an arm on Julia's shoulder and asked:

"What are you celebrating, kid?"

"*Le Figaro* reports that the world remains round," I said.

"Astounding! Have you cabled the news to Toronto?"

"And to Vancouver, for Burdock's sake."

"Yes, he's fond of Vancouver. Perhaps because Stella comes from Australia," Julia said.

"How stupid of me not to see it!" Wad looked at the others again. "I think Tolstoi should pay, you know, Arlette. He was *your* partner. And he's up on the evening. What do you say, Michaeleen?"

"Sorry, I don't know how you bet on bridge. If Arlette was the big winner, maybe she should pay."

"Ah, M. Ward, you are *un salaud*." She tried to entangle me in the smile that accompanied the remark. She was pretty enough: tall, poised, well-dressed, ironic as hell, but she looked complicated. She was about five years older than I was.

"You are a hard man, McWardo," Waddington said.

"I say, I don't mind paying for the first round," said Tolstoi. He did, and we toasted the Russian Steppes.

"Let's celebrate them one by one," Wad said, lifting his glass. "Ladies and gentlemen, I give you —"

"Please," said Arlette, "I don't see any ladies." Tolstoi gave her a friendly jab.

"Gentlemen, I give you Steppe Number Six!" We clapped and drank.

"On behalf of Steppe Number Six, I accept," said Tolstoi. He spilled part of his drink as he made a grand flourish with his hand, glancing from one face to the next, looking for assurances that he had caught the proper spirit of fun. He seemed a little behind the others in picking up cues. Tolstoi was a compact but well-built Englishman with a public school accent, rather worn clothes and a dissipated manner. He had a face that hadn't been lived in, the male equivalent of a virgin at a bacchanal. Wad told me privately that he was being paid by his parents to stay away from the family acres near King's Lynn in Norfolk.

"He's been on the dope," Wad said. "Whenever he threatens to come home, the family raises his allowance. The dope-peddlers at the Hole in the Wall couldn't ask for a more obliging customer."

We continued to toast Russian geographical landmarks and institutions. Dr. Tyler had a deep understanding of Russian geography and the drinks were disappearing quickly. A skinny, hollow-chested man, just under six feet tall, Tyler had large teeth protruding from under his military-looking moustache. His greenish eyes were hooded; his nose jutted out like the pointer on a sundial. His tailoring was without fault, and he didn't seem to care a damn about it.

"Here's to Tchaikovski, the Tennyson of composers," he said.

"Here's to Schubert, the Keats of composers," said Wad.

"Schubert's not Russian."

"He is from here," Wad protested.

While they fought it out, I turned to Julia, who had

hardly said a word since she came into the bar. She'd been watching Biz with the men swarming around her across the room. Biz didn't seem to be missing the fellow who brought her.

"You weren't playing bridge?" I asked Julia.

"Oh, I'm too good for this bunch. They won't let me play. It isn't fair."

"I'll bet Wad would let you put on the gloves with him."

"That's all I can look forward to. He won't play tennis with me again. Not since I beat him with a sprained ankle."

"That slowed him down, did it?"

"Don't be absurd!" she said. "It was *my* ankle!" She enjoyed the joke, and we laughed as we both imagined Wad's face on being beaten in such circumstances.

"Are you one of the characters in this Spanish novel he's been working on?"

"Certainly not," she said, managing to put as much southern inflection as it is possible to put on two words. "Waddington knows the name of my father's law firm. They scan the daily papers looking for opportunities to sue, bless their little hearts. But he isn't really putting people we know in the novel, is he?"

"That's the talk around the Quarter. Ask him."

When we looked over at the others, Tolstoi was trying to think of a Russian composer who might be described as the Browning of Russian composers. Anson suggested Rimsky-Korsakov.

"Of the five Russian composers of the last century, only Rimsky-Korsakov was able to throw off his amateur standing. He was a perfectionist, not the musical equivalent of a Sunday painter, Tolstoi. By God, Korsakov had standards! What mastery of form! Forget his lyricism for a moment — it just gets in the way, as Browning's does —

just think of his opulence, his output, his command of his orchestra."

"You're not related, are you, Anson?" Arlette asked with a smile. "I wish someone would endorse me as strongly. I might get somewhere."

"He was the consummate professional. As a professional myself, I have to salute him," the Doctor said.

"I think you need another drink, Anson. Let's toast both Browning and Rish-ky . . . *Rim*sky-Korsakov," said Tolstoi.

"Julia," I said, turning back to her, "can you tell me why Tolstoi is Tolstoi? Has he published much about the retreat from Moscow or women who walk the wrong way on railway tracks?"

"Oh, Mike, I thought you knew! His name is really Warren Pease. Now, honestly, who could resist the temptation to play with that?"

Wad certainly couldn't resist the compulsion to bestow a nickname. After years of being "Michael" or "Mike," I was resigned to being "Wardo" or "McWardo" and "Michaeleen" as long as Wad remained in the Quarter. I glanced over at him, looking unshaven and heavy in his Fair Isle sweater. Next to him, the Doctor looked almost dapper. Anson Tyler had been listening to our conversation with more than half an ear. Julia leaned over towards him, picking off a mote of make-believe lint from his jacket.

"Mike was asking about the Spanish book."

Anson raised his eyebrows. "That's the big question," he said. "Everybody wants to get a look at it. Lawyers on two continents are sharpening their pencils." He grinned at his exaggeration. There was a small tuft of whiskers in the cleft of his chin. His face was reddening with drink, or perhaps it was reflecting mine.

"Why don't we get Wad to tell us about it?" I asked.

"There are a few rules in the Quarter, Mr. Ward —"

"Mike, please."

"Although we survive on rations of gossip, the direct question is frowned upon as unsubtle. All mystery wilts before the question direct. In a way, Paris is like an island. You may see a whispered exchange across the floor. There's no need to bend an ear or move closer. Someone will tell you what was going on before the week is over. That's the way it is in an expatriate community."

"You sound as though you've studied in Vienna."

"No, but I'm in touch with the literature. Actually, I'm a general surgeon at the American Hospital in Neuilly. For my sins, which are beyond numbering, I remove gallstones from American tourists who have eaten too much pâté while 'exploring' the Dordogne. I have quite a collection of them."

"Does that mean you've been here for some time?"

"My boy," he said, ignoring the prohibition on direct questions, "I was here before Gaul was divided into three parts. I'm beginning to think it's a life sentence."

"And you live in the Quarter?"

"I live exactly between the Right and Left Banks. I'll explain that to you one day." He gave me a friendly but rather superior, rabbity grin. "I've been in France on and off since the war."

"Apart from me, you're practically the only person I've met with a real job to go to in the morning."

"Hey, you fellows, I resent that!" Julia put in. "*Vogue* pays me a salary every month! I'm not to be considered part of the décor. I'm a working girl and my daddy's proud of me."

"A thousand pardons, Miss Lowry. I'm still not used to the idea of women working for a living. That comes of living in a backwater like Toronto."

"He said Vancouver, didn't he?" said Wad, putting a clumsy hand on Julia's tiny shoulder. She took the paw in her small hand and held it.

"In Toronto, the Blue Laws are made from choice indigo. Imported by supporters of the Lord's Day Alliance and defended by all those who disapprove of tobogganing in High Park on Sundays."

"You're both changing the subject," scolded Julia. "I work for a living."

"Julie's the editor's right-hand man; Paul Poiret, the designer, won't take a step without consulting Julie. She's made herself indispensable."

"Hash devours Paris *Vogue* every chance she gets. On the news-stands mostly. We're too broke to buy it. Tell me, Pudding, do you ever actually *write* for the magazine?"

"*Write*? Waddington, darling, I bloody well *translate* most of it! And I don't mean from French. My specialty is going from broken to standard English."

"The editor's hired some so-called writers he's lured out of Brooklyn and the Bronx with pieces of raw meat," Wad added. "Julie has to change all their Vs to Ws."

"Listen, Vaddinkstein, you could do verse than vorkink for *Vogue*," Tolstoi said with a funny accent.

"I think he's out to pinch my job," said Julia.

"Pudding! How can you even think such a thing?"

"Wad doesn't know anything about fashion," Arlette said. "He can't tell an out-seam from an in-seam. And what about those new fasteners? What do you call them?"

"Zippers," Julia said, with an air of superiority. "They will put buttons out to pasture."

"Oh! I just had a painful thought," said Waddington, pulling his knees up.

"You're more interested in what's going on behind the fashions," said Julia.

"Or under them," added the Doctor.

"Now boys! You're wandering away from the libretto," Arlette said. "We need to see where they put the drinks we requested."

I looked around and found Biz still seated at the bar. She was talking to the bartender, who was nodding slowly, then shaking his head. She was still surrounded but no longer being spoken to. Wad was now sitting with his back towards her. He didn't look in her direction.

When the *fines* arrived, we let the old fag-ends of conversation die a natural death.

"Here's rain on your cotton!" said Julia, and we drank to that in case she'd meant it for a toast. For a few minutes, we talked about Jack the Ripper of Paris. Wad was very good at getting into the mind of the killer. He should have been seconded to the *Sûreté*. Then I saw Hal Leopold come into the Dingo. He was looking grim. Wad saw him too as he walked through the tables to where Biz was still sitting at the bar. He took the stool that Biz had been holding for me and my recovered sense of duty. He moved her bag to the bar and spoke with the bartender briefly.

"I knew he'd show up if Biz was here. They have an instinct for trouble." Wad pulled himself out of his chair. The legs squeaked as he got up.

"Ah, lay off, Wad. He's a he-man at least. He may only be thirsty," I said.

"Right. Thirst is a great lev-leveller. I once found myself drinking out of the same stream as a water moccasin. Kike bastard!"

"Christ, Wad! 'Hath not a Jew eyes?'"

"What business has he with Lady Biz?"

"Wad, you're drunk! How many girls do you want?"

"Shut up, kid. You don't know what you're talking about."

"Come on, Waddington, sit down. There's a good fellow," said Tolstoi. Wad did as he was told, but finished his cognac to show that he was sober.

"You know," said Arlette, who hadn't said much because her English wasn't perfect and she was shy in company, "I am surprised at you Americans and English who come here. You pretend to be poor, you pretend that you are artists, you think you are better than the tourists. You make me very cross, you know. You *are* tourists. You don't ride a charabanc, but you are no better than the people who go home with a Tour Eiffel paperweight and a bottle of Napoléon brandy." The group stared at Arlette for a full minute.

"Arlette! What's wrong?" Anson demanded. "Why are you talking this way? What have we done to hurt you, dear girl?"

"It's not you. It's everybody. Maybe I'm sick of this town. Maybe I wish more of you went home to your roast potatoes and apple pie."

"Steady on, old girl! We're not without feelings. Don't be so hard on us," said Tolstoi.

"Yes, what can we do about it?" asked Julia.

"You treat us all as the background, the cyclorama — is that what you call the back curtain in a theatre? — for your pretending. Do you know that France is going crazy? The franc is falling every day. Everywhere the prices are going up. Everyone blames the government, the bankers, the Jews. *Sans blague*! How many of you know this? How many of you have ever been away from your language for even a day? You don't care about us except as supernumeraries in your little dreams."

"Come on, Arlette, that's a bit thick. We know you, don't we?"

"I'm sorry. I wasn't going to say anything. I apologize."

"I think you've had a drop too much, kid," Wad said.

"I am going to the Water," she said as though it were the announcement of the succession to the British throne, and got up carefully.

Over at the bar, Lady Biz was now arguing with Leopold. It looked as though he wanted her to leave with him and she didn't want to go. He had a hand on her arm. Wad was on his feet. I got up and started over. But, before I got there, Wad had pulled one of the men away from Biz and almost at the same moment had taken a poke at Leopold.

"Damn!" said Anson Tyler. "He thinks he's Jack Dempsey!"

"God! Did you see it?" Hal Leopold had gone over backwards to the floor, taking one of the stools with him. A few customers got to their feet. Leopold was rubbing his chin with one hand and feeling along the floor to make contact with his fallen eyeglasses. The men at the bar had gone white and silent. I gave Hal a hand and he stood up in slow stages. Colour had drained from Biz's face. Wad was leaning back against the bar as though he'd just shot a lion. There was blood on Hal's face.

"Let a professional sawbones have a look at that," Anson said, putting his thumb under Hal's eye. We gave the Doctor room and Hal allowed Anson's hands to move his head around. After a moment, they grinned at one another. "Nothing to make medical history here," Anson announced as he got to his feet.

"Wad, what the hell was that for?" Hal asked, fitting his spectacles in place and straightening his bow tie.

"It doesn't pay to bother a lady. You should have seen she didn't want to go with you."

"And what business is that of yours?"

"You can't get away with that sort of thing around

here," Wad said, evasively. "Maybe it's time you shoved off."

Leopold had taken off his eyeglasses again and was wiping them with a handkerchief. Sweat was shining on Wad's face.

"Last time I heard, the Dingo was still a public place, Wad. Are you still sore about Spain? I thought we were all through with Spain. Do you want to come outside into the street to settle this?"

"Sure," Wad said. "I'm at your disposal." He made a little bow, as though they were talking about pistols in the Bois at dawn.

"Come on, you two," I said, coming between them. "Let's have a drink and forget this. Come on, Biz, join the party. Your friends can spare you for a few minutes."

"You're like one of those minor bullfighters, Mike. You come between the matador and the bull at just the right time," Biz said.

"He's going to get gored one of these days," Wad said, but he joined Biz and the rest of us in returning to the table. Julia shifted a few chairs from where she was sitting; Tolstoi, less usefully, stood up. Leopold hung back, waiting for a special invitation. It was easy to see why Wad disliked him. He was pouting like a schoolboy.

"Come on, Hal! Have a drink and forget about this."

"Have you chaps arranged this encore of one of our Pamplona evenings for my benefit?" Biz asked. "I could have done without it, really. You try too hard to amuse me. I'm not worth it." She failed in her attempt to lighten the heavy feeling at the table. Waddington was still sweating as though he had already done fifteen rounds with Hal. I called for another round of *fines*. Cognac might take the sharp edge off all of us, and at two francs each, they were almost within my means.

"Wish somebody'd fight over me," Julia said. "I haven't had such a fuss made over me since I left Arkansas." Arlette returned to the table. She threw a curious look over the party, as though trying to decode it. We were wearing some of what she had missed on our faces.

"Would you have come outside with me, Wad?" Hal asked. "If Mike hadn't come along?"

"It's all rot talking about it," Wad said, without looking at Hal. "The thing is, you do it, you don't talk about doing it." He looked as though he had more to say on the subject, but Tolstoi suddenly stood up, shouting:

"George! Am I seeing things or is it you?"

A tanned, lean, sturdy-looking man with red-rimmed eyes and tweeds stood just inside the doorway. Except for Biz, we all turned to see.

"Oh, hello George," Biz drawled as though the family dog had wandered in with the company. She returned to her drink as George shook hands with the nearest of his friends.

"Hel-lo, Wad! Hel-lo, hel-lo! I'm afraid I'm a bit tight. Is that a capital offence at this table? I've confessed, you know; now you can't say I didn't warn you." He was now standing behind Lady Biz's chair. "An undischarged bankrupt can't be too careful. Hel-lo, Tolstoi, old man! Good to see you!"

"Mike," Wad said, "this is Biz's on-again, off-again fiancé, George Gordon. George, this is a Canadian friend, Mike Ward."

"You did that without a stumble, Wad," Biz said, smiling at him with eyes that also seemed to be calling for help. "You're getting better at it."

"Wad has wonderful manners!" Julia interjected.

George and I shook hands. His was a less than vice-like grip. He had the face of a serious drunk. It was a nice face, generous, humorous, ironic even, but it was the face of a drunk.

"Sit down, George. Have a drink." Wad was apparently delighted to welcome George into our little group, if only because it made Hal Leopold look more uneasy than ever. Another admirer for Lady Biz Leighton.

"Like nothing better, nothing better, but I've left a friend out in the street while I popped in to see if you were here. I'll be back at a gallop." He let go of the back of Biz's chair without Biz having looked at him. Quickly he was out the door, after nearly tripping over the doctor's umbrella.

He returned almost at once with a tall, big-boned blonde woman in a dress that was based on a classical Greek design. The dress was beltless and the figure under it was unfashionably voluptuous. Her hair was not bobbed according to the very newest fashions but worn loose, hanging almost to her shoulders. Her eyebrows were dark and her mouth showed white teeth behind full lips. Hers was a new face to me, but most of the people at the table recognized her.

"*Bonsoir, tout le monde!*" she said in a low, rather masculine voice. Her smile was generous and read the expressions on all our faces. I decided that her evening make-up had been applied too heavily, but I could find no other fault. I was in fact glad that it was the chair next to me that was cleared of our personal rubble and into which she settled, showing rather a lot of silk stocking in the process.

"Mike, do you know Laure Duclos?" Wad asked, trying to catch the passing waiter's eye at the same time. Although Laure Duclos was smiling warmly around her, the answering smiles were frosty.

"So, you're a Canadian?" George said to me across the table. "The Prince has a ranch out your way."

"That's a good deal west of where I come from. The only time I saw the Prince, he asked me to get out of his way. We are less than intimate. Not the best of friends."

The waiter arrived. Laure ordered Pernod and George made a fuss about the Dingo's supply of Scotch. He settled finally for a double shot of something with a cock grouse on the bottle. I was the only one drinking the Bavarian beer that the place was famous for. But I was a tourist still. I had a lot of learning to do.

Before the drinks arrived, I escaped to the Water Closet. It was one of the primitive kinds with two foot-stands rising out of a cesspool and a rusty chain that had lost its knob before the Armistice. On my way out, after escaping the flood that followed my pulling the chain, I ran into George patiently waiting his turn.

"Have nightmares about these things," George said, bobbing his head at the WC. "I see you were quite taken by Laure, old man."

"She's a good-looking woman, and my blood is still faintly red."

"Go to it, my dear chap. But be warned: she's more complicated than she looks."

"She seemed to lower the temperature at the table when she came in."

"Lower . . . ? Oh, I see what you mean." George took his hand from the handle of the door to the WC. "Laure — how should I put it? — has no casual relationships. That gets the women in a stew. Won't play by the rules of the game. I've always liked her, and I must be the only man at the table she hasn't run off with. Back when I first met her, she was Anson's ball-and-chain. That was 1922. I was new to Paris then. Checked into a hotel and told everybody its name was 'Hôtel Meublé.' Everybody thought I was pulling their legs."

"What else does she do?"

"She's a teacher of French, old man. She's also a type-writer. That alone makes her indispensable in the Quarter. So many writers about, don't you know. She made a fair copy of Waddington's first book for Robert McAlmon. She turns up everywhere. But not in here, I hope." Again his attention shifted to the WC, and I rejoined the others.

Fresh drinks had arrived. Everybody was talking. I felt rather privileged to take part, if only by listening. At his end of the table, Hal Leopold stood up with a glass in his hand. He didn't look drunk but rather like a junior lecturer in the safety of his faculty club. "I'd just like to say . . ." he said and then said it again, "that I want to congratulate my erstwhile sparring partner, Jason Waddington. Not for his punch — it was a lucky punch, Wad — but for the fact that I learned today in a letter from Boni and Liveright in New York that they are going to publish not only my new novel — some of you knew about that — but Wad's as well!"

The table went wild with congratulations. Julia and Biz kissed Wad, and Arlette and Laure did as much for Hal, but while Hal was all grins and boyish charm, poking holes in the clouds of smoke that hovered over the table with his pipe, Wad looked like he'd just read a withering rejection notice.

"What's the matter, Waddington?" Tolstoi asked. "You look as though your partner had failed to see that you were holding a grand slam."

"Yes," said Biz, examining his brooding face. "You do look as though you've been sipping hemlock again."

"Liveright's offered him a three-book contract," Hal added.

"But that's marvellous!" said Laure. "And the precious lamb didn't even mention it."

"It's old news," said Wad. "The contract's been signed

for months. I saw the book jacket in August." Wad began waving his arms around. They looked as though they were undecided about whether they were shadow-boxing or manipulating a bullfighter's cape.

George rejoined the party. Biz whispered the news to him before he sat down.

"When do we get to see the first of the books, old man?" George asked. "I'll mortgage my birthright to the Jews and buy fifty copies."

"It's the same book that was published here. Almost. Damned thing will be out in a couple of weeks. Let's change the subject."

"But Waddington, this one will be read in your own country. Big difference there, I think."

"I'll keep you posted, George, on the news from the good ol' Jew S.A." Wad looked at Hal and added, "Sorry, Hal. No offence intended."

"Is the next book to be the Spanish novel, Wad?" I asked.

"The Spanish novel?" Laure asked. "What Spanish novel? Have you been holding out on your old comrades in arms, Waddington?" Wad shook his head and gave me a dirty look for introducing the subject. George and Biz exchanged glances. Hal looked from one face to another, smiling a pained smile. I discovered that I was developing a peculiar interest in this novel Wad was writing.

"Leopold, old chap, I don't see what you're so chipper about. You were there as well, remember." George turned to see the other end of the table. "We were all this raw material, damn it all! Should get royalties, what?" Wad appeared about to make a dash for the tiny, dirty toilet at the back; all in all a better place to be at the moment. George was shaking his head at the unpleasant memory.

"None of us behaved well. I know I was not at my best. We were all tight most of the week."

"I just thought that Wad would like all of you to know," Hal said. "Thought it was good news. Sorry. I don't see why you're hanging crêpe around the walls."

"Let's just not talk about it, damn it!"

Julia took his big right hand in both her tiny hands again. "He was only trying to be kind, Wad. He thought we'd all like to share the good news." She leaned closer and almost brushed his cheek with hers. "Let me tell you what they were saying about you at *Vogue* this afternoon." She began whispering. Wad nodded and smiled. He put his free arm around Julia's waist. Soon he was looking less like a whipped schoolboy.

George was whispering to Biz now as well. They looked serious. Perhaps Biz was angry that George had brought Laure along. Poor Leopold was sitting well into the suburbs of the table watching our bending author and Lady Biz. He had tried to strike a spark, but it had fizzled. If he had taken out a book to read or had gone home, no one would have noticed. I felt sorry for Hal, but not too sorry. He wasn't having a good night.

Laure leaned over towards me, touching my hand as she asked for a cigarette. She held onto my hand to steady it while I held the match. I liked her fragrance. And, just as I thought that, she looked across at me as though she had overheard the thought and it was a secret between us, something not to be shared with the others. She took a puff, letting her cheeks go quite hollow as the smoke found its way out of sight beneath the elaborate folds of her Greek dress. During the next few minutes, without my noticing it, I found that she had moved her chair closer to mine and that our legs brushed under the table. It wasn't like a kick under the table, a warning from a friend to change the subject. This was a brushing, and it could have been an accident the first time. But soon I knew that Laure was touching me with her silk-stockinged leg for reasons which had nothing to do with the conversation. I tried to convey my understanding through pressure of my own. Soon my attention to the conversation faded and my interests were invested below the table.

CHAPTER 5

The evening ended some time after that. George and Biz were the first to leave, and then Hal Leopold ten minutes after that. It was late when I found myself in the street with the others. Freddy, the bartender, locked the door behind us. People waved as they left in opposite directions. Wad saw Julia to a taxi. His big shoulders followed her into the back seat, where I imagined a drunken kiss. He watched the taxi motor down the boulevard, then crossed the street, almost stumbling on the streetcar tracks.

I found myself walking down Montparnasse with Laure Duclos on my arm. Even as we were walking up the rue Delambre to the boulevard, I couldn't quite understand my luck. There was something about the pressure of her arm on mine that gave me not only hope but confidence. After she kissed me in front of the shuttered florists on Montparnasse, I pulled her closer to me as we walked.

Of course I'd had a lot to drink. My head was swimming because of a late change from beer to cognac. Laure, too, had had a full evening with George before she'd appeared at the Dingo. For both of us, it was one of those silly, rash acts in the making. She led me through a maze of streets that I didn't know. There were freight sheds behind the Gare Montparnasse. I remember seeing some folded tables and awnings against a wall: a dismantled, temporary covered market. I kissed her once more against a spiked ornamental fence that protected the inside angle of a high

wall from the insults of the incontinent, in spite of the stencilled warning: *DÉFENSE D'URINER*. I held her close,
and Laure directed my hand as it explored the vibrant body
beneath her dark cloak and tightly pleated Greek chiton.
Her breath was hot on my ear and her mouth on mine was
wonderfully sour from drink and cigarettes as we kissed
again and again with hard intensity.

She said little as we walked. I was now completely lost
in this web of streets; there were only pools of light and
darkness. The silver clasps of Laure's cloak shone as we
passed under the arc lamps. She was holding my hand now.
Our heads were close. When we reached her door, she rang,
and we waited for the concierge to pull the cordon to open
the lock. The door slammed loudly behind us as we stepped
into a cobblestone courtyard. From there, she led the way
up a spiral of drunken stairs, uncovered by drugget after the
first floor, to the top of the house. She handed me her
leather bag, where I fumbled for the key. Her hand was on
my arm as I opened the door, and we were inside.

I could see some light coming in through a small window, touching curtains, the fabric of the bedclothes and the
outlines of a bookshelf. She made no move to turn on the
gaslight, but I felt her hands loosening my necktie before I
had sloughed my topcoat. I tried to undo the silver clasps of
her cloak as I pulled her towards the bed, unprotesting. I
could hear her breathing and my own as I pulled the fillets
of cloth that held her dress together. She hunched her
shoulders into me as the dress fell away from her. In the
darkness of the room, I could only see her eyes and feel our
hot mouths on one another. Without taking our hands away
from each other's body, we managed to struggle out of our
clothes and into the bed.

Perfect lassitude. I could now see better in the dark: the
hump our bodies made in the bed, the cracks in the high

ceiling, a distorted rectangle of light pulled across the wall, moving over the irregularities of a picture frame and clothes draped over the open door of an armoire. She was next to me. In fact my nearly numb hand was still closed around one of her breasts. I turned and moved my arm from where it was trapped beneath her and she shifted langorously into a new position, losing herself in and around my limbs. I touched her cheek lightly with my other hand. She took it in her own, cupped it and held it to her mouth. I heard the word "*chéri*" whispered in a husky, lazy voice. She was warm against me, and I felt the lassitude slipping, giving way to renewed caresses and urgency.

When we had slept for some time, we smoked a shared cigarette.

"I know next to nothing about you," I said, thinking aloud, and louder than I'd intended.

"Shh," she said, putting a finger over my mouth. "You don't want to know."

"I do, you know. I suddenly want to know all about you."

"All you need to know is that we were together. Before that and after that, we were two people with nothing in common, I think."

"We don't even know that. I'm Canadian; you're French."

"Half-French. My mother was Irish. I grew up in Passy and Dublin. Do you know Dublin?"

"No. But I've visited Balzac's house in Passy." She laughed and took the cigarette from my mouth, placing it in hers.

"Wad says that you're a rich man," Laure said.

"I have no money of my own," I said. "My father's a surgeon, but he comes from a family that runs department stores in three cities. We are poor relations who are invited to spend Christmas with our betters."

"You look like a little boy when you try to sound bitter. Do you resent not having money to spend?"

"We've never gone hungry. I shouldn't paint too bleak a picture. My mother saw to it that my father sent me to the right schools and made sure I had the right advantages. I didn't rebel. I didn't know I was supposed to rebel. I saw no necessity for rebellion until I went to work for a newspaper. I met people there who taught me about the advantages I'd had without being aware of them. It never occurred to me when I was at Trinity that everybody wasn't as welcome as I was. The questions never formed themselves."

"My father was a soldier who was always getting into trouble. He was a great intriguer. Luckily, the war came along and he galloped away at the head of a regiment of cavalry. That was before the General Staff knew what barbed wire could do to cavalry."

"I'm sorry."

"Why should you be? I'm not. He was *un salaud*, that one. He . . . well, never mind what he did. Take my word, *chéri*. Trust me, he was a bastard." Again she put her face close to mine and I felt her warmth everywhere, and I slept again.

When I woke, the room was larger than it had appeared in the dark. It was also empty. I gathered my clothes together and climbed into them. In my stocking feet I padded around the worn carpet that covered the terracotta tiles of the floor. There was no recess, no hidden alcove, behind which I might find Laure. I sat in a Louis XV chair badly in need of re-covering, and put on my shoes. I didn't hurry, since Laure's absence might have been temporary. But once my necktie had been knotted anew around my wrinkled shirt collar and my topcoat buttoned, there seemed little to do except go. I was curious to see what treasures her room contained, but I was secure enough in the hope that I would see it again that I was reluctant to extend my solitary stay. I was finally induced to leave by a need to find the nearest WC. It was hidden behind a concave panel on the landing between floors. I didn't return to the room afterwards. Instead, I went down the stairs, through the cobbled courtyard and into the busy morning street.

I crossed the street to take a good look at the building where I'd spent the night. It was a brave imitation of the sturdy apartment houses of the Faubourg St-Germain, only falling slightly into decay. Then I corrected myself: it was the sort of older city building that the Faubourg imitated and elaborated for the families of the middle class. Here, with the *abattoirs de la Rive Gauche* on one side of the street and La Ruche, a beehive of artists' studios built like a rising soufflé or an abandoned wheel of Brie on the other, Laure was safe from the prying eyes of respectable people. I made a note of the address, the passage de Dantzig, before finding a tobacconist's to replenish my cigarette case. That done, I found the nearest café.

There sat Laure, huddled over a *café-crème* in the corner and reflected several times in the dirty mirrors that surrounded her. In spite of our recent intimacy, or perhaps because of it, she was the last person in the world I wanted to see. I felt unwashed and gritty. When she saw me, I think she saw something of my reluctance in my face. Perhaps her own feelings echoed my own.

"Oh, hello," she said, as though we were fellow tellers at the Guaranty Trust, encountered by chance on the weekend. "I'm not talkative in the morning, I hope you are not wanting to talk."

"My head will only permit rudimentary communications, I'm afraid. May I join you?" She didn't change her expression. I sat down across from her. The waiter in shirtsleeves took my order and brought coffee. We sipped in silence and nibbled at a stale brioche.

I watched the beet sugar melt and crumble in my spoon as I lowered it into my cup and brought it out again. The hangover was now fully established, though I hadn't been aware of it until I spoke. Laure was dressed conservatively and carried a leather briefcase. With her hair up, she was altogether the French schoolmistress on her way to meet her first class of the day. Since the imposition of the "no talking" rule, my head was filling with questions I wanted to ask her. I was also certain that I did not wish to appear to be the young lad from the country anxious about the pleasures of the night before and curious about when he might reasonably look forward to their repetition. I understood enough to recognize the code that governed the etiquette of the morning after the night before. I sipped my coffee.

At last she opened her leather handbag and examined the change inside. "I've left myself a bit short, Mike," she said, smiling at me for the first time with her eyes. "Could you help me out?"

"Of course," I said, pulling out my billfold and opening it. I took out thirty francs, which would be enough for a couple of good meals, but she reached across and took two fifty-franc banknotes from me. I was astounded, but tried to contain my surprise. She had taken half of what the billfold contained.

"You're a dear," she said, putting her hand on mine and brushing my unwashed face with hers as she got to her feet. She put the money away in her bag. "*A tout à l'heure*, Mike," she said. I'd heard that phrase before. It didn't mean "goodbye" but simply "until later." I could get through the rest of the day with that, I thought, as I watched her leave the café.

CHAPTER 6

It was a time when one day and one hangover blended into the next. Was it only a few days later that I found myself inside the Select with nearly the same people I'd met that night at the Dingo? We had been drinking and it was late. Chairs were already piled up on top of the tables on the terrace in front of the windows. Mme. Select was beginning to look anxious, but she put up with a good deal from her American and British clientele.

"Did you see the piece in *Le Figaro* about Fargue?" Laure asked Wad in French. Waddington nodded and told her that he thought Fargue was all washed up.

"All that surrealist stuff's going up the chimney," he said.

"Wad!" Julia protested, with smiling eyes. "Some of my best friends are surrealists! What about Duchamp and Villon and Man Ray? They have something."

"I'm not talking about the artists. It's people like Tzara, Fargue and Cocteau. They make me sore."

"Your drink is showing, darling Wad," said Biz, removing a longish cigarette end from her cigarette-holder and replacing it with a fresh one. Biz was always bored by literary conversations. "Why don't we take a cab up to Bricktop's? I'd like to hear some music after all this talk."

"She's got a great nigger band from New York," Julia added. I began to feel uneasy, as I did whenever it was suggested that we uproot ourselves.

"It's worth the trip just to see Bricktop's hair," Anson said. "The last time she had it dyed, it went quite blonde. After watching her two nights ago, I realized that she reminded me of a pint of Guinness."

"Oh, Anson!" Julia said. "Do you say such terrible things about people one knows, as well?"

"My dear child, I'm essentially a truth-teller. My role in life is to run through it as though it were a masked ball and I were in charge of taking off all the masks."

"You're too serious, Anson," Julia said, her eyes glinting in the semi-darkness. "Except when you're pulling the wings off social butterflies."

"Going to take lessons in being frivolous. I thought coming to Montparnasse was pretty frivolous, but I see my high seriousness is rubbing off on Tolstoi. Isn't it, old sport? What do you think? Should we change the Quarter? Should we venture forth?" Anson asked.

Julia and Biz scanned our faces, but no enthusiasm for crossing the river at this time of night was written there. Instead, we promised Mme. Select that we would leave quietly after one more round of drinks. She looked doubtful that we would keep our word but served the drinks anyway.

"I'm going home to bed," Hal Leopold announced, as though there were some novelty in the idea. No one protested. Biz took the newly fitted cigarette from her holder and replaced it in her case.

"I'll come along with you," she said to Hal, and then to the table at large. "Don't get up, please." All the men got up.

Once Biz had left the Select with Hal, the party began to break up in earnest. Wad was muttering something about Leopold, but I didn't catch it. His disapproval of Biz cadging a ride home with Hal was clear, but he never offered to lend her the fare. Of course, he was on short rations himself.

I felt an arm encircle my waist. I knew it was Laure before I turned around. "Be a dear and let me have thirty francs, *chéri*. I'm in a fix and you're the only one I can trust." Her smile was warm and promising. I didn't dispute her need. I could feel her body against mine as I took out my billfold. Once again she took it from me and removed the money herself. "You are a darling, you know! Dear Mike." She patted my cheek and kissed it in a sisterly way before disentangling her arms from me.

"I'll see you home," I said, picking up my beret from the chair. "I don't want Jack to come up behind you in the dark."

"You are a dear, Mike, but I'll be quite safe in a taxi."

"But —!"

Laure moved away from me, still smiling, and announced to the group that she was leaving. I could no longer get her to look at me. At the door, when she turned to wave, I was included in her brittle "Good night." I glanced at the others, who were already collecting their belongings from the brass rack above the banquette for their own departure. No one looked at me. Was I exaggerating my feelings? Certainly not enough for any of my friends to spare me a reassuring smile. When I came to pay for my share of the bill, I discovered that Laure had taken something in excess of thirty francs.

I began to think about what to do next as I started across rue Vavin. I had got only half way when Wad caught up to me. "I've got half a bottle of good wine back at the apartment," he said.

"What about Hash and Snick?"

"Just for a few minutes. Hash won't mind, and I have to change Snick anyway."

"Why not?" I said. "Waddington, I am here." We walked up the boulevard towards the intersection where it becomes Port-Royal and then skirted the Closerie des Lilas, with its chairs sitting on top of the tables on the *terrasse*.

"I'm going to have to read your stuff," I said to Wad. "It's getting embarrassing to know you and maintain my native ignorance." We walked into the apartment on top of the carpenter's loft on the rue Notre-Dame-des-Champs. The concierge swore audibly as she pulled the cordon that let us in. On our way up, we made no more noise than the sounds of the stairs themselves. We relieved ourselves in the WC on the landing, bowing elaborately and saying, "After you, my dear Alphonse." We ignored the shushing noises.

It was dark inside and Waddington lit the gas. I removed a teddy bear from a chair as I sat down, beginning to feel my drink. I made a noise misjudging the distance between me and the bottom of the chair. It was hardly louder than the sound of the cork as Wad pulled it. A door opened and a tousled auburn head came around the corner of the frame.

"Tatie, is that you?"

"Go back to sleep, Hash. I'll see to Snick. I've got Mike with me."

"Good night, Mike," she said, stretching as she turned. "Don't let him keep you up all night."

Wad handed me some wine and a slim volume with the title *Ten Stories and Three Poems*. I liked the feel of it in my hand. The titles of the selections were printed on the cover as well in the same sanserif type.

"This must make you feel good."

"Like a warm-up bout with a middleweight. Gets your blood moving but you don't raise a sweat."

"You're going for bigger game?"

"I've bagged it already. I've got a publisher I want to get rid of and three others that want to take me on. They all want my book."

"That's the Spanish book?"

"Yup."

"And these aren't French publishers?"

"Hell, no!" he said a little too loudly, and then he repeated it in a whisper.

"So that's why you had such a strange reaction to Hal Leopold's news the other night?"

"Now everybody in town knows. Damn it!"

"Is Laure Duclos in it?"

"I thought you knew something about writing, kid?" I shrugged and couldn't find an answer. It was one of Wad's trick questions. "Well, damn it, you should know a fool question before you ask it. A novel is a long fiction. And fiction is what you make up."

"We both know that's only partly true. You don't need Mencken to tell you that. We've both read *Huckleberry Finn*, so let's be honest."

"This is fragile stuff, Michaeleen."

"And the book is written?"

"Thank God for that! Shit, I did it in a few weeks. Started in mid-July and finished it on the twenty-first of September."

"You like it?"

"Hell, that's a damned funny question! Yeah, I like a lot of it. A lot of it will have to do, and some of it is close to the way it should be."

"This is a fifteen-round bout?"

"More like eight, but eight good ones. The kind that gives you a good feeling afterwards. The kind you want to have a big meal after. But let's shut up about the book, okay, Mike? Talking about it can spook it for me and I need this one. What are you doing? Have you got a novel going? Almost everybody has."

"Nope," I lied. "I just write my share of the cables and

keep the wire humming. I'll leave fiction to you, for now, anyway." I took out my watch; it was nearly four in the morning. "I should be getting back," I said.

"Just stay another minute. We'll finish this bottle. Why'd you ask about Laure?"

"She's right out of Michael Arlen, isn't she?"

"She could show that rug merchant something. She was living with Tolstoi until a month ago. There were no kisses exchanged when they parted."

"I heard she was with the Doctor?"

"Ancient history. She might be working her way through the Chamber of Deputies for all I know."

"How interested is she in George? I thought he was wearing the Leighton colours."

"George is going to be a wealthy man one day soon, unless he's put in jail first for skipping out on a few hotel bills. In Spain . . ."

"Yes? In Spain, what?"

"Never mind. It's just that George doesn't know what year it is where women are concerned. But what is he to do when Laure plays up to him? I think he enjoys making the Countess jealous."

"The Countess?"

"Biz. That's what they call her here in the Quarter."

"I can't see George and Biz. Can you?"

"When there's a fortune to be made, I can see more every day. It's called education. For instance, that Laure has a nasty side, Mike. She can play rough."

"There are no secrets in the Quarter, are there?"

"Not to my knowledge. You be careful, kid. She's like a character out of Laclos. You know who I mean?"

"Yeah. *Les Liaisons Dangereuses*, right? Yeah, I know the stuff. It's all letters, right?"

"Well, Laure can be as bad as the Marquise de

Merteuil with all of Valmont thrown in. They're both wrapped around inside Laure like a pair of rattlers. She's worse than a mischief-maker — there are plenty of those in the Quarter, along with the time-wasters — but Laure can be evil, Mike. Take my word for it, kid."

"Really?"

"Take it from me, Mike: Laure's poison."

CHAPTER 7

I didn't see Waddington or any of the rest of that gang of his for a few weeks. Work at the agency had piled up and I began to earn my pay. In the evening, I started eating at Michaud's in the rue des Saints-Pères, on the chance that one night I might catch a glimpse of James Joyce, who was said to dine there all the time. Three nights' vigil snuffed that canard.

I didn't want to *meet* Joyce, I just wanted to see him. My admiration for *Ulysses* and *Dubliners* was such that I wouldn't dare present myself as another stammering votary. I imagined that one day we might exchange a knowing glance that would encapsulate all I would have liked to say but, because of his perfect understanding, I need not try to express.

Waddington's questions about what I was working on had got me thinking. Handling his book made the thought visible. I had to admit to myself that I was not without literary ambitions, but the stories I had left with Cyril Burdock were older than I liked to say. "What had I written recently?" was the question I had to address. The answer goaded my desire to become more than a journalist. I wanted my name on the cover of a book. To this end, I began to make some notes and even went so far as to buy several small blue notebooks at the Librairie Joseph Gibert on boulevard St-Michel. I sat for an hour at a back table in a nearby brasserie with a succession of *cafés-crèmes* and tried to think of something to say. It wasn't easy. I tried to tell myself that the time spent sitting was an important early step to writing fiction, but I only half believed it. When my hour was up, I went for a walk in the Luxembourg Gardens and watched the children sailing their boats in the octagonal pond. Maybe I could write something about them.

The ivy on the drooping garlands that bordered the Médicis Fountain had started turning brown. The water had been turned off for the season. A group of women were standing around a tripod, being instructed by a small, black-bearded man in a smock in the alchemy of photography. The women stood well back, away from the camera, as though it might explode. I watched the instructor overcome their timidity, and indeed soon he was inviting each of the women to share with him under the black cloth an inverted view of the *grande allée* leading to the pond.

Recalled from this distraction by a tugging at the cuff of my trousers, I turned away from the photography lesson to find a white poodle busy at work on my left leg. The moment he stopped tugging at it, he started entwining his forepaws tightly around my calf, mistaking me for one of his own kind.

"*Viens ici! Dépêche-toi!*" This was the voice of the dog's owner, I presumed, as I tried to shake off this unwelcome attention.

"Get down, dog. You need glasses if you think I'm a bitch! Get away from me!" The dog continued in spite of my turning and shaking.

"*Madame, ce chien manque de politesse,*" I said. "*C'est pas poli de faire comme ça,*" I added, in what I hoped translated into a tone of rebuke in French.

"Basket! Get down!" she said. "Basket, come here at once!" By now I could see that the owner was a thin, tiny woman with an olive complexion and a forbidding countenance. I pulled the dog off me and picked him up. He was a well-fed mutt and heavy.

"Madam, your dog," I said, dropping into English and feeling abashed at my outburst in a language in which I did not believe I would be understood.

"Basket, you naughty, naughty dog!" she said. She did not look up at me. I was by now feeling doubly ruffled. The dog had abused me and now I was being cut by its owner for my outburst. The woman kept her dark, rather Spanish eyes on her dog, petting and embracing him. After a few moments of this, she stood up again.

"*Monsieur,*" she said in French, although she had heard my English, "*Je suis vraiment désolée. Viens, Basket, nous sommes déja en retard,*" she said with little feeling. I was glad to hear that she valued her time as I tried to deal with the curtness of her apology. By the time I had brushed off my trousers, the dog, who was really a very clean dog, had had a leash attached to his collar and was hurrying away down the *grande allée* pulling his mistress behind him. I watched them until they began a turn around the pond. Maybe I could write something about them, too, I thought.

I left the park through the gates leading into the Place Edmond Rostand and found an empty table in a café. I sat down and surveyed the damage to my trousers. It was visible, but required no immediate attention. Thinking about that odd woman with her dog, I ordered a *demi*. I thought of her foreign-looking face, then laughed to myself at my audacity: here I was, a displaced Canadian sitting in a Paris café, daring to call people foreign.

I finished the beer and ordered another, passing the time with a discarded copy of *Le Matin*. When I looked up from time to time, the green-and-cream-coloured streetcars were still skirting the statue in the middle of the square. I settled into an account of a meeting held the previous night to protest the lack of progress being made in the hunt for the killer of six unaccompanied young women in the Montparnasse area, for the most part within the last thirteen weeks. *Monsieur le Préfet de police* was having a hard time both with the press and with groups of angry citizens demanding immediate action. He announced both that he was exploring every lead, questioning several suspects, and that he had nothing to announce at the moment. He said that he expected an early break in the case. The paper did not report whether any of his fingers were crossed when he said this. The Prefect is a political appointee, required to be more of a politician than a policeman. But Paris is more tightly controlled than a North American city: the concierges report unusual comings and goings; hotel-keepers report all changes in residence; informers ply a profitable trade in the cafés on both sides of the river. The *terrasse* of La Rotonde was said to be alive with police informers. Nevertheless, it remained the "political" café of the Quarter, where revolutions were being plotted from dawn till well after midnight. That was to be expected.

Having finished with the news, I turned the paper over to the back page, where I found the usual puzzle: two apparently identical drawings, but with seven subtle differences which I began trying to find. Working through *Les sept erreurs* had become an important part of my day, a reward I gave myself for reading through the business pages and editorials. I had begun to notice myself setting up small rewards for completing unpleasant tasks. Was it a sign of my uprooted condition? Should I try to seek out my drinking friends again? Would that hold back the insidious creep of middle age over my bones? I didn't know, nor did I get a chance to think about it further, because, just then, as I'd located the third error, the shape of Hal Leopold came between me and the sun.

"May I sit down?" he asked, in the act of doing so.

"Sure. How are you?"

"I want to get out of this town," he said.

"From what I saw of it the other night, you lead a complex life. How's the Countess?"

"I haven't seen her. I hear she's been sick. She drinks too much. That's her trouble."

"She had a rotten war."

"She wears it like a badge."

"It killed her husband, isn't that enough?"

"It didn't kill him, Mike, it turned him into a drunk, a dangerous drunk. She had to get out of that."

"And why do you want to get away from Paris? Seems like a grand place from what I've seen this last month and a half."

"You don't understand the way it can close in on you. Too many people want a permanent place in my life. I just want to be free of that. Ever since my book came out, people are after me. Everybody's standing with his hand out. Everybody wants me to help start a magazine, or find a new place to stay, or lend enough to buy clothes, or paint, or canvas. It never ends. And it's not just women. They're harder to get rid of, that's all."

"Have you seen any of the gang from the Dingo?"

"Not since I last saw you. Nothing decent ever happens to me in the Dingo. Have you seen Wad?"

"No, but I've been thinking about him, trying to figure him out."

"Aw, Mike, he's just a bully. Has to be a tough guy. And he's a braggart, too. He hasn't done half the things he says he has."

"Oh, I'm catching on to that. I'm trying to think why he does it."

"He keeps saying I was the middleweight boxing

champion of the Princeton boxing team when there isn't a Princeton boxing team. He'll say it until it becomes the truth."

"What kind of war did he have?"

"He got blown up in Italy on the Austrian Front. You've seen his legs on the courts. He's not making that up."

"Why'd he tell me he was a boxer from Chicago's North Side? Why'd he put on this story about living in hobo jungles, riding the rods and getting pitched off freight trains? We both come from the same sort of middle-class home. Both our fathers are doctors. It doesn't make sense."

"It took me a while to find out he came from Oak Park. He tries that out on everybody. Wants to wash those tree-lined streets and big houses out of his system. He's always making changes. Hash is going to be next, if he gets his courage up."

"Hash?"

"Sure. He's trying to leave her."

"But she's a wonderful woman! And there's Snick! He couldn't leave them. And who'd he leave 'em for? The Countess? Julia? I don't follow your thinking, Hal."

"He hasn't been able to love Hash since she lost his manuscripts. Wad doesn't know how to forgive people. He just strikes them off his list."

"You must be sore at him to say a thing like that. This is something between the two of you." Leopold stared at me, smiling at my thick-headedness. "Leave Hash, indeed! Hash isn't people, she's his wife. She does everything for him. She even puts up with that harem he runs around with. Not many women would tolerate that. He'd never leave her."

"Open up your eyes, Mike. It's the way he is. Those stories meant the world to him. Over two years of solid work! And she lost all of it."

"I heard something about that from Stella Burdock a few weeks ago. What actually happened?"

"Wad was covering a peace conference at Lausanne for the International News Service and the Universal Service, for Hearst."

"I thought he was working for the Toronto *Star*? I know he was a *Star* correspondent."

"I don't know about that, but I'm sure he was working for the two Hearst agencies. Maybe he was double-crossing his Toronto employers. It wouldn't be the first time. Maybe he gambled that the Toronto people never saw an American paper? Who knows? Anyway, Hash and Wad were supposed to have gone to Lausanne together, but Hash had a bad cold and was sick in bed when he had to leave. When she recovered, she thought it would be a good idea to take the stories he'd been working on with her. Trouble was, she brought *everything*. Roughs, carbons, early drafts, notes, *everything*. It was just a few days before Christmas in 1922. The Gare de Lyon was busy with people leaving on holiday. After she got her things installed in a compartment, she went out for a paper, according to Wad, or to check to see whether the valise with their winter clothes was being loaded into the baggage car, according to Hash. Anyway, when she got back, the suitcase with the manuscripts in it was gone. Before the train had even left the station."

"Every writer's nightmare!" I said, thinking of my own stories.

"Wad won't say exactly what was inside the suitcase. It may have been stories and poems. It may have been a big part of a novel. He says he never talks about casualties."

"He may not talk about them, but, from what you say, he never forgets about them either. Didn't Carlyle have to rewrite the first volume of *The French Revolution* when it got burned by accident?"

"You got me there. I only know that Wad is actively and at times not very subtly scouting about for Hash's successor. He may not even *know* he's doing it, but he is."

"You think it's Julia Lowry?"

Hal smiled across at me, then shrugged. "He's been seen with Lady Biz and Laure Duclos as well. Take your pick."

"It won't be Biz; she doesn't have any money. Wad may like the lady's title, but that will disappear in the divorce court. Julia's a better bet."

"Now you're talking. She's rich as Croesus. Or at least her uncle is. She could support him until his writing catches on. She's thick with that crowd down on the Riviera, too. Once he's in with them he won't have to double-cross editors anymore. He'll never have to work again, except at his stories."

"And Laure?" I was interested in Hal's assessment of Laure for my own reasons.

"Not sure about her. People are afraid of her. Nobody has the nerve to tell her to shove off," Hal said. "She lived with Tolstoi for a long time, and there were others before and after him. Her father was shot as a French traitor during the war. Did you know that?"

"I'd heard that he was dead. That's all," I lied.

"Laure's a major source of the gossip you hear around the Quarter. Some of it is hare-brained. She once said that Waddington was going to run off with Gertrude Stein."

"I didn't even know they knew one another. He's never mentioned her to me."

"Wad likes to keep his friends in separate pens. He doesn't like them to know one another unless it's through him. He likes to be in control. Gertrude has been a big help to him in his writing. That's what Wad used to say. I haven't heard that lately. It irks him to admit a debt."

"What's that supposed to mean?" I asked, jumping to the defence of my friend.

"There was a time when Wad had a good word to say for all of the people who'd either helped him or given him some good models: Sherwood Anderson, Ring Lardner and Miss Stein. But not nowadays. He is less than generous, Mike. I've heard him go out of his way to slam Lardner and Anderson. He heard about Spain from Miss Stein and McAlmon; now you'd think he thought the place up all by himself."

"You have to crawl out from behind your influences."

"Is that it? Maybe."

"Speaking of Spain, what went on down there this summer? What happened?"

Hal ran a knuckle around the edge of his mouth before answering. "I'm not the one to tell you about it, Mike. I had a rotten time and ended up . . . You ask Wad about it. I'm still too mad to talk about it."

"Does it have anything to do with Biz?"

"Goddamn it, it has everything to do with dear Lady Biz. I'll tell you that for nothing!"

"And this book of Wad's?"

"It'd better be barroom talk, Mike. It damn well better be like the rest of Waddington's lies. If he's telling the truth for once, he's stirring up a hive of wasps."

I asked Hal to join me for a drink and then dinner, but he said that he had to meet someone at the Crillon in less than two hours. I was beginning to love it the way the Quarter was a playground for some people; they put on their old clothes here, drank cheap draft beer and made jottings in blue notebooks in cafés. Then they got dressed up and spent a fortune at the bar of the Ritz or Crillon. I thought about that while we each paid our share to redeem the saucers on the table. Hal was quiet. Was he brooding over what had happened in Spain? Or was it Wad and his novel? When we parted, he could spare only a limp handshake and a courteous inclination of his head.

I watched him walk across the square, in his compact, self-possessed way, thinking that I'd follow him across the river to see what distraction I could find in Place Pigalle. A sudden thought of Laure Duclos held me back. My fingers were almost tingling at the image of her. It was too early to begin searching for her in Montparnasse. Later on, I would have more luck. It was perhaps silly of me, but I needed to talk to her. Anyway, it made more sense than following Hal Leopold across the Seine.

CHAPTER 8

That night, I saw Joyce at Michaud's. He was sitting there with his family, looking like a rather shabby dandy, with a velvet jacket and a brocaded waistcoat. A monocle was attached to a watch fob by a thin black ribbon. He quizzed the waiter about the menu as though he were a police inspector questioning a suspect at the commissariat opposite St-Sulpice, all the while letting his fingers play arpeggios on his ash-plant walking stick as though it were a knobbly peasant's flute. His son, Giorgio, sat across from him, dressed like a junior banker. Giorgio's sister was ignoring the men and deeply engaged in a dispute with Nora, her handsome mother, whose fine, dark hair framed her face. When the waiter had retired to the kitchen with the order, Joyce began drumming on the table with his many-ringed fingers, obviously quite happy with the selections he had made. I felt peculiar taking my eyes off such objects to look at the menu and make my own decisions about dinner.

When I looked across at the Joyces a few minutes later, there were tall, green bottles on the table, as well as a new face across from the writer. Giorgio had been displaced by a long, stoop-shouldered man with a craggy face and a red beard. Nora Joyce was lecturing him, and, from the look on his face, he couldn't wait for her to stop; he hadn't come here to listen to Mrs. James Joyce. In the end, Joyce himself interrupted so that the redheaded Bohemian was able to get his oar in. I call him a Bohemian because he wore no necktie or cravat of any kind and the trousers of his suit didn't match the double-breasted jacket he was wearing. I wrote him off as a painter. The Quarter was full of them, famous for them in fact, although they didn't often find their way to Michaud's. Since the death a couple of years ago of Modigliani, painters had made Chez Rosalie on the rue Campagne-Première a holy shrine. Others hung about the small restaurants near the studios on the Grande-Chaumière, where horsemeat steaks could be bought at reasonable prices. Whoever this painter was, he was speaking English with an American accent. His talk was animated and could be heard across the room.

"Listen, Jimmy, Mussolini ain't as *noir* as he's been limned. Come on down to Rapallo; see for yourself. I'm livin' in a cookie jar, Jim, goin' like sixty and hittin' on all six cylinders." He spoke as Huckleberry Finn himself might have spoken. The spirit of Mark Twain was perhaps riding on his shoulder. I leaned closer when my soup plate had been removed.

"Hell, I'm damned sorry about the studio. I thought we could get the tenant out. She was subletting from me, damn it! I didn't know she was going to take in a Worthy Oriental Gentleman, did I? But she won't be budged. She's still got my traps in it, furniture I made myself. *Maledictione*! as Verdi says. Still, I'm glad I came back to see if I could help. She's four times as stubborn as the froggywogs. These damned Americans should stay at the George V."

Giorgio Joyce moved his chair beyond the reach of the speaker's demonstrative arm, after being clipped in the ear with a soup spoon. I tried to imagine who might be insensitive enough to harangue the author of *Ulysses* in this gauche manner. He had interrupted Joyce several times, correcting him and scolding! It couldn't have been more disrespectful. As soon as the word "disrespectful" passed through my head, I suddenly knew the identity of the unruly American. It was Ezra Pound, the *avant-garde* poet and editor. He had recently moved off to Italy, Wad had told me, leaving a studio flat on Notre-Dame-des-Champs, the same street he lived on.

"I finally got the lowdown on those la-dee-daw Greeks, Jim. Catullus is the key to the whole doggamn thing. He had it all figured out. Best modern brain of antiquity, saving your reverence."

Later, Joyce was speaking quietly to Pound, whose head was wagging like a redheaded terrier's and with the same awkwardness as a growing pup. Joyce, on the other hand, was speaking in a steady, low voice I couldn't catch. He looked like a bishop reprimanding a fallen woman. A monsignor at the very least. And all the while, his rings flashed as he moved his long fingers up and down his walking stick. There was something almost evil about his intensity. At that moment he looked capable of burning Joan of Arc. Then he spoiled it with a joke, for they began to fall about one another laughing. Although he had said relatively little, it was plain to see that Pound was impressed. The Ten Commandments of the new age might have been dictated during this short talk. Meanwhile Joyce's daughter began complaining in Italian about her *pommes pailles*, which she declined to either eat or translate. I continued to eat a nice *côte rôtie* along with a bottle of Hermitage Belle Roche. Across from me, the conversation was taken up by the younger generation, and I concentrated on Monsieur Raulo's cooking.

Later, after the table across from me had been taken by some journalists who had the idea of eating hors-d'oeuvre and drinking, I thanked Monsieur Raulo and paid my bill. He had been a war hero and was proudly wearing the rosettes on his lapel that represented his two medals. Most of the time they were hidden under the bib of his apron. On leaving Michaud's, I walked down rue des Saints-Pères to the river. The dark shape of the Louvre lay on the far shore. As I walked along the quay, keeping the closed green boxes of the book and map vendors to my left, I passed Sommeliers, the dealer in artists' supplies, and the dome of the Institute. I buttoned up my jacket and turned up the collar as the squat mass of Notre Dame appeared to the right of the Palais de Justice. I thought of taking a walk on the island but turned away, moving instead up the rue des Grands-Augustins, across the boulevard and up the rue de Tournon to the high ground where Vaugirard skirts the Luxembourg Gardens. It was too late to cross the park, so I kept to Vaugirard until I hit familiar territory. The cafés on Montparnasse were bright under the electric lights. Vaguely, I was looking over the faces on the *terrasses* for one I knew. Keeping away from the cafés had been good for my liver, but I was beginning to feel the need for bad company.

I searched all of the usual places: the Rotonde, with its squabbling Norwegians and Russians, the Select and the Dôme. There I found familiar faces and some hands waving me to join them, but I didn't see the object of my quest. I walked past the lumber yard on the south side of the boulevard and turned into the rue Montparnasse, where I went into a few of the bars I knew. I spent half an hour at The Jockey, drinking expensive beer and listening to Kiki sing one of her incomparably dirty songs while whipping her skirts about her and lifting them provocatively. Before I went into The Jockey, I had wanted to find Laure. Now I needed to.

I found her at last at the place where I should have started. She was sitting in the Dingo with Cyril Burdock.

"Ah, Ward," he said. "I've been on the look-out for you!" He moved his coat from the chair opposite their encampment on the banquette. "I must say I'm rather keen on the story at the bicycle races. Almost made me feel I was right there, old chap, and I'm not much of an athlete, you know. Ask Laure.- She'll tell you what a lazy-guts I am."

"Hello, Mike," said Laure, without returning my look. Her eyes were on the large form of her companion. In fact, she was leaning towards him with her left arm resting on the back of the banquette. I sat down, trying to recall whether I'd been asked. I was looking forward to a *fine à l'eau*. I hadn't known that I wanted one, and then I needed it rather a lot.

"Tell me what a lazy-guts Mr. Burdock is, Laure," I said.

"He's hunting for insults, poor lamb. He's worse than a woman looking for compliments, aren't you, you funny man?"

"I protest I'm innocent of all guile where you're concerned, my dear." He looked at her in a way I hadn't seen since I saw the villain in *The Drunkard* rub his hands together. But perhaps I was an unreliable witness.

"You must make a habit of dropping around to our rooms on the island, my dear chap. We have stimulating talk, and sometimes other stimulants. We have a merry old time, no holds barred."

"I'll remember that."

"We can go over your story. There are just a few things I'd like to talk to you about. Trifles, bagatelles."

"I'd be honoured to have Conrad's collaborator take an interest in my little story." I could see the chilly effect of what I was saying as it hit the table. I didn't seem to have any control over what I said. I was glad when the *fine* arrived. I saluted both of them over my glass and drank off most of the contents.

Laure was wearing a cloche hat and a cloth coat with a fur collar draped over her nearly bare shoulders. She was smoking one cigarette after the other in a long holder. Her long arms were white in the smoky haze that hung in the room about eye-level.

"You haven't been in the bar for a few weeks, have you?" At least she was going to give me hell. That's better than nothing.

"I've settled into French life so successfully I've even developed a bad liver. Can a foreigner do more?"

"An impressive tribute, to be sure," Laure said. "I've missed seeing your face."

"Among so many others? You flatter me. Dare I ask why?"

"Ah, Mike! Always so . . . so serious. You should get yourself a girl, you know."

"I thought I had one. I was reasonably sure."

"In this town, Mike, you can never really be sure. People change. Moods change. The moment passes."

"And I suppose that that moment won't be along again, like the number 91 tram?"

"Dear Mike, I wouldn't count on it. But there will be others. Not the same, but others. You won't have any trouble. Believe me. Meanwhile, one tries not to be boring."

"Thank you for this solicitude, Laure. It's really more than I deserve."

"I say, Ward, you haven't started writing a novel, have you?" Burdock wasn't trying to change the subject. He seemed mystified by what had passed between us and was simply trying to move the ball back into play. "You don't have to answer that, dear boy. I'm just casting about, you know. Though if you have one, you should talk to me or

Bill Bird about it. Unless you have your own Canadian connections."

It was only a few minutes after that that I put some money on the table and left. Outside, in the rue Delambre, the air felt cold and sharp in my lungs. I walked home to the rue Bonaparte kicking at pebbles and stones that lay in the way of my feet. I kept one stone rolling ahead of me for at least three long blocks.

I was just about to ring the bell when I knew it would be wrong to go in without putting up more of a fight. I had no desire to face my bed in this mood. I walked into St-Germain-des-Prés to the taxi rank, went to the *tête de station* and took the first car. I gave the driver the address and listened to him on the subject of what the Communists and Jews were doing to France. I was too tired to give him an argument, but it got me thinking about poor Hal Leopold again. Although he was doing a good deal of damage to himself, I couldn't see that France was in any danger from him.

When I got to the passage de Dantzig, I paid the driver and gave him the minimum for his service. He then reminded me of the night tariff, which I'd neglected. I left the cab in a temper, then found the café where Laure and I had had a silent breakfast and went in. Two men with caps on their heads and elbows heavily placed on the zinc bar looked over at me. The proprietor dusted crumbs from the table near the window as I pulled up a chair. The men were drinking a pale-green drink to which they added water: Pernod, perhaps, or a cheaper stand-in. I had nothing to read with me, so I took out a scrap of paper and began writing down a list of things that I wanted to accomplish during the next month or so. At intervals, I looked out into the street to see whether Laure was returning to her room. I consulted my pocket-watch and concluded that it was still early enough that she hadn't reached home before me.

I ordered a *demi* and immediately regretted it. It was too cold for drinking beer. It stuck in my throat, and I was reduced to sipping it. The *patron* joined the two men, talking with them in low voices from his side of the bar. He poured himself a glass of what the others were drinking. The light in the café was bright enough so that I would have trouble seeing anyone walking along the far side of the street, except where he or she passed under one of the arc lamps. Sitting by the window, there was a pool of light that gave me a respectable chance of catching Laure, even out of the corner of my eye.

It was a long half-hour. I'd corrected my first choice of a beverage, amending it to red wine, which went down more easily. The *patron* and the two men at the bar continued to talk. I caught the gist of what they were saying. One was accusing the young son of Charles of the Ritz with having escaped to America to avoid the war. The *patron* insisted that there was no harm in that since the young man had completed his military service first. The third voice tended to side first with the *patron* and then with his friend about whether the lad had betrayed his country or not. My interest in following this died suddenly when I caught a shadow moving through the pool of light outside my window. I'd already prepared for the necessity of a quick leave-taking; my money was already on the table when I walked quickly out into the street.

"Laure!" I called. I repeated it before she turned.

"Hello Mike. What are you doing here?"

"There was a party at La Ruche," I lied.

"That's all it is over there: one long, boring party."

"I want to talk to you, Laure."

"Now, look at me, Mike. I hope that you aren't getting foolish notions about me?" She had taken hold of the sleeve of my coat. I wanted to hold her close to me and let that be my argument, but she kept her arm stiff, as though preventing my pulling her to me was her reason for taking my arm.

"I live a hell of a mixed-up life, Mike. You don't know anything about me. It's disgusting, really, and I'm disgusted with it myself. But what can I do about it? I have no will to change anything. I'm exhausted just making myself presentable. You want to keep clear of me."

"Can't we go somewhere and talk? Can I come up?"

"No, dear Mike. The best advice I can give you is to find yourself a girl."

"I thought you were my girl."

"Really? That's absurd!" She repeated what I'd said and started to laugh. I couldn't stand that.

"Stop it! Laure, be reasonable!" She released her grip on my arm and started to back away from me. She nearly collided with the two men from the café, who had obviously called it a night. She began moving to her door.

"Laure, you have to talk to me. You can't just break the connection."

"There is no connection! Now you are beginning to bore me. Stop following me and go home and soak your head." She had her room key in her hand and I went to her to help with the door, but she pulled the cordon herself.

"Get away from me!" She screamed this and pushed me away from her.

"I was only . . ." The door opened and she had fled behind it. I ran to the door, but it had closed and locked behind her. I banged on the door with my fists, more to expel the anger that had been building up within me than to bring her running back to let me in. When I turned, I couldn't avoid the looks of the two men from the café. They said nothing to me, but their remarks to one another were neither friendly nor anything that I could argue with without getting pushed into the gutter with a broken nose.

I turned my back on them and walked past the now dark café in the direction of La Ruche, where I found an all-night party in one of the studios. I don't remember much about it. Pascin was there, and so was Foujita, who was still wearing the remnants of fancy dress. His face was heavily rouged, but there was nothing in the least effeminate about his play with two beautiful women, who looked like sisters. There was a cask of wine in the middle of the floor with a paint can under the bung to catch the drips. I found a discarded glass and began drinking in earnest.

A grey day was just beginning when I found myself on a cot with one of the sisters. I have no recollection of how she got there. I disengaged myself and steered a course around the sleeping bodies scattered on the floor. Foujita had passed out in the model's chair on a rostrum in the middle of the studio. Pascin had pulled his hat over his eyes before falling asleep. Apart from the sounds of slow breathing and the odd snore, the room was remarkably quiet. Far off, I could hear bells that reminded me of the countryside. I left the studio door open as I found it.

On the ground floor, not far from the ornate entrance, which had been part of the 1900 Paris Exposition, I heard a gentle moaning in another of the studios. I looked in. Here were the left-overs from another party, or so it looked at first, for there again were bodies lying on straw-filled pallets. There was a sticky, heavy odour that hung about the room. Had they been smoking hashish, I wondered? On a wooden chest that was being used as a table, I found a long-stemmed pipe with an alcohol lamp covered with a glass chimney. Open near it was a tin of what looked like paste. I sniffed and knew at once what it was.

A figure in a dark corner groaned. Would she be wanting another sniff of the poppy? I turned to leave as quietly as I could, but before I'd reached the door she called out to me.

"Mike, oh my little sweet woolly lamb!" It was Laure, who was half-staggering to her feet. Her hair was falling loose around her shoulders. "Be a dear, Mike, and help me back to my room," she said.

Without a glance at the figure of the man who had had his arm around Laure's waist when I first saw her, she accepted my arm, and we went out into the early morning light together. A parade of goats was coming down the passage de Dantzig as we crossed the street.

She walked up the stairs more lightly than I would have expected. I found her key and helped her into the untidy room. Laure sat on the edge of the bed, watching me try to return the key to her bag.

"You may give that to me, Mike," she said in a heavy voice. I handed it over, but her outstretched arm fell as she failed to grip it. She rolled her head back on her neck, as though to balance it more easily. "You'd better get out of here," she said without emotion. I picked up the key from the floor.

"Are you ——?"

"Just get out, Mike! Leave me alone! *Va te faire fiche!*"

For a moment she looked as though she was going to fall off the bed. Instead, she got up, stood close and raked her fingers over my face. I felt the burn of her nails and sat her down roughly on the bed.

"Will you leave me alone now?" she said, leaning on one arm for support.

"I'm going, Laure. I just hope you'll be all right."

"Go away!" she said, taking off a shoe and throwing it at me. "Just go!" she said, throwing its mate. She was reaching for a book on her night table to shy at me next as I closed the door behind me.

There were no further sounds of goats or of goat bells in the passage de Dantzig as I returned to the street.

CHAPTER 9

Again I tried to stay away from Montparnasse. I went to see a play at the Comédie Française and didn't like it; I went to see Josephine Baker's "Revue Nègre" and even followed one of the performers back to the Hôtel Istria, where the troupe was staying. I liked Josephine Baker a lot, but so did all of Paris. Most evenings, I stayed in my room and worked on stories. I didn't have it right, not by a long chalk, but working regularly was making it better. Wad had told me that and now I believed him.

The Rotonde was one of the handsomest cafés in the Quarter, but hardly any of the people I knew frequented it. Maybe that's why I chose it that night in late October. I looked around me to see if the paid police informers were easily recognizable. Were they all reading copies of *L'Action Française*, the right-wing newspaper? There were certainly lots of copies of *L'Humanité* in evidence, but I wasn't surprised to see a communist paper in this setting of conspiring would-be revolutionaries. If I were a stool-pigeon for the police, I would see to it that I carried *L'Humanité*. In that setting it would be an asset. However, even the newspapers didn't help. I couldn't tell the *mouchards* from the regular customers.

I drank off my *fine* too quickly. I had not learned the fine art of timing a solitary drink. In the winter, I'd heard, one drink, especially an expensive one, buys a lot of sitting time. During the hot summer days when the *terrasses* are full and tourists are as thick as pigeons around a statue, the clock on one's sitting time runs more quickly. I brought out a page of something I'd been writing and looked it over. It was very depressing, a description of my encounter in the Luxembourg with the swarthy lady and her poodle. Had I been successful in describing her fussy, correct manner, her studied insolence at my rebuke of the dog? Maybe it required a greater subtlety than I could manage.

Across the boulevard, I thought I glimpsed a familiar figure just as the view was cut off by a streetcar. After the cream-and-green tram had moved, I could see Laure Duclos just entering the Café du Dôme on the corner opposite. Quickly I paid my bill and crossed the road to join her, hoping that she might have forgotten our last meeting. Perhaps I should have questioned my precipitousness, especially when I saw Laure speak to the waiter, who then consulted his pocket-watch. But the sight of the woman who had been on my mind did away with good sense.

Laure gave me a wary smile as I came towards her through the nests of tables and chairs. It was caution bordering on alarm, but she gave me her hand. "I hope you're not expecting anybody?" I asked, hoping to be asked to sit down. Laure was looking wonderfully well. She was wearing a dark coat with a white fur collar and cuffs. Her lips and eyes had been made up as carefully as her fingernails, which glistened as she drew back her hand. Her navy-blue frock, with a small white tie at her throat, reached down to her knees. There were silver buckles on her high-heeled shoes.

"It's very boring, Mike, but the bald fact is that I *am* meeting someone. But why don't you buy us a quick drink, poor lamb, after the way I've treated you. I'm a quarter of an hour early. I need a witness. It's never been said that I'm the promptest woman in the Quarter."

I sat down and pulled the chair close. Our knees were almost touching under the table. Laure flagged down the waiter and we both ordered: she a *vin blanc* and I a local beer. Considering Laure across from me now, indifferent, smiling, but, within reason, friendly, it was easier to see her as the *femme fatale* of the stories I'd been hearing. At that moment, she'd decided to be irrelevant and teasing, but impersonal. I wished she would stop moving her finger from the tip of her chin to the top of the tie. I wanted to tell her to stop, but even in my state I recognized that the problem was mine and not hers.

Laure talked about a book-signing she had just come from. Cocteau had been there with his following from the Boeuf sur le Toit, his regular place of permanent exhibition. She was quite wickedly delightful in her descriptions of the fuss they had made. "He's quite out of mourning for Radiguet now. He has even shed his black armband. Until recently, he dressed like a mortician. Cocteau in mourning could out-Hamlet Hamlet."

She listened to what I told her about my life, which I tried to dramatize with what cunning I possessed, but her eyes made a regular survey of the passing throng on the sidewalk. She asked me about Waddington and the rest of that flock, none of whom I'd seen. "Everybody is reading Wilson O'Donnell's new book," she said. For a few minutes we discussed O'Donnell and his work. Luckily, I'd been given a copy of the novel by a colleague from the *Star* to read on the boat. O'Donnell was one of my favourite writers. In the papers they called him "the Father of the Jazz Age," as though he had discovered a way of burning his candle even faster than Miss Millay. Of all the writers I knew, his seemed to be the most accurate voice of a generation that had come home from the battlefields, damaged and exhausted.

Laure had that French intensity when she spoke. O'Donnell seemed very real as she discussed him. She had read the novel with an eye far more acute than my own, but I could imagine her discussing the proper tearing of lettuce with the same grave face. The French people I'd met treated all subjects with an equal seriousness. The location of a street not found on my map occupied an interrupted pedestrian as fully as a discussion of the sinking value of the franc or the talk of German rearmament schemes. I didn't think that Laure was an intellectual, by any means, but she had acquired the intellectual method.

It was starting to rain again, not heavily, but what in England would be called a Scotch mist. Out of it came four or five art students in bright costumes. They were in high spirits as they began to bedeck the customers with a fine gold confetti while they passed out leaflets. They missed me but caught Laure with a near-direct hit. She looked like a statue cast in gold. It was quite a wonderful moment. The gold clung to her forehead and clothes in an extraordinary way, as though Zeus himself had taken a sudden interest in Laure and had cleverly beaten my time with her in yet another of his ingenious ways. Laure touched the gold on her arm. It was a powder rather than paper, as I first had thought: gold-dust or the dry making of gold paint. Perhaps it had come from a picture-framer's supply of gilt. The gold came off in her fingers and she touched my forehead with it.

"Here's something for you, Mike. Let me share my sudden wealth."

"*Allez-vous-en! Allez-vous-en!*" It was Père Chambon, the proprietor of the café, shouting to the young people at the top of his guttural voice. He came after them, his moustaches terrible, his bald pate shining under the electric light. Two waiters gathered up the students at the other end of the enclosed *terrasse* and ejected them into the night and the fine rain. As they passed our window, we could see that their spirits weren't in the least dampened, either by their reception in the café or by the weather.

"Poor dears," said Laure, watching them cross the boulevard to the Rotonde. "They'll get a worse reception there."

Paul Chambon hurried over to our table and to those of others who had been dusted by the students. He picked up fallen leaflets advertising the sale of students' works at the Ecole des Beaux-Arts, panting as he got to his feet and holding his back. "Last year a woman got some of that in her eyes!" he said trying to catch his breath. "And who do you think had to pay the hospital bills, eh?"

Laure wiped the gold flecks from her face with a handkerchief. As she looked at the metallic stain, she saw that I was watching her and for a moment returned my look.

"Poor lamb, you've got it bad, haven't you?" She took my hand in one of her gilded hands. "I'm sorry I'm such a raffish bitch. Really, I am. You're far better off to be shut of me."

"I'm sure you're right," I said, looking her in the eye. It took all my strength, but I even smiled.

At the end of ten minutes, I paid for the drinks and took my leave. She bussed me on both cheeks in the French manner and we parted. I concentrated on what I had heard about her from the others. I was going to take her advice and get myself a girl of my own. But in the meantime, I was still curious about the identity of the lucky dog who was meeting her. After walking along the boulevard for a few hundred yards, I crossed over to the other side and found another table under the marquee of the Rotonde. This time I ordered whisky with a siphon. But the thought of discovering who it was that Laure had planned to meet proved to be more warming than the drink.

After about ten minutes, Jason Waddington crossed Montparnasse, coming from the direction of the *gare*. He had started crossing before he'd reached the *terrasse* of Le Select. A number 91 tram coming from Port Royal, marked "Montparnasse-Bastille," interrupted his crossing. Wad stood back from the tracks, letting the car nearly touch him. It was an imitation of a bullfighter allowing the horns to get as close to him as his suit of lights. The arc lamps picked out the pass and the streetcar continued out of sight down the boulevard. Wad went by the Dôme without going in. He crossed to the display of *fruits de mer*, sitting on a bed of kelp, outside a restaurant on the far corner, then retraced his steps, this time going up to Laure's table and joining her.

There was something rather formal about their greeting, as far as I could judge. There was certainly no bussing, just a conventional shaking of hands. The waiter brought them something to drink and they talked, leaning towards one another for five minutes. Laure brought a piece of paper from her purse and showed it to Wad, who half stood up when he saw it. He took it in both hands and read it. In a moment, he let his hand drop. Laure reached for the paper, with Wad for a moment unwilling to return it. In the end he held it out to her, and Laure returned it to her bag. They talked for another ten minutes, then Laure got up and left the café, walking off in the direction of the Dingo, up the rue Delambre and out of sight.

Wad sat for another minute, then reached into his pocket to pull out enough money to cover their drinks and the *service non compris*. He looked as if he were trying to catch up with Laure as he rounded the wedge-shaped end of the Dôme and headed up Delambre. Something was going on, and my curiosity was such that I redeemed my saucers immediately and crossed the street.

The usual haunts along the rue Delambre were crowded and smoky. The din and subdued lighting made a sharp contrast to what was going on out of doors. I saw Arlette and Anson in the Dingo and Biz and George in the place around the corner. They tried to get me to join them, but I hurried on as soon as it was clear that neither Laure nor Wad was present. When I came out again into the night air, I was out of breath. Why was I running after them? What did I hope to discover?

After another short block, I slowed down. The silliness of my chase had become evident. I turned around and cut across the street. I had never liked the back streets behind Montparnasse. The cemetery along boulevard Edgar Quinet bothered me. Above the high walls, leafless black branches clawed at the sky. I thought of Baudelaire buried on the other side of the wall and hurried on. Rounding a corner that I hoped would return me to the boulevard, I passed a rundown café with tables full of scruffy artists, one of whom was in the act of pocketing sugar as I moved beyond the yellow light and tobacco smoke.

Montparnasse was looking friendly and bright from the glimpse I had of it half-way up rue Campagne-Première. A streetcar silently crossed the top of the street. When I reached the corner, I turned back in the direction of the Dôme. There was a dark stretch to cross before I would come into the full illumination of the *carrefour*. Perhaps my eyes were already adapting to the stronger light, because they spotted something bright in the gutter. For a moment my feet failed to stop, and I nearly fell. Catching my balance, I went back to see what could have had such power over my progress. It was a woman's handbag, made of soft leather and held together by a bright metal rim with fasteners at the top. I picked it up and brushed away the rain and dirt from the underside. I felt like an imbecile holding onto a woman's handbag, but then, I was on Montparnasse, where these things are not perhaps as strange as elsewhere. I moved back in the direction from which I'd come, stopping under the street lamp. My fingers clicked the bag open; I began to rummage through it to see if there was a name and address to help the police find the owner. I found a rather good fountain pen and a lace handkerchief. Under a silver cigarette case, I discovered a postcard with the following name and address:

Mlle. Laure Duclos
14, rue de Tilsitt
Paris, 17^e

The message from the Côte d'Azur was friendly, with some Mack Sennett bathing beauties on the other side. It was signed *Françoise*. I decided that I had better find a place to sit down. My eyes stayed in the gutter as I moved towards the light. There lay cigarette ends, a twisted bicycle spoke and hub, a familiar broadsheet advertising a forthcoming Beaux-Arts sale of art and a discarded, broken umbrella.

CHAPTER 10

M ike, what the hell's the matter with you?"

"What?"

"I'm talking to you, that's what!"

"Sorry, Quent, I was wool-gathering."

I was having lunch at our usual little restaurant a few streets from the agency. Quentin Bryson, who worked with me, was staring at me from across the table. He'd been in Paris a year longer than I had and was drawing a larger salary. A serious fellow from Montreal, with an early bald spot growing through his fair hair, Quent could talk about nothing but the office until he had had three *demis*. Then the intimacies came in a torrent: his father, the brute; his mother, the brow-beaten victim; his wife, who did not understand him; his daughter, who had suddenly and suspiciously stopped hating this posting. He had a motor-car and, when he was not taking it apart and putting it together again, he motored up to Senlis with his wife and daughter. He had vaguely suggested on several occasions that an invitation to dinner was on its way, but it never arrived.

Wool-gathering, I had said. It was not strictly true. I had withstood a few shocks since I'd discovered Laure's purse in the gutter the night before. First and foremost, when I reached the office the next morning, I learned that Jack de Paris had been busy again overnight. His seventh victim had been discovered not far from the place where I'd

found Laure's handbag. It was with more than routine interest, then, that I'd pursued my inquiries at the commissariat
about the identity of the murdered woman.

"Mike! Damn it, there you go again!"

"Sorry, Quent," I said, digging into the last of my leek-
and-potato soup. "I was thinking about the murders."

Quent was cleaning up the last traces of soup from the
sides of his bowl. He was clean-shaven, tall and round-
shouldered. He was stooping now over his soup, as a mediaeval monk might have over an illuminated manuscript or
as he did at the office, over his Royal typewriter. He finally
put down his spoon with a clatter.

"You sent off all we know about the seventh killing
this morning. What's bothering you about it?"

"She was found in my own backyard, Quent. All of
them were. I use those streets every day. It's all right for
you out in St-Mandé."

"Charenton," he corrected. "Where was this one?"

"Rue Léopold Robert, a block away from the Dôme."

"Yeah, I see what you mean. They don't know her
name?"

"They may, but they wouldn't tell me. All I got from
the commissariat was this: 'When there is a statement to be
made, it will be made by Monsieur le Préfet.'"

"Wonderful!"

Our main courses had arrived and for awhile talking
was unnecessary. I couldn't share my anxiety over Laure
with Quentin. I'd been nearly incapable of doing my job all
morning. As soon as I read the report on my desk, I went to
the finger-marked wall map to check the location of the
street. It was the very intersection where I'd stumbled on
Laure's purse. Could her body have been there all the time?
Had it been lying in the deep shadows of the buildings
along that dark stretch of Montparnasse?

But it was more than I knew to say that the body belonged to Laure Duclos. There was even some question about whether the handbag I had found belonged to her. The name was right but the address was wrong. I looked up the rue de Tilsitt on the wall map. It was in the Étoile district, close to the Arc de Triomphe, a solidly middle-class area. It couldn't be Laure. For all I knew, Laure had finished her evening in her own bed in the passage de Dantzig. Or in another. But certainly not in the gutters of rue Léopold Robert.

One thing was sure, I had to find out quickly or there would be no sleep for me tonight. The quicker I could deliver the handbag over to its owner the better. And if, stretching the probabilities, just supposing, the murdered woman was Laure, then the sooner I sent the bag around to the authorities the better it would be for all concerned. I had been with Laure last night. Had I been seen? Was I now a suspect? All of this was premature. I should keep my speculations confined to the cheese tray which would follow my main course.

"What do you know about Jack the Ripper, Quent?"

"Not a great deal. He murdered prostitutes in London's East End in the late 1880s. He was said to be a surgeon gone wrong and at least as crazy as this killer here in Paris. But our man isn't trying to rid the world of whores; he's content to prey on artists' models for the most part. Both of them kept to a single district in their cities. Jack never struck outside Whitechapel, and our man is happy in Montparnasse.

"There have been all sorts of theories about Jack's identity. Some of them come close to the British royal family, and others are just as far-fetched. Someone named General Booth of the Salvation Army, if you can believe it! One murderer admitted to being Jack, but he didn't elaborate."

"What do you mean?"

"He was standing on the gallows at the time, and the hangman dropped him through before he could enlarge upon his theme."

"Not very helpful to the investigation. Do you think our Jack is mad?"

"As a hatter. Our man is closer to Jack than he is to another French killer, like Landru. Ah, that was before you arrived, Mike. He went to the national barber three years ago. They called him Bluebeard. He killed women all right, but all his cases involved some aspect of fraud. The murders were secondary. At his trial, Landru had everybody laughing, even while he refused to admit a single fact presented against him. You know how formal a French court of law is? Well, one day a woman came into the courtroom and couldn't find a seat. Landru got up politely and offered to let her have his seat in the prisoner's dock."

"Our man kills these women without having known them at all. The *flics* won't say whether or not they have been interfered with."

"Glad to see you've read the style book on reporting rape."

Mme. Bonnet came to our table with her inevitable tray of cheeses. As usual, the coffee filter on my cup refused to function until the water was so cold I had no further interest in it. Quentin watched me peeling an elderly piece of Camembert, which Madame explained had "abandoned itself." I was acquiring a taste for it, but I confess it still reminded me of the odour that lingers at the ends of third-class coaches on French trains.

We went back to the office for another three hours. I was working on several stories and wasn't happy with any of them. I couldn't concentrate. How should I have been able to do so, with Laure's leather bag lying where I had carelessly flung it on coming back to my room the night before?

Before leaving the office at the end of the day, I hefted the heavy Paris directory, the *Bottin*, to my desk. I checked 14, rue de Tilsitt. There was no one named Duclos listed. I telephoned one of Quentin's friends at the commissariat in the Étoile neighbourhood and asked if he had more recent information about the tenants at number 14 than was printed in the *Bottin*. This brought the second big surprise of the day. One of the apartments had been let to the American writer and novelist Wilson O'Donnell and his wife. Laure and I had just been talking about his new book! What would the King of the Jazz Age want with Laure Duclos? Was there a connection? If Laure knew O'Donnell personally, why hadn't she mentioned it? There were too many absurdities here to reflect upon. What on earth would a famous writer like O'Donnell have in common with Laure, or any of our friends on this side of the river? O'Donnell had made himself wealthy with his novels. We were all struggling around the bottom of the ladder he had climbed so easily.

I ran down the steps into the Métro at the Champs-Élysées, waited endlessly for the second train to come to the Châtelet station, then pushed against the crowd descending into the St-Germain-des-Prés station on my way out. On my way to my room, the concierge handed me some letters and postcards. I arranged with her to have a bath drawn; it was part of the bargain I'd made with her. She told me that she would knock on my door when it was ready. Once inside the room under the slate roof, I locked the door behind me and checked to see whether the bag was where I had left it. It was.

This time I opened it without the excuse that I was in search of a clue to the owner. There was a certain desperation in my fingers as I spread out the contents on the plain wooden table that served both as a wash-stand and a desk. I found my notebook and opened it to a fresh page. Here I listed:

1 handkerchief (gold flecks)	1 box matches
1 cigarette case (silver)	5,237.85 francs in bills and coins
1 postcard (Françoise)	1 compact with make-up
1 Parker pen	
1 notebook	1 identity card from Berlitz School
2 aspirins	
1 page of typewriting	1 pair kid gloves

I examined all of these things again: the postcard from Françoise with the Tilsitt address, the perfumed handkerchief with the gold flecks Laure had wiped from her face after the students had been chased from the Dôme, the expensive fountain pen and cigarette case and her gloves. Without looking further, I wondered how I could have raised a moment's doubt about the owner of the bag. Of course, it was the implication! In addition to these items that I recognized, a notebook, written in closely-packed French that I couldn't decipher, was no help to me. But a page, a yellowing page of newsprint paper, the same sort we use at the agency, attracted my attention. On it I read the following, in blurry, typewritten sentences:

> *They hanged the three whores in the marketplace*
> *after lunch. The fat one with the broken shoe*
> *hobbled up the steps and had to be held...*

The whole passage ran to under a dozen lines. It was centred on the page so that I was sure that this was the entire piece; there was no second page. It didn't seem to be part of anything, simply an isolated event written in stark, realistic terms as though by an eyewitness. As I refolded the paper, a bent corner fell off onto the table. In this condition, it could not have survived in Laure's purse for very long. Could this have been the piece of paper she showed Waddington at the Dôme?

As I stared at the list in my notebook and the short prose piece on the yellow newsprint, I became acutely aware of my position should I be discovered with this purse in my possession. I would have a difficult time in a back room of the commissariat, trying to explain myself and my relationship to the dead woman. No wonder my every nerve and fibre rebelled against identifying Laure with the latest victim of Jack de Paris. As if to confirm my anxiety, I dropped Laure's notebook to the floor when the concierge knocked upon my door to tell me that the bath had been drawn and the bathroom now awaited me. Quickly, I put the contents of the bag back together and clicked the clasp.

An hour and a half later, I rang the bell at Laure's building to attract her concierge. When she came to the door, which she opened no more than she had to, she told me that Laure, "that one," as she described her, "had not been seen all day." She launched into a diatribe against young women today and I nodded until I could properly take my leave.

It cost me just a franc to hire a boy outside St-Sulpice. I gave him the handbag and instructed him to take it into the *commissariat du Sixième Arrondissement*. I watched him long enough over the sculptured horses in the fountain to see that he went inside. Then I quickly walked into the rue Madame and tried to make as much speed as I could before I came to the rue d'Assas, where a translator I'd met lived. It was a good moment for a call, so I paid him a short visit and enjoyed the drink he poured me more than he could have known. It felt good to be rid of the handbag, but I was now plagued by the thought that somehow it would be traced back to me. The French police were astute when they chose to be. My fingerprints were all over the bag and the papers within it. Could they read fingerprints left on leather or paper? I didn't know. The only thought that gave me peace was the fact that my fingerprints had never been taken and so were not in the files of the French police. That calmed me considerably, as did the invitation from my translator friend to taste some cherries preserved in alcohol.

Later, when my host had walked with me to the Dôme, I sat with him watching the pedestrians walking by, holding their coats around them.

"It was a terrible summer," my friend said. "Now it's coming on winter. Maybe I'll escape to Italy. If it gets worse, I'll definitely go south."

Fine for him, I thought. Some of us have little choice. After he left me, I continued to watch the moving throng outside. Tonight it looked sad. Poor deluded tourists! Didn't they know they'd come too late to the City of Light? I worked it out; we were all five years too late. All the truly great painters had either died or moved away. Modigliani was dead, and so were Cormon and Bannat. John Singer Sargent never understood Vorticism; now they both were dead. Picasso was seldom seen on Montparnasse. Matisse had moved to the south. Proust and Apollinaire were gone, gathered to their ancestors. I'd even missed the visiting revolutionaries from Russia. Was it Lenin or Trotsky who had plotted on the *terrasse* at the Rotonde? Perhaps both. Now all these café chairs were occupied by Vlamincks, Soutines and other lesser talents like Pascin, Gris and Denis. Did they think they could take the places of the Montparnasse originals? I was entertaining this thought while watching a fellow I knew as Kisling count out his change twice before leaving most of it beside his two saucers and empty glass. When he got up and left, I saw Cendrars, looking like the *mutilé de guerre* he was, with his empty sleeve pinned up. A spent force, I thought.

"Hello, Michaeleen! What are you looking so glum about?" It was Waddington, of course. I didn't even have to look up.

"Hello yourself. Sit down." When I looked up, I caught him glancing at the other tables near mine, perhaps looking for a more agreeable companion. He must have been working on something: his beard was a two- or three-day growth. He was wearing an open shirt over a sweatshirt, all nearly hidden by a double-breasted suit badly in need of a flat iron. I didn't mind him watching me examine him. I'd seen him examine me often enough.

"I can see that you have served in the Indian Army, were wounded in the heel of your left foot and are left-handed on your mother's side. I can see that you have been shearing sheep out of season. But what is that to gentlemen of the world?"

"Hell, my left heel is about the only place I wasn't hit. Took a piece of metal out of my knee yesterday morning. Stuff keeps working its way out." Wad bunched himself down into the wicker chair opposite me.

"If the metal is zinc, you can open a bar."

"A lot of Americans have washed up on zinc beaches, Wardo."

"What have you seen of the old gang?"

"That bunch of worthless characters? I've been avoiding them since I started working again. Rewriting and cutting. It's nearly ready to send to New York," he said, pretending to give me a left and then a right jab over my saucer and coffee.

"You call them characters because they're all in the book, I presume. Maybe one of them will come looking for you with a gun."

"I'm not saying that I've put anybody you know in the book. But, kid, you should know that nobody ever recognizes himself in a book. Everybody knows that."

"Have you seen Laure Duclos in the last few days?" I tried to make the question as casual as I could, but I could see that it put him on edge. A muscle in his cheek twitched, stretching his mouth into a half-smile.

"Told you, I've been working. When I work, Michaeleen, I curtail the social commitments to three meals a day and a good night's sleep."

"So, you've not been seen on the boulevard?"

"I told you, Mike! Do I have to chew my cabbage twice?"

"Hey! Don't get sore! I'm sitting here having a swell time and suddenly Anger shows his ruddy face! Did you join me for a drink or an argument?"

Waddington grinned and sat back, glancing over his shoulder to see whether the waiter was working his way in our direction.

"Are you playing tennis these days, Mike?"

"When I get a chance. Mornings are tough for me. Late afternoons are easier."

"Good! I can't make it in the morning either. Sorry I growled at you, Michaeleen. Laure's not my favourite character."

"No?"

"Hell, it's the way she infiltrates the American lines. Like she's a French spy. Like Mata Hari, whom I met once, but that's another story —"

"'And besides, the wench is dead.'"

"What?" Wad was on his feet and looking shocked.

"Mata Hari was shot eight years ago. It's hardly news. Were you in France in 1917?"

Wad made a face and sat down again. "Oh, shove it along, Mike! I thought you meant. . . . How the hell does anybody talk to you?" He wiped both sides of his moustache with a curved index finger. "How do you know for sure that I didn't meet the lady?"

"You're talking about Mata Hari again, are you?"

He didn't bother to nod. "Maybe it was in a shabby room with a high ceiling in the Seventh Arrondissement, some place near the Champs-de-Mars? Maybe it was an afternoon, and the light through the shutters painted stripes on the wall and bed?"

He was making me lose my grip on the facts such as I knew them. I'd just done a piece on Mata, so I was sound there, but I was short on facts about Jason Waddington.

"You couldn't have been much older than eighteen then, Wad. What was your special appeal for the lady?"

"She found out through the Allied General Staff that I was singularly well-endowed. She was sent to investigate on behalf of the German High Command in the name of the German People."

"Highly democratic. And?"

"Mata Hari did her duty."

"You've got it bad, Waddington! I've worked in paddocks with less of what you're shovelling."

"You wound me, Mike. Cynicism like that led to the fall of Rome. I preserve a tender memory of dear Mata. She paid a high price for our night of bliss."

"Uncle! Uncle!" I cried. "You win, I lose! Only stop!" We both laughed, and Wad ordered a beer for himself. I decided to switch to beer as well. The waiter was preoccupied and sweaty; I wondered what was happening in his life. When the drinks came, I tried to get back to our earlier discussion.

"You said that Laure infiltrated the American lines like your dear friend Mata Hari. I'm interested in her, Wad. I might put her in a sketch I'm thinking of. Unless you've done her already?"

"Hell, no!" he said, taking a cigarette from my case. "Help yourself." He was showing a shine on his forehead and drank off his beer as soon as it came to the table. "Shouldn't talk about what you're working on, Wardo. It'll spook the work as sure as sunrise. The Quarter's full of writers who talk about what they're going to do, or are planning to do, or plotting to do. In the meantime, all they do is build pagodas of saucers on tables like this one. I call people like that scum."

"Thanks, I'll remember that," I said, adding, "and what about Laure?"

Wad frowned and pulled at the corner of his moustache. "Laure, Michaeleen, is out for learning. It's as though she was studying her friends to get her manners perfect or something. She's fly about what's in and what's out of fashion. That's why she hangs around with Julia Lowry. Because of Paris *Vogue*. She tips off the French press about American trends. She soaks up information and always manages to turn it to her advantage. She's learned a lot from the men she's lived with, especially Wilson O'Donnell."

"What?" I couldn't believe what Wad had just said.

"O'Donnell's a born teacher. Information, the buying and selling of, that's Laure's stock in trade."

"No, I meant about them living together. I want to hear."

"Hell, I thought you knew. Laure gets around."

"No, I didn't know. I suppose everyone else does?"

"This is not for one of your cables, old man. It could hurt Wilson professionally and get him in dutch with that crazy wife of his. Georgia is more than a little jealous. She asks where he's been when he goes out to buy a cigar."

"You seem to know a lot about Laure and the O'Donnells."

"Met Wilson in the Dingo a few months ago. He passed out in my arms. Wilson's always passing out. He was born a couple of drinks below par."

"And Laure? Was she under orders of the Allied High Command?"

"Ah, kid. Let's lay off Laure, huh? She's somebody to keep a paddle-length away from."

I was wondering whether to share my suspicions about Laure's possible fate with Wad. I was worried about her. Several times a day I had to blink back the image of her handbag lying in the gutter. But her death was still such a far-fetched idea, even to me, that I decided not to speak of it. I would have given a lot to see Wad's reaction, although I didn't completely trust him on this subject. I knew he had seen her the night she disappeared. I didn't want him to know that I had reasons for suspecting she might have been Jack's latest victim.

In the back of my mind, I'd decided to try to get a story about Wilson O'Donnell for the agency. It would give me a chance to see him from across a table. I wanted to clear up the mystery of 14, rue de Tilsitt. French café tables are smaller than tables at home, and faces are consequently thrust closer together. In some cases the intimacy is welcome. I don't know what I expected to find in the face of Wilson O'Donnell.

When I put my mind back into focus, Wad was talking about his life in Toronto. "On Sundays, Hash and I used to go out to Woodbine to watch the horses work out on the track."

"But there are no races on Sundays, Wad. Are you pulling my leg again?"

"Hell, kid, in those days we were too poor to bet most of the time. And the horses have to be worked whether they are racing or not. Horses don't know it's Sunday."

It was late when we got up and headed down the rue Vavin. I left Wad where his long narrow street crossed my slightly longer way back to the rue Bonaparte.

CHAPTER 11

They were taking pictures outside Sylvia Beach's bookshop on the rue de l'Odéon. A young man with blond bangs was pretending to climb down from a second-floor window to the not-very-secure helping hand held up to him. The hand belonged to the bob-headed proprietor herself, who was admonishing the young man to be careful. When enough exposures had been made, the photographer, a woman with a plain round face and a long woollen skirt with a vest, took her camera into the bookstore at number 12. Sylvia Beach and I followed. I apologized for spoiling one of the pictures by blundering into the scene.

"Don't be silly, young man," Miss Beach said, "it may turn out to be the best on the roll." She introduced herself and her friend, the photographer, Adrienne Monnier, who ran the French bookshop across the street at number 7. I didn't mention that this was not my first visit to the rue de l'Odéon. I had stopped by for a few minutes during my first week in Paris, to see with my own eyes the place that Morley Callaghan had told me about. Of course, Morley's information came from Waddington, who was a friend of Callaghan's in Toronto. I explained to Miss Beach that I was expecting to meet Wilson O'Donnell at the shop for an interview I was doing for the news service.

"Then you'd better have a chair, you know," she said. "I once lost half a day waiting for Wilson to keep an appointment. And I'm not the only one he's kept dangling."

"No indeed," Adrienne Monnier agreed, in inflections strikingly similar to Miss Beach's.

"Have you seen his new book?"

"Yes," I said. "I read it on the boat on my way over from Canada."

"Ah, another Canadian!"

"You mean there are more of us?"

"Oh dear, yes," Miss Beach said. "The most famous poet in the world lives in the Place du Panthéon." She exchanged a wry look with her friend.

"But T.S. Eliot is in London and is an American."

"But I'm talking about Robert W. Service, who wrote 'The Shooting of Dangerous Dan McGrew.'"

"Canada has a great deal to answer for," I said.

"Oh, don't be a snob, Mr. Ward. Bob's a very good fellow and all the real poets love him dearly."

"Especially James Stephens," added Mlle. Monnier.

"Dear me, yes! They go about like a pair of vaudeville soft-shoe dancers. They're great friends. Bob's been trying to learn how to paint."

I took out my watch and looked at it while Miss Beach poured a cup of coffee for me from a well-used pot. O'Donnell was half an hour late. I accepted the coffee and complimented Miss Beach and her friend on their locations; I'd been watching the pedestrian traffic moving up the slight rise in the direction of the Odéon, the Theatre of France. When I brought the conversation around to Waddington, they both smiled at the mention of his name. I asked if there was a copy of Wad's stories, *for all time*, in the shop.

"Indeed there is! Far too many of them. But for a first book, it is doing very well. Would you like to see it?" I said I would, and she led me to the "Waddington section," which consisted of two dozen copies of *for all time* and about the same number of the Paris-printed book Wad had shown me, *Ten Stories and Three Poems*. There was also a stack of mail held together like a sheaf of love letters by a length of red ribbon.

"We've been his post office since he first came to Paris in 1922," Miss Beach said. "He was very shy in those days. I think he still is a shy man underneath. All that shadow-boxing is just play-acting. Although he *did* box for a while when he was younger. Of all the people who have come to see us here on the rue de l'Odéon, Wad is one of our favourites."

I paid for a copy of each of his books and sipped my coffee until long after it had become cold. As a newspaperman, cold coffee was nothing new to me, but I was beginning to feel that my presence in the store waiting for O'Donnell meant that they had to continue to entertain me. I answered their questions about my Canadian background, and accepted Adrienne's compliments on my French, which we now slipped into and continued speaking in until a title or an American name spun us back into English again. After a tour of the store, during which Miss Beach showed me the authors' photographs on the wall and told me the circumstances of each of them, the young man with blond bangs entered the shop. He was introduced as George Antheil, the composer of the *Jazz Symphony*. He and his new wife lived on the second floor. I was lining him up for an interview when Wilson O'Donnell came in looking rather pale and tousled. His hair stood up from a centre parting in two fair horns, but his blue eyes were smiling as he hugged Sylvia and Adrienne. When he got around to me, he put on a wide grin and mimed abject embarrassment by flinging his arms around and pretending to grovel.

"Damned sorry to leave you hanging out to dry like that, old man, but I was up until six this morning with a sick friend."

"Wilson!"

"No, honestly. Georgia and I were up at Bricktop's and one of the singers had an attack of — we thought it was gas at first — but she ended up getting her appendix out at the American Hospital. My good friend Dr. Anson Tyler did the honours."

"Really, Wilson, you are the limit!" Sylvia said. At this, O'Donnell put his hand into the inside pocket of his jacket and brought out a small bottle. There was something floating in the liquid in the bottle.

"*Voilà*!" he said. "The defence rests." The bottle was passed from hand to hand, and, after looking again, I gave it back to its present owner.

"So, that's an appendix. It looks like a little finger with the bone removed." I couldn't look at it without thinking of the body in the morgue. Without my mentioning it, Miss Beach began talking about the Montparnasse murders and about how close some of the victims had lived to the rue de l'Odéon. O'Donnell listened without comment, then observed that a tiny piece of tissue floating in alcohol was a powerful promoter of morbid conversation. In order to change the subject, I said:

"I know your friend, the surgeon, by the way."

"Anson Tyler?" Wilson replied.

"I've run into him from time to time at the Dingo."

"Oh, Mr. Ward, you should stay away from such places!"

"You never tell *me* that, Sylvia," O'Donnell said, showing mild surprise.

"You, Wilson? Oh, you're hopeless. You never do what anybody says. You're allergic to good advice, you are."

Everybody laughed, including O'Donnell, who began his abject apologetic show once again. When that had been played out, I asked him if he'd had lunch yet. He said he hadn't. I told him that it went with the interview. He smiled, and, as soon as we had made our goodbyes, we were walking down the rue de l'Odéon into the *carrefour*.

"Where should we go?" he asked, looking at the statue of the revolutionary figure Danton.

"The Procope's just across the street. It's reasonable and the food is good."

"Never heard of it. I was thinking of a simple luncheon, but a good one."

"The Procope is where Benjamin Franklin used to eat. It's the oldest place in town. Voltaire dined there. So did Danton, Robespierre, Talleyrand and Bonaparte. Writers like George Sand, Balzac and Verlaine —"

"Sounds terrible. I've got a very simple meal in mind. Nothing fancy."

"The Procope's been serving simple meals since the seventeenth century."

"Are you touting for the place, Ward, or what? Let's get a cab and find a quiet place in the Bois."

"I think we have different ideas about 'simple,' Mr. O'Donnell."

"Please. Call me anything but 'Mister.' I'll even answer to Calvin Coolidge, but never 'Mister.'"

"Look, Wilson, if we go all the way to the Bois to eat, we won't be finished until dark. There are lots of places here in the Quarter that I don't get a touting fee from. The important thing is to talk, isn't it?"

"Okay, we'll compromise. Let's hurry over to the Tour d'Argent for a duck. I haven't been there since the old man died."

"I can't afford to take you there! I work for a news service, not the Morgan Bank. I can offer you a modest luncheon. What about the Chope Danton over there?"

"Mike, old man, I'm buying. I won't even argue with you. So don't look green when I say the Tour d'Argent." Wilson wanted to try to get a taxi, but I convinced him that it would be faster to walk. He looked at me as though walking were a dirty word. In the end he agreed, probably because it would make a good story. He could tell his friends on the other side of the Seine that he had actually walked from the rue de l'Odéon to the Quai de la Tournelle.

My first victory was to get O'Donnell to trust my knowledge of the streets of the Quarter. He wanted to buy a map. In the end, I convinced him that the rue Racine would take us to the rue des Écoles, and that we could have a pleasant time walking past the windows of second-hand bookstores and watching the Sorbonne students.

It wasn't the shortest route, but the visual distractions made it seem so. O'Donnell was out of shape. He was puffing by the time we got to the Place de l'Odéon and the downhill run from there to St-Michel was not much better. He wanted to stop in a café for a drink and to catch his breath, which seemed like a good idea to me, since the place he picked also served a small menu for lunch. But he wouldn't be put off with an omelette or some pâté or even the *moules marinières* that the waiter recommended. Wilson's mind had fixed on the duck he was going to order at the Tour d'Argent. I tried to tell him that it was getting very late, but he began questioning me over the whisky and soda he had ordered. I kept pulling my watch out and looking at it. Each time I did it less subtly than the time before. The omelette being served at the neighbouring table looked like a work of art. O'Donnell was not softened.

"So all of your family comes from Toronto?"

"Most of it. There are a few farmers north and east of Toronto who answer to 'Uncle Charley' and 'Uncle

Vernon.' The war thinned the family out. I lost some cousins and more uncles at Passchendaele and Vimy."

"I was in the army, but I didn't get over to this side," he said. "You were too young to get into it?" I nodded. "Have you ever been to a place called Orillia?" he asked.

"Orillia? Sure. My family has a summer home near there at Uptergrove. I'm surprised you've ever heard of Orillia. That's where Stephen Leacock lives in the summer."

"Leacock's funnier than Will Rogers."

"Granted. But, please, I want to know how you know about Orillia."

"I spent some weeks there in the summer of 1907. Camp Chatham. It was run by a rather cloying woman named Mrs. Upton. There were several counsellors and they all wore whistles around their necks on cords. As a little fellow, I was quite helpless in their hands. They taught me how to swim. I'll give them that. I've got a letter to my mother, which she saved to show me what a little snob I'd already become by the time I was ten."

"I'm finding it a little hard to digest this. I never imagined you closer to the border than Great Neck, Long Island."

"Well, old man, just don't let it get around," he said. "I don't suppose they would let us buy some French frieds, would they?" He looked hopeful.

"I shouldn't be surprised." I called the waiter over and asked about the potatoes, and Wilson asked for a salad to accompany his. I went directly for the mussels and wasn't sorry. A half bottle of Alsatian white wine was brought from the cellar for Wilson to inspect and we settled for that and its brother and sister. O'Donnell was a cautious eater. He trimmed the spines from the Romaine lettuce and left them, as though they were discarded chicken bones. The remainder of the meal, with the exception of the wine, he picked at rather than feasted upon.

While we were eating I asked him the questions that would help make the luncheon profitable for my employers. I interviewed him about the new novel and its reception in America. He was willing to talk about it, but not with much enthusiasm. He saved that for the American and British writers who had made Paris their home. He discussed Joyce and Gertrude Stein in reverential tones. Then, after mentioning some of the others, he gave Jason Waddington a big endorsement. "He's instinctively in touch with everything new and exciting about the modern movement. His novel, which will be published next year by a major American publisher, will set new standards on both sides of the Atlantic."

When I thought I had given the agency value for its luncheon money, I began to ask Wilson about the difficulty of moving around the world with a young family. Georgia and Wilson were accompanied almost everywhere by their charming three-year-old daughter, Willie.

"Willie was born in a steamer trunk, or very nearly," he said. "She's just a perfect travelling companion. Whenever Georgia's nursing a headache, Willie is there with an ice-pack, if you can believe it. And she's only three!"

"You're living at 14, rue de Tilsitt right now, isn't that right?"

"Sure. But for God's sake don't put the address in your copy or I'll start getting manuscripts sent to me again. They follow me like Banquo's ghost wherever I go. It used to be that every time the doorbell rang, there'd be a sob-story standing on the doorstep. Be a pal, Mike, and forget about where we're staying."

"You sublet the place from the real tenant, is that right?"

"Sure. They're the originals of Lord Tarlyon and his wife in that Michael Arlen book of last year or so. What was it called? *Piracy,* that's right."

"And you in turn sublet the apartment when you're going away from Paris?"

"Yes, that's right. Where is this leading, Mike? You sound like a tax lawyer trying to account for my wasted millions."

"I ran across a woman named Laure Duclos, a friend of some people I know at the Dingo. She gave your address."

"Oh, Laure. Yes, Georgia let her have our place while we were down with the Murphys on the Côte d'Azur."

"She's quite a woman, this Laure Duclos."

"Yes, I've put her into a story or two."

"Damn. That's too bad. I was thinking of using her myself."

"Don't tell me she's caught you in that tangle of blond hair, Mike? She collects men. You'd better know that."

"Well, at the moment I'm on the shelf, Wilson. I'm alone in a strange town. Besides, I'm a little worried about her. She seems to have disappeared."

"Forget it!" he said, finally deciding to remove his heavy navy-blue overcoat. "Laure can take care of herself. She'll turn up, you'll see." A waiter carefully took the overcoat and hung it up. "Art and games are one thing, Ward; Laure's another. When I tell you to keep away from her, I'm doing you a favour, old man. I'm not running it out. This is the crystalline truth. Don't get involved. That's the best advice I can give you."

"Are you still carrying the torch?"

"I don't know what you think you know, Mike, but back away from that angle, please. I'm a happily harassed husband and wish to remain so. I was trying to give you a piece of advice."

"I don't mean to pry. I know it's none of my business, but I'd like to find out as much as I can about Mlle Duclos.

And, by the way, you noticed, I hope, that I put my notebook and pen away some time ago."

"I suspect that you've got a bad case. You have my sympathy. Hell, I thought she was a hell of a girl myself, so don't go blaming yourself. There's nothing picayune about Laure. She could give the old boys who take a nap on the courthouse lawn at home a rude awakening, to coin a phrase."

"She can be nice. I admit that."

"Original party girl, incarnate. Damn it, she jumps out of everything I've ever written."

"And when she's not so nice?" I asked. "I'd better hear it all."

"Has she been getting that way with you, Mike?"

"I won't know until I hear about it."

"She has a way of reminding one of a compromising situation just before she remembers that she's short of rent money. Funny, how it works out that way."

"Did she use pressure on you to get the apartment this summer?"

"She didn't actually say she'd tell Georgia about a momentary lapse of mine. She only hinted. And since Georgia's very fond of her, I couldn't see the harm. Any available oil to calm the raging sea. I try not to get into a fight with Georgia. She wouldn't understand."

"Has she ever asked for rather a lot of money?"

"A couple of nights ago."

"What did you tell her? I assume she threatened you after her fashion?"

"She was a little balder than usual. A lot of steel showing under the velvet glove. I told her that I'd have to think it over. She said she'd give me overnight and that's all."

"And?"

"I haven't heard a word. Every time the telephone rings at the apartment, I think it's going to be her."

"Do you think Georgia suspects anything?"

"God! No! She can't know! She thinks I've never been with anyone but her. Georgia mustn't find out. Ever!"

"I see the delicacy of your position."

"You don't begin to see," O'Donnell said, his fingers white against the edge of the table. "If Georgia found out about Laure, I wouldn't give ten francs for either of our hides. Georgia's a complex and delicately balanced woman. I wouldn't even want to guess what might happen if Georgia ever found out about Laure and me." O'Donnell emptied his glass. That was when I saw that he was beginning to look scared.

CHAPTER 12

The morning papers cleared up the mystery of why Laure Duclos hadn't been in her room when I'd called again, just before I began looking for a place to eat dinner. Again I'd talked to her concierge, and again I'd not been given any information other than that she had not been seen. According to all the morning papers, Laure had not been seen because she had been lying in the Institut Médico-Légal, the new morgue in the Place Mazas. Although I'd been fearing the worst since the moment I discovered her bag in the gutter, I was shocked to read about Laure's death in the paper, as though the printing of the news created, not simply confirmed, the fact. As a newspaperman, I knew only too well the fallibility of the press, but this was in all the dailies. The body found in the rue Léopold Robert the night I came upon the handbag was that of Laure Duclos. Even in English, the words seemed to suggest that there was a Laure alive somewhere who was the owner of this body, even as she was the owner of the handbag and the tenant of the room in the passage de Dantzig. It was a trick of the way the languages worked, I know, and whatever the words seemed to say, the message was that the lovely, provocative, perhaps evil Laure Duclos was dead.

I was reading and eating breakfast at the Café Lipp, which was just around the corner from my room. The waiters in their waistcoats and shirtsleeves were dealing informally with the few early customers. The black jackets would be donned closer to noon and the informality, the banter with the morning regulars, would slip into more formal modes of address. I sipped my coffee and pulled a croissant to pieces, daubing them liberally with butter and jam from the *pot à confitures*. To an observer, I might have lavished more attention on these things than they deserved. But, to be honest, I was shaken by the news. I needed to grasp ordinary things to reconfirm the fact that the world around me still functioned, still responded to all the normal laws of nature.

I had an appointment to play tennis with Wad. Should one cancel the match out of respect for Laure? It was hard to tell what was the right thing to do. Would Wad have heard the news? As I walked back along St-Germain to the tram stop, I tried not to look at the display of medical instruments in a window; stainless-steel clamps, retractors and scalpels. I shut my eyes hard against them and the thought of the Institut Médico-Légal.

The number 14 tram took me from St-Germain-des-Prés to the Quai d'Orsay. The seats reserved for *femmes enceintes et mutilés de guerre* were occupied by three men with walking sticks. One wore his medal on his jacket. It had the look of having been pinned on by some loved one. Across from them, my duffel bag, with its racket, was an embarrassment to me, a reproach. I buried the bag under my coat and left it in the cloakroom at the office.

I filed two or three stories, took them by taxi to the Gare St-Lazare to see them off on the boat-train and did an interview with an actor who had just won some award or other, while we ate lunch at a place off rue Byron. He was singularly proud of his honour; there wasn't a shred of false modesty. When I had completed my assignments, I took the Métro from Étoile to Denfert-Rochereau and hurried with my bag up the boulevard Arago to the clay courts. I arrived five minutes late. Wad was already there, changed and trying to hold onto the court. He was twirling his racket and looking mean. He was in no mood for talk, so we got at it.

I won the first game easily. Wad was too cross to concentrate. He slammed the ball as hard as he could and missed the first shot of each of his serves. He took the second game using the same tactics but with more control, and I took the last one, probably because his legs were tiring. He wore an elastic bandage around his right knee. It was hard not to take advantage of his disability. After all, he could claim a seat on the Métro while I couldn't. We let another couple play and then reclaimed the red clay court for a last set. Again I beat him, but it was a better, more evenly matched game. We headed for the showers.

"You've heard about Laure?" I asked.

"I heard last night in the Dingo that it was Laure. Freddy, the bartender there, knows a bigwig on the Quai des Orfèvres. *Flics* have been asking questions all around the Quarter since she was killed."

"The papers say that it was Jack. Is that what the police think?"

"Sure. Why not? It was just Laure's bad luck to be walking home that night alone."

"Do you think it was Jack, Wad?"

"What's getting into you, McWardo?"

Steam was filling the room, which was already dim with the fading of the light. We had to raise our voices to be heard above the sound of the water.

I hadn't thought much about it, but I had a feeling that Laure's death could not simply be written off as another of Jack de Paris's random murders. It might have been because Laure was still so real to me that I needed a murderer with a motive and a personal contact with Laure.

That Laure was a casual victim of a madman seemed unjust. It was not a bit like Laure.

In the locker room we climbed back into our clothes. Wad ran a comb carefully through his hair, showing a vanity I hadn't suspected.

"If Jack didn't kill Laure, Mike, who do you think did? What was his reason?"

"Look, Wad, you know as well as I do that she had enemies. If the police ever begin searching beyond the possibility of an insane street marauder, they might take a look at Wilson O'Donnell, or me — or you."

"Me! I hardly knew the woman! She was a drinking friend, that's all. I know almost nothing about her." He was tying the laces of his boots now with a worried face.

"Laure was the sort of woman who gets murdered, Wad. She was playing a dangerous game. She collected enemies as well as lovers. She was a notorious user of people."

"Who do you think you are, Michaeleen? Hawkshaw the Detective? Sherlock Holmes? What are you getting mixed up in?"

"If the *flics* think Jack did it, that's just fine. But we know that it wasn't simply her bad luck in being in the wrong place at the wrong time. Laure was killed because she was a blackmailer."

"Spit it out! Go ahead! You think I did it? You think I took a pair of scissors to her? You pale Canadian turd!"

"You were talking to her at the Dôme the night she was killed. I saw you myself from across the street. After she got up and left, you followed her."

"You flat-faced son of a bitch!"

"Calling me names isn't an answer. Another thing: even before it was known that the body found in the rue Léopold Robert was Laure's, you told me you hadn't seen her. That was a goddamned lie. You not only met and talked to her, but she showed you something that upset you. Hell, Wad, I could see it all the way from the Rotonde! She —"

"You bastard!"

"I know you can swear, Waddington. I know you can probably knock me down the way you knocked Hal Leopold down. But that won't change anything. Don't you see, if the police begin looking for a fall guy who isn't Jack de Paris, both of us are prime suspects?"

"You? Don't talk wild."

"I went home with her. I was seen with her in her neighbourhood. She got tired of me and dumped me. I was angry about that, not enough to kill her, but that's a question the examining magistrate might not be convinced on."

"One minute you sound like a fucking stool-pigeon and now you're trying to say you're a potential killer. Get your lines straight, kid." Wad wrapped his shorts, jockstrap and racket in his shirt with some skill and left the locker room without another word. I followed him outside, where the air was sharp and cold on my arms. He was already half a block down the road when I caught up to him.

"Wad, listen to me! I'm not trying to pin this murder on you. But I'm sure Laure wasn't killed by that madman. She was murdered because of what she was and what she's done to you and Wilson O'Donnell. Damn it, you must see that she was pushing one of her blackmail victims too hard. If it wasn't because of what she had on you, then it was one of the rest of us. It has to have been somebody here in the Quarter."

Wad slowed down to a walk and I was able to keep up to him. He didn't say anything for a long time.

"You see that," he said, stopping suddenly and pointing at a massive doorway just around the corner. "That's where the condemned man gets his first glimpse of the guillotine. It's only a few steps from the door to the *bascule*."

"Charming," I said. "I didn't know it was still a public show."

"They pick an early hour and the date is a well-kept secret, even from the condemned. Yes, Mike, this is where the Third Republic devours its children."

"They say it's a highly democratic device."

"A month ago I was here to see two men shortened before breakfast. Took less than thirty seconds each." Wad was trying out new fiction.

"Jack is giving the Republic a run for its money. He's credited with seven — how many can the Republic claim?"

"Jack preys on women exclusively. The Republic must be more circumspect. Democracy has been tempered by public opinion. Few fair heads have fallen in the boulevard Arago."

"What does that spell for democracy?"

"We'd better have a drink to consider the question. What do you think, old man?" He wasn't going to apologize, but he was showing his friendly side again.

"Long live the Republic!"

"As you say, Citizen. I know a little place around the corner."

I followed Wad, who led me three blocks away from the Santé Prison and into a small boîte with tables near a window looking out on a corner of the avenue de l'Observatoire. We installed ourselves and ordered Alsatian beer. When it came, Wad indicated the heavily moustached waiter.

"He's one of the assistants of Monsieur de Paris, that fellow." When I looked blank, he added, "He's the assistant chopper, Michaeleen. He holds the condemned so he doesn't succeed in depriving the state of its rightful portion of neck."

"What are you talking about?"

"Look, once you've got your neck locked between the

upper and lower portions of the *lunette*, you might try to pull your head back into your shoulders. This makes for messy democracy. Therefore, the assistant, dressed in somber black and wearing the traditional derby hat, pulls the ears or hair of the patient at the last moment. It's supposed to distract the condemned. What do you think?"

I shrugged. I had no appetite for this information, since Wad was using it to keep us from discussing more pressing things. He called the waiter over and together they discussed the fine art of decapitation. The waiter nodded seriously and answered Wad's questions directly.

"It is better, messieurs, from every point of view, if the patient's neck is severed in the middle and not at the base of the skull. What I say is the distillation of over one hundred years of experience, messieurs, although I, personally, have only only assisted to *enfourner* but a dozen souls."

"Why do you say you 'put them in the oven'?" I asked, interested in spite of myself.

"It is an expression, monsieur," he said with a shrug. "I did not invent it."

When the waiter went back to his zinc counter, where he was making a Welsh rarebit, Wad and I lifted our *demis* in a toast to democracy and to the glorious Third Republic.

"Sorry I jumped on your back there, Wardo." I was surprised that Wad admitted error. "I thought you thought that I did it."

"I don't know that you didn't." A cloud crossed his face. "But if you had, I think you would have taken away that piece of paper she showed you. You didn't, so maybe yours'll be just another innocent head in the basket."

"You were watching us, that night?"

"I was in love with her, Wad. I wanted to see who she was meeting, where she was spending her time. I was a little unhinged."

"Who appointed you guardian?"

"I couldn't stand by with my arms folded."

"A neat phrase. I may borrow it."

"Look, Wad, will you help me? The sooner the murderer is caught, the sooner we can get back to everyday life. We both know there is a murderer loose on Montparnasse, and his name isn't Jack de Paris. Aren't you even curious? It's nearly killing me. I want to find out what happened. Don't you? Hell, we may be next."

Wad finished his *demi* and called for two more. When they arrived, he looked over at me with a serious expression. What was under it, I'll never know. But he got the look right. "What do you want to know?"

"What was on that piece of paper?"

He stared at the saucers and then at the amber beer in the tall glasses. "Something I wrote a long time ago."

"Was it something you didn't want anyone to see?"

"What? No! Of course not! It was a short description I wrote back in the fall of 1922. It disappeared. I haven't seen it since Hash lost the suitcase with it and a lot of other stuff in it."

"So, if Laure had that fragment, does that mean she has the other missing things?"

"I don't know. She showed me that one page and asked me what I thought. I asked her where she got it and she just smiled, wouldn't say anything. She wanted to know what it was worth to me."

"Are you talking about the manuscripts that Hash lost on the train at the Gare de Lyon?"

"Yes. I don't go losing things all the time, for Christ's sake!"

"Then you think the suitcase has been recovered from whoever took it in the first place?"

"Damn it, Mike, I don't know what to think. I don't like to save my rejection slips. I don't count casualties. I keep my attention on the page in front of me. Otherwise I'd go crazy. When Hash lost that stuff, I thought I'd been blown up all over again. But I got over it. It's the only way to survive. Survival is the most important match on the card, kid. So, I got back to work and I forgot what was in that suitcase because it was the heart, bone and blood of two years' work. Then, out of the blue, Laure shows up with one of the pages. I like it the way she just shows up with it! It had to have come from one of the manilla envelopes with all my stuff."

"You still sound bitter about it."

"Look, Michaeleen, I don't pretend to be a crystal-gazer. Too much entrail-reading is bad for a writer. You end up in a cork-lined room like that fellow Proust. If I peer too closely at what I'm doing, it goes bad. I know this. I try to prevent it. All I care about is behaviour, what people do. Not what they think or what they would like to do, but what they do in changing circumstances. I can almost handle that. I miss, God knows by how far I miss! But that's my turf. That's where I'm at home. I work bloody hard, Mike. Bloody hard."

"And Hash?"

"I owe that woman everything, kid. She's supported both of us. All three of us, since I stopped doing journalism. A man couldn't wish for a better wife."

"And yet . . .?"

"And yet nothing! She's a wonderful girl. I'd never think of leaving her."

For a moment, he sat there a little surprised at what he'd said, as though the thought, even expressed negatively, had opened a door into a new chamber of his consciousness.

CHAPTER 13

Before I left Waddington, he told me about a party at a studio where Biz had been living. He thought that it was probably going to turn into a wake for Laure, but he couldn't be sure.

"I was planning to go hear Valéry Larbaud read on the rue de l'Odéon," I said.

"Who the hell's Larbaud?"

"Important French writer, Wad. He loves you Americans."

"Never heard of him," he said, as though that wiped Larbaud off the face of history.

"I'll remember that," I said.

"If you decide to come, call around to the carpenter's loft after dinner and we'll all go in a taxi together."

When I got to the Waddington apartment, Mme. Rohrbach, Snick's usual night-time custodian, was getting last-minute instructions from Hash, while Wad paced the floor eager to be away. We walked to the taxi rank in front of the Dôme feeling the sharp mist on our faces. It wasn't a long drive to the rue Broca, but it seemed cosy and even luxurious on a chilly night. I had long ago got used to the idea of taking taxis only for business reasons, so I had to wonder how the Waddingtons were able to afford such luxuries. I shouldn't have worried about that, because I ended up paying myself. Wad said he'd match me for it when we next met for tennis.

On the way up the curving staircase that somehow seemed to bring the outdoors inside, we could hear more and more music coming from the studio above us. It was after nine o'clock and the noise from the open doorway was already impressive. Music came from a gramophone sitting on a piano stool. Behind it was a round table bending under the weight of litres of wine bought in bulk, probably from the country relatives of the concierge for a small commission.

The room was a cube, with a single large window that I feared was not on the preferred north wall. Opposite the window, the roughly plastered wall supported a balcony, which overhung a quarter of the room. The stairs leading up to it were already occupied by various members of the congregation.

Lady Biz came hurrying through the crowd of people in the main room to greet the Waddingtons. She held my hand formally for a moment, too, and offered me a powdered cheek to kiss. Waving her arms in the direction of the round table, she urged me to find some wine for myself.

"It's one for all and all for one, chaps, with a little of every man for himself. There are glasses in the crate under the table. Do help yourselves."

The walls of the studio were hung with unframed canvases, some of startling size, showing some flair but no huge talent. There were also maquettes of sculptures and even some architectural friezes, mounted low enough to be used as shelves for some dishes and a clock. The music I recognized as Rossini as it came to an end. It was replaced by Chevalier singing in his fruity tenor. Biz was off across the room like an express train before I could properly ask any questions. I felt overdressed in my suit and tie. Some of the painters were dressed in worn suits with old ties knotted around the collars of colourful flannel shirts. Most of them were wearing sweaters and peasant blouses, which a number of artists were affecting this year.

I went over to the table and found a glass in a wooden crate divided into sections. Wine was poured into my glass while I was still trying to decide which of the bottles looked the least lethal. I turned to see a woman with a mole on her cheek and dark hair. Her skin was clear and uncomfortably white.

"You are not a painter?" She looked at me, perhaps hoping I was J.P. Morgan's wayward son.

"That's true, but I like paintings."

She looked at me as though I had said something clever that she had not understood. She frowned.

"Everybody's a painter around here. A canvas merchant could grow rich. You're not English?"

"No, I'm Canadian."

"So that's why you speak French."

"I'm from English Canada, but I wanted to learn the language."

Already the woman was scanning the new faces coming into the studio and making assessments.

"It's a rotten language," she said. "It'll keep me poor. I think German's a better language. Germans always have money."

"What do you do?"

"I rent my skin, what do you think? These painters around here are crazy for me. But most of them can't pay, and the rest won't. Still," she said with a shrug, "it's better than my sister Étiennette in the Place de Clichy. And I don't have to give most of what I make to some goddamned pimp. It's honest work. Why are you in the Quarter?"

"I've got a cheap room, where I'm trying to write. In the daytime I work for a news service across the river."

"So you come here to find some girl?" She was looking at me as simply as though she'd asked me the time. I found it chilling at first, and then refreshing.

"Probably," I said, matching her candour.

Biz was greeting the O'Donnells, who had just come in. You could hear the din abate as they stood looking for familiar faces. Georgia was wearing a flame-coloured dress with an irregular slashed hem that was supposed to look like tongues of fire. Wilson took off an impeccable grey felt hat and finely tailored overcoat. He handed it to someone without looking. I watched the progress of the coat up the stairs, dislodging entwined couples, to a bed on the balcony.

"You think I'm pretty?" the girl beside me asked.

"You are very attractive. What's your name?"

"Justine. It's a terrible name, don't you think?"

"No. I like it. It suits you."

"The artists all think it's some dirty joke when I tell them. That's another reason why I'm sick of this stinking town. How are you called?"

"Michael."

"Like the archangel. I like that. My father was religious. My mother was a socialist, and a lot of good it did her."

"Where do you do your modelling?" I asked the question in all innocence, but quickly she made me reach up to loosen my tie.

"You want to come and see?" I protested, but she went right on as though I hadn't spoken. "Don't worry, I'll get you a ticket. You must come over to La Ruche. If I'm not with Foujita or Vlaminck, I'll be there. You know it? La Ruche, the beehive?"

"I know it," I said, as though simply knowing the address were already the first button unbuttoned, the first ribbon untied.

Wilson O'Donnell's white face was moving over to the table near where we were standing.

"Hello, Mike! How are you? Crushing the grape, I see."

"This vintage hasn't been cooled a long age in the deep-delved earth, I fear, but it burns well enough, I think."

"Don't tell me! A damned scholar hiding behind a typewriter!"

"Just don't tell anybody. Justine, I'd like to introduce my friend, Wilson. Wilson, this is my old friend Justine, who is a model by trade." I immediately felt ashamed of the introduction. Maybe I had been crushing too many grapes. But I didn't know Justine's last name.

"You're an American?" Justine asked, with a smile that could already taste the dollars. She poured a glass for Wilson, brightening, almost shimmering, as she handed the glass to the writer. Her eyes were now fully open.

"What's going on here, youse guys?" It was Georgia O'Donnell, putting on a tough accent. She grabbed Wilson's arm so that the wine spilled on the studio floor, where it would never be noticed.

For years I'd been reading about the great beauty of Georgia O'Donnell, the original flapper, the chain-smoking new woman of the Jazz Age. She didn't in any way look like a drawing by John Held, Jr. She was rounder, for one thing, more traditionally feminine, more like the girl down the street than a movie queen. Her smile was certainly electric, but her eyes seemed to change from moment to moment, now smiling and joking, a second later, heavy, dark and troubled. Sometimes they were wide open and alive, the next, hooded and deep-set. Hers was by far the more interesting face of the couple. Wilson looked a little like Harry Langdon, a face waiting for its character to be stamped on. Georgia's hair was not the spun-gold of legend but akin to her husband's in colour. Wilson introduced us, giving last names with ease, except when he came to Justine.

"Vaux," she said. "Justine Vaux." She gave me a look as she did this, a small reproof for my earlier sloppy introduction to Wilson.

"Don't tell me, I just know you are a genuine artist's model!"

"All the world are artists' models, Madame." Her enthusiasm for Wilson began to chill when she saw Georgia's proprietary hand on her husband's arm. There was a flicker of a smile as yet another of her horses failed to finish.

I felt Georgia assessing me, measuring me against Wilson's account of our recent lunch.

"And you're the writer who was so understanding when Goofo was late for your luncheon."

"Just a reporter, Mrs. O'Donnell. And he wasn't very late."

"Spoken like a sport!" chimed in Wilson. "Georgia, do you have some gin in that bag of yours or are you carrying it out of pure affectation?"

"There's gin within," she said, laughed, and repeated it in a louder voice. "Get some glasses. That wine looks positively revolting! I bet it would polish silver." Georgia poured gin into the clutch of glasses Wilson brought over. "They say it almost amounts to a sin against the Holy Ghost to drink pure gin, but there's not a thing on the table to mix with it. Not even varnish. You'd think they would keep varnish, wouldn't you?" Georgia raised her glass high above her head and waved it as though it were a banner. "Well, here's how!"

Both the O'Donnells drained their glasses swiftly. I looked at Justine over the brim of mine. It was plain that she thought that we were all quite mad. Her last words to me were abrupt and cruel, and a painful reminder of Laure:

"You want to find yourself some girl, you know, Michael." It was the only time she used my first name. "There are lots of them, more *sympathique* than others, you know."

Then she lost herself in the crowd of painters over in one corner. They were trying to take a photograph with a saucer full of magnesium. After several attempts they abandoned the project, leaving the room full of smoke. A painter who had been sitting inside a large gilt picture frame got up from his cramped position and executed a frog-walk across the floor, while those nearby laughed and shouted out unflattering remarks.

Meanwhile, the Waddingtons had been sitting near the large window with George Gordon, Biz, Dr. Anson Tyler and Tolstoi. Tolstoi was rather drunk.

"The simple fact is," he was saying, "that actually I didn't see Laure again after that night. Actually, I hadn't seen much of her since the great parting of the ways. Actually —"

"Tell us, Anson, what sort of a man is it that kills helpless women that way? Is he human?" Lady Biz looked interested.

"The doctors in Vienna would have a name for him," Hash said brightly, her round face glowing with the wine she'd been drinking and her red hair glinting under the fringed electric light above her head.

"'Crazy' is good enough for me," George said.

"You should read Mrs. Lowndes's novel, *The Lodger*," the Doctor said. "She probes the mind of an insane criminal, not too different from the man the French police are looking for, with great skill."

"Who gets time to read anything? Do you chaps read? I used to, didn't I, George? I was a great reader. But things are too complicated nowadays. Perhaps it was the war."

"You blame everything on the war, Biz. It's become your whipping-boy."

"Well, I say, George, can you think of a better one? The war is probably what twisted Jack's mind. Although why he should take it out on defenceless women I can't imagine." Biz, who was not usually a great talker, was warming to her theme. "Wad, you're a clever chap; why would anyone want to kill a chap like Laure? I mean, if he didn't know her. *We* knew her all too well, but he didn't have a reason for *this*."

"He was probably trying to kill his mother," Waddington said. "He's killed her seven times now, maybe it will soon give him peace. Some mothers are hard to kill. Now my mother —"

"Wad! I won't hear one word against mothers!" It was Georgia, who had been listening to this island of English in a sea of French. "You'll support me in this, won't you Cilla?" Hash smiled, but said nothing. I suppose she knew her mother-in-law, and Georgia O'Donnell did not.

"My mother is a collector of *cojones*," Wad said. "She keeps my father's in a yellow leather pouch in a drawer." Those who knew Spanish laughed.

"I declare," Georgia went on, "the police would have the head of the killer in a big brown bag already if it was a woman who went around killing men at random. Nobody cares about the deaths of seven women. Nobody will care when he's killed a dozen. Because you men, filthy beasts that you are, all get a little jab of pleasure when a woman gets her throat cut. No! Don't bother to deny it, because it's true, it's true. You know it's true!" There was a storm of protest.

"That's plain crazy!" said Wad.

"Every woman knows it," Georgia insisted. "Speak up, Cilla. Tell them."

Wad shrugged and looked at me.

"I have a hard enough time discovering what's in one man's head, Georgia," Hash said. "I'd never presume to talk about all men. I don't think I'd want to."

"Damn it all, Georgia," George Gordon said, "I haven't cut a throat in weeks."

"And I, only one or two," said Anson with a smile. "But that was in the line of business."

Arlette joined the group, her dark hair beautifully sculptured, carrying glasses of wine. She kissed all the men, including me. Biz quickly briefed her about the conversation.

"People do terrible things to one another. Doesn't matter which sex," she said, as though this were a self-evident fact.

"Cilla," Georgia said, picking up her original thought, "are we going to sit here and listen to these evasions? I swear we should treat men the way the women do in that Greek play. What's it's name? *Lysi*-something. You know the one I mean, Goofo?"

"*Lysistrata*," said O'Donnell.

"Here we go!" said Waddington, looking at Georgia, as though she was a bomb about to go off. Georgia ignored him, as she often did.

"Yes," she said, drawing out the word. "The women in the play deny their husbands all conjugal rights until . . . until . . . I forgot what."

"Well, I for one think it's a jolly good idea," said Biz, "on general principles. Men are beastly, the way they hang about, waiting for favours. I don't mean you, George. You're a prince among men."

"Which isn't saying much, according to you, old girl,"

George said. "Being the best of a thoroughly bad lot is nothing to write home about. Be fair."

"Don't 'old girl' me, you degenerate beast," Biz said, taking George's big head in her arms, giving George a sheepdog look.

"I don't know this *Lysi* — the play, you know — but you can't take these Greeks seriously. They're not like us. Don't like cricket, for a start. And they're too damned fond of their sheep."

Hash, who was holding on to Wad's arm, gave it a tug. They exchanged a grin.

"Oh, George!" Biz said. "I've never seen you at a cricket match! You always give away your Lord's tickets to your tailor so he won't dun you."

"Hasn't helped much. I suppose, on second thoughts, I could live quite reasonably in Greece. Wear one of those tutu things, live in a ruin, learn to take photographs of tourists, that sort of thing. I'd do that before going back into the army."

"If they'd have you!"

"Yes, well, there's that."

"I think it would be a cute idea if all we girls got serious and started denying privileges to our boys. We could make out with appropriately shaped vegetables until this killer is brought to justice."

"Really, Georgia, you go too far!"

"It's *all* in the play! Goofo, don't you think it's a cute idea?"

"Now, darling, how could I approve of such a thing? I'd be a traitor to my sex."

"It's a very cute idea," said Wad. "Like the Volstead Act."

"Or the Repeal of the Corn Laws," I suggested.

"Or banning *Ulysses* at home. All cute ideas," Wad

said. It had become a little too broad, and I was now sorry I'd made a contribution.

Georgia said, "When the game gets serious, the men get clannish."

"Who began it, may I ask? Who began speaking of *Lysistrata* and vegetables?" Wad inquired.

"We were talking about poor Laure," said Tolstoi, who had decided that he was inconsolable but was having a hard time holding on to centre stage. "I hadn't seen her since that night in the Dingo."

"You told me you lunched, *chéri*," Arlette put in, then added, "Sorry."

"No, not after that night at the Dingo."

"Let's all shut up about Laure, chaps. It's too, too ironic that she should be dead and we should be sitting here around her coffin, as it were."

"Where is the irony, Biz?" I asked. "You see, I didn't really know her." Like Tolstoi, I wasn't admitting everything.

"Laure was —"

"*De mortuis nil nisi bonum*," George quoted, with a look at Biz.

"I'll say what I like. That's what comes of not educating girls, George. We don't know Greek."

"Latin," Tolstoi corrected from fifty fathoms down.

"The police still have no idea who has been doing these things. At least, they are keeping very quiet if they do know something."

"Aw, come on, Michaeleen," Wad said, "when they find him, they'll announce to the world that a third-class bank clerk from Crédit Lyonnais or a sweeper of antiquities in the Louvre has turned himself in or done away with himself. It will be the first occasion his name will appear in print."

"But, as a writer, don't you find it interesting, old man?"

"No, George, it isn't interesting. It would be cute if he wasn't a madman. Then you'd have something."

"What do you mean? I don't quite follow you." George tried to fix Wad with a look, but he couldn't quite focus his eyes.

"If the killer is mad, then you have a very ordinary fellow who gives himself up to crazy impulses from time to time. Maybe when his mother tells him to clean up his room or to go out and get work, or maybe whenever he eats beetroot or sees the Eiffel Tower."

"*Pace*, Alexandre Gustave, *pace*," said Dr. Tyler. "Who wouldn't feel inadequate?"

Wad continued after giving Anson a grin. "In order to make his bad feeling go away, he finds some innocent woman and kills her when nobody is looking. That will hold him until the bad feeling comes back."

"What you're saying, Wad, is perfectly sound from a medical point of view. But why do you say that it's dull?"

"I didn't say it was dull, I said it was uninteresting. From a writer's angle."

"I think I see. I've written enough to know that novelty counts a good deal," said Anson, who now produced a small flask from an inside pocket and passed it to Wad, who took it and splashed an ounce or so into his glass.

"Novelty plays a part — don't you agree, Wilson? — but it's not the whole *corrida*. If the murderer were sane, it would be a more interesting mind for a writer to probe."

"But Waddington," Georgia asked, "how could he be sane?"

Wad made his forehead into a ploughed field. "I don't know. But it wouldn't be dull and it wouldn't be cute."

"What would it be like," Georgia said, "to go out in the evening with the idea that you are going to kill someone?"

"Oh, Georgia, let's turn the page! Honestly!" said her husband.

"You begin to sound like De Quincey: 'Murder Considered as One of the Fine Arts,'" I contributed.

"Some people argued that in the Landru case," said Georgia, her eyes sparkling.

"Ah, Bluebeard! The chap who killed his wives. Our fellow is covering his trail better. He hasn't been married to his victims," George said.

"I don't think I'd like to write about Jack, Wad. To me it doesn't make much difference if he's mad or not. What about you, Mike?"

I was flattered by having Wilson O'Donnell ask my opinion on a question of writing. I was beginning to feel like a fellow professional instead of a news service hack. It was a swell feeling.

"I've already filed a few sticks on Jack de Paris, based on police reports. I hadn't thought of putting him into a story. Do you see me as a latter-day Edgar Allan Poe? I neither write nor drink in his league." That came out more stuffily than I'd intended, more consciously literary. I bit my tongue. "Most of my writing is still in the box waiting to be unwrapped." I hoped that that improved things, but nobody seemed to be listening.

"I say, Wad, you should slip our friend Jack into that book about this summer in Spain."

"I don't think Jack will travel, George. Besides, the book is finished."

"But you only began it after the fiesta!" said Biz. "I say, you are a sly puss, Waddington. When you sit down to work, you're a prodigious whirlwind, aren't you? Who would have thought?"

"That's right, everybody talks a good book in Paris, but didn't they tell you, Wad, that nobody actually writes one?" Anson, like the others, was suddenly very interested in this news. "When did you finish it, old man?"

"Second last week of September, as close as I can recollect. I celebrated by taking a dip in the river. Tore a ligament, but the water was so cold I didn't feel it until the next morning when my right foot wouldn't support my weight."

"That's less than a month ago!"

"You put us all to shame, Waddington. I can stare all day at a jar full of dirty brushes," said Biz.

"So, maybe next year you'll be in the best-seller lists, Wad," said Wilson, rather more expansively than he'd intended.

"Yes, it's time somebody gave G.B. Stern and Janet Fairbank a run for their money. And what about Michael Arlen and Margaret Kennedy? Maybe it's time to teach Somerset Maugham what Paris is really like." Wad had added a snarl to his voice, and that was a new side of him for me. I hadn't actually imagined that he even looked at the best-seller lists. But I was forgetting his competitive side. And he was forgetting that Wilson's novel was also holding its own in the best-seller lists.

"I say, Wad, is there a chance that we might have a look at your Pamplona opus? I hope you didn't put me in it," George said, taking a last sip from his glass. "I didn't cover myself with roses down there. I don't think I behaved quite well. Especially towards your friend Leopold."

"That's water over the falls, George," said Wad.

"Still . . ."

"As a matter of record, George," suggested Lady Biz, "you behaved abominably. But we all did. Everybody but Hash. Hash was the one and truly only lady of Spain."

"I say, Wad, I think she's just given you a title!" said George, missing the point.

"Yes, if I say it myself, I think I rather like that.

Perhaps I should give up painting, which is so messy, and try fiction. I'll have that title back for a start, Waddington. You can find your own title. Try the Bible. The Bible is full of titles."

"Biz is good at finding titles," Georgia said slyly. Nobody reacted, so she said it again: "Lady Biz is good at finding titles."

Biz smiled this time and looked at her. "The title's fine, Georgia. The problem is I haven't a pocketbook or bankbook to put it on."

Tolstoi put his arm around Biz's shoulders. "I will be glad to share my millions with you, my dear."

"Ah! At last! A true gentleman. I knew they couldn't have perished to a man in the war."

"I still say that Hash was the only one of us to come out of Spain with nothing to regret," George added, trying to bring the conversation back to his own obvious interest.

"Let's shut up about Spain, shall we?" Biz suggested.

"I'll second that," said Wad.

"Do you think I could become a writer, Waddington, or does it take years and years and years?" asked Biz, none too seriously.

"You just need one true sentence after the other," he said. "That's the trick of it."

"I've got some wonderful stories from my time in the army," said George. "Wonderful stories! I just haven't had the time to write them down."

"Everybody says that, George. It's just another way of saying you're not a writer. Why don't people recognize that? George, I wouldn't presume to tell you about the army, so why do you think you've got a writer buried inside you?"

"Easy, Wad," I said. "Last time I looked, George was still a friend of ours." Waddington gave me a dirty grin. There was no fun behind it.

"You used to write, Anson?" Hash said quickly. "Why don't you talk about it anymore?"

"I've had to give it all up. Life at the American Hospital in Neuilly is too ripe for fiction."

"I liked the way you and Tatie used to talk about what you were working on."

"Maybe I'm a reformed writer, Hash. I haven't had a drop in nearly three years."

"Well, how about another drop from your gin supply, Goofo?" said Georgia. Wilson poured out a ration into the extended glasses, finishing the bottle's last few ounces himself.

"I say," said Georgia, "have any of you ever climbed the Eiffel Tower at night?"

"It's closed. Hours ago," said her husband.

"We can break in, can't we? First, we'll get something to drink. What about some champagne?"

"Do you know what you're talking about? Think of the stairs!"

"Oh, you leaden minds, you scrap-iron imaginations! Goofo, it's time to change the Quarter. Get your coat and get your hat."

Georgia went into an emotional nosedive as soon as her crazy scheme was questioned. She was taking the plan's first critic with her, but that was not her chief concern. During the scuffle to send someone through the French-speaking hordes upstairs to retrieve the coats, Wilson had suddenly gone very pale and had stopped talking.

"Before you go, Georgia," Wad said, giving her a smile that only partly disguised the savage look under it, "I think you ought to know that Mike, here, has his own theory about the murders we were talking about."

"Wad!" I said. "I don't think this is the moment —"

"Yes, Michaeleen, here, with his wily Canadian

appetite for news, has had an idea about Laure's death that might interest you."

"Shut up about that, Wad! I was only thinking out loud."

"McWardo thinks that her death wasn't the work of a madman —"

"Damn it all!"

" — he thinks that she was killed by one of us. Cut her throat hoping the police would take it for the work of Jack de Paris. How do you read those aces?"

"Good night, nurse!" said Tolstoi. "If one of us did do it, Wad, you sure as hell have given him his next victim on a silver platter."

CHAPTER 14

Our quarter of the room was still digesting Tolstoi's observation, when a new interruption punctured the party atmosphere.

"Oh, my God! Goofo!" Georgia screamed. We all looked in the direction of the great author in time to see him sink to his knees and fall over on his face. My last glimpse of him, as he fell, was of a face devoid of colour and eyes rolling back sightless.

"Give him air!" George called. "Stand away from him!"

"Anson! He needs a doctor!"

I was certain he must be having a heart attack, but Anson's face was calm as he kneeled on the floor by the body. Georgia quickly recovered herself. "Goofo, oh Goofo, you'll drive me to distraction!" She collected her smoking things and announced that it was time to send a second runner for their coats. Since Anson was doing what medical things had to be done, which didn't seem to be much, I went up the stairs into the balcony to retrieve our coats and hats. Entwined couples parted like the Red Sea as I came downstairs with my burden of fur and camel-hair. The music now was something by Gershwin: "Lady Be Good," I think.

When I returned to the main party near the window, Georgia was lighting a cigarette from the one in Biz's holder. I decided then that it was not unfeeling to maintain a calm exterior. Wad, Anson and I pulled Wilson to his feet. He was dead weight. Someone had to run out to fetch a taxi, and it was waiting for us by the time we'd got him down five flights of stairs. We were luckily able to pass a few of the doors without the tenant coming out to tell us what he thought of us and the late hours we kept: Didn't we understand that working people needed their sleep? Was I unaware that there were laws that protected tenants from people like us? We let Arlette deal with these men in worn carpet slippers and women in paper curlers and mouse-coloured bathrobes. One woman was wearing a vest made from cat-pelts. I wondered whether they were her own, or simply the kind you buy at the drug store. Arlette was very good at soothing everybody. On the whole, it was wise of us non-French-natives to keep our mouths shut. That would have been all the situation needed: a new dimension for sharp tongues to wag in.

The driver of the taxi declared that he was not about to let all the world mount into his cab. We were instructed to think of his poor springs. In the end, without a dainty leave-taking, I went in the taxi with Anson and the O'Donnells to help carry Wilson into the apartment. Wad, Hash and the others waved us away, looking as if they were on their way to another party. As we drove off, I had a glimpse of Mr. and Mrs. Burdock coming around the corner searching for the party we'd just left. He resembled Lord Plushbottom in the Sunday papers at home.

"The more I see of him, the less I can abide that posturing fake of a man," Georgia said through the driver's speaking-tube behind the glass in the front seat. I was to discover that Georgia almost always travelled across town next to the driver. If she noticed the driver at all, she was sure to turn him into a slave for life.

"What?"

"Who do you mean? Not Burdock, just now?"

"No! I mean that bogus he-man, Jason Waddington. Oh! He makes me so cross!"

"Wasn't he nice to you, Georgia? I think he and Hash both think the world of both of you."

"At home we'd call her a doormat. She has no spunk, no mind of her own. All she lives for is to please the lord and master. Who does she think she's married to, Tarzan of the Apes?"

It was very late. Montparnasse was nearly quiet, the boulevard wide and empty. The taxi took the avenue Bosquet to the Pont de l'Alma, moving a little faster as the gentle hump of the bridge came closer. The river was dark, almost invisible beneath us. We circled the *place* to avenue Marceau and its ramparts of apartment houses, then spun around the Étoile to the avenue du Bois de Boulogne, where the driver turned into the impressive rue de Tilsitt. Number 14 hardly separated itself out from its spacious fellows. I paid the driver, who, though charmed by Georgia, did not fail to add in the night tariff. I tipped him, hoping I would see the money again when Wilson sobered up. With Georgia holding open the doors, we got him into the building and then into the lift, as I was beginning to call the elevator because of the number of English people I'd been talking to recently.

There were no signs of life from O'Donnell as we laid him out on the bed. Anson removed his shoes, while Georgia crossed his hands on his chest and placed a silk rose there for good measure.

"There," she said, "nothing will wake him now until morning." She spoke in a normal voice, where most people would have whispered. We followed her out of the room. Anson closed the door behind him.

"Do you think he'll need anything for the morning?" he asked, searching in his pocket for a notepad.

"You mean a prescription? No, Anson, Goofo's got a trunk full of medicine. We don't need any more. But you're a dear to ask."

"Are you sure we shouldn't put him to bed?" I asked.

"He'll be right as rain in the morning. Except for the headache. If he went to mass, he wouldn't even have that. But do you think I can get him to go?"

Ten minutes later, Anson Tyler and I were walking under the Arc de Triomphe. Leaves were blowing about in the great empty space beneath. There were no taxis in view.

"Do you feel like walking?" Anson asked.

"At Châtelet we could catch an all-night bus."

"I'll walk with you that far. My boat is in the river near there." We set out down the Champs-Élysées, with the wide sidewalks all to ourselves. The electric signs had been turned off except in the showroom of an automobile firm on the Rond Point. From there, we walked under the chestnut trees that ran in two long lines on our side of the street.

"Did I understand correctly that you live on a boat?"

"A barge, really. It's not a yacht. Nothing grand, but I wouldn't trade it for that studio we were in tonight."

Anson Tyler moved with a quick military stride. We covered the distance to the river in less than twenty minutes. Tacitly, I'd given up the hope of a night bus. I wanted to have a look at this barge on the Seine. I'd seen strings of barges moving up and down the river before, usually offering a glimpse of a woman hanging out washing on a clothesline or the captain changing the baby. It was another world on the river. The trips on the *bateaux-mouches* don't quite catch it.

We crossed an empty Place de la Concorde. The globes of the street lamps glowed. The mist in the air made the classical fronts of the buildings on the other side look like a painted backdrop for a stage setting. One of the fountains was draped in canvas while some restoration work was going on; it made the other, uncovered fountains look austere and naked. The obelisk in the centre of the square divided the night sky in two. The water under the bridge was moving quickly, with occasional eddies to illustrate the power of the river held in check.

The barge, wide and low in the water, was tied between the Pont de la Concorde and the Pont de Solferino. It nestled into a curve of the quay and looked battened down for a squall. There was a fenced-in square of deck space with a view of the best of Paris, if from a low angle. I was about to say good night and shove off when a hatch opened in the deck and a head with a pipe in its mouth poked through.

"You make enough noise for the German army!" the head said in French.

"Sorry, Georges. Are you off?"

"Yes, I worked until about half an hour ago. Now, I go for a walk in Les Halles. Maybe I can find myself a good northern breakfast."

Anson introduced me to Georges Sim, who shared the barge with him. Georges, who came from Liège, spent the day writing pot-boilers on the barge. He had a wife somewhere in the city, but he came to the barge when he wanted to work. Tonight he had taken advantage of Anson's being away to get a few more hours of writing done.

"He turns them out the way Ford does in Detroit," Anson said.

"There's coffee made," Georges said, opening up the rest of the hatch cover.

"Won't you stay and have some?" I suggested. He shrugged and went below. We followed.

Sim's writing desk was bare except for a pot of paste and a pair of scissors. His portable typewriter was in its case. He saw me looking and smiled, taking his pipe out of his mouth as he spoke.

"What I do will never pass for literature," he said, "but I try to keep it tidy. Years from now I'll get the *Légion d'Honneur* for spelling and neatness."

"I try to keep my office neat, too, but there are too many other people using the space."

"Oh, don't tell me! Another writer! Anson, where do you find them?" He took the remaining clean cup and poured coffee into it. There was a bowl of sugar but no milk. I took the first sip and passed the cup on. The coffee had been boiled.

The main cabin was low-ceilinged with gas lamps in weighted balances mounted on the walls. There was a double bunk built into one of the bulkheads. Hooks along one wall carried caps and a couple of dark jackets, one with a tracery of gold flecks on the shoulders. One of the caps was fixed with gold braid in front of the jutting, dark peak. The cabin was altogether a tidy place to lay one's head, if you ignored the galley.

"What sorts of things do you write?" I asked Georges. "I'm sure Anson was pulling my leg when he said they were pot-boilers."

"No, not at all. They're pot-boilers all right. People keep asking me when I'm going to write a real novel, a big novel, a serious *magnum opus*. Ha! That's an easy question. Maybe the sum of all my pot-boilers will be my big novel. I used to think I was writing them for practice; now, I accept them as what I do. It's a sort of *métier*, or a *métier* of a sort."

"Have you ever done a detective story?"

"Never. I'm easily confused by puzzles. I'd make a hash of it."

"Detective stories?" Anson said with a superior smile.

"Why waste time writing that sort of rubbish? You'll turn your mind to jelly."

"Ah," said Georges, "you say that *now*! I remember when you were trying to write one yourself, *mon ami*." Georges laughed as though he had just declared checkmate on his companion.

"Yes, I tried to write one once. As an experiment. Georges was no help at all. But it wasn't his fault; it's the form. They're trash, a truant occupation. There's no room for literary interest. In fact, it's almost breaking the rules to put in anything but the puzzle." Anson had climbed out of his coat and jacket and was now in his shirtsleeves. The front of his shirt showed expensive studs.

"But the detective story doesn't have to be a puzzle like the English mysteries," I said. "It could be about real people with their backs against the wall." Georges cocked his large head as though to examine the proposition from a new angle. "Most murderers aren't master criminals. They are ordinary people caught on the wrong foot."

"*A bout de souffle*? At the end of one's tether?" Georges said, knocking his inverted pipe against his boot. "I hadn't considered that. Maybe it's a thought I should put in my pipe to think about." He got up smiling and shook hands with both of us. "In the meantime, I have a wife who expects me to bring some meat and vegetables from the market. I'll leave my mistress —" Here he nodded at the table and the portable typewriter " — in your custody." He said goodbye, and we could hear the sound of his boots on the deck overhead as he went ashore.

"Georges is a nice fellow," I said, hoping to hear more about him from my host.

"He's a demon for work," Anson said. "I could never keep up with him. He can finish a book less than three weeks after he's started it. And he's getting faster!"

"Anson, you're being too hard on yourself. How could you keep up with Georges? You're at the hospital all day. Be fair with yourself. Didn't Wad quit journalism before he started writing seriously? I can't see how anyone can do two jobs. I know I'm usually too tired at the end of the day to do more than find a good place to have dinner. If I had a place like this, I'd be too tired to keep it clean."

"Well, you can see that our ideas on housekeeping are similar." Anson had removed his shirt and was pulling on a cotton sweatshirt. "The last time I found the broom, it had cobwebs growing on it."

"But don't you find your work at Neuilly fully rewarding?" I asked, having taken the liberty of pouring more coffee into the single cup. "I should have thought that, with medicine, you wouldn't need to look for . . ."

"Fulfilment? A reason for not cutting my throat?"

"Well, let's just say another string to your bow."

"Mike, I'd say that I'm a good doctor, a good surgeon; I can handle the traffic in the operating room. They call me a good clinician. I have a sixth sense when it comes to diagnosis. But when I think that I might still be taking out gallbladders and tonsils twenty years from now, I begin to wonder whether I've not taken a wrong turn somewhere. Maybe I should have taken a run at politics back home, or — hell, I don't know." Anson had slipped out of his trousers and pulled on some dungarees. He tightened the belt with care.

"That's why I came over here, Mike. America wasn't in the war yet, but I wanted to escape from filling sample jars with tonsils and prostates for the pathologist."

"I see," I said inadequately.

"I was in a good practice; everything was going well. I was a member of the country club. I was learning to sail."

"But you came over to do medicine in the front lines."

"I enjoyed that." He gave me a large grin that showed his front teeth at their rabbity best. "I'll never tell anyone I had a rotten war. People left me alone. No interference. Once America came into it, I had to fight my own people, who found my freelance status embarrassing to them. I wasn't in the right pigeon-hole, they said. They wanted me out of there. I was fighting on two fronts. By day there was the fight in the advance medical units against gangrene and blood-loss and shock, and, by night the writing of letters to so-called superior officers protesting my re-posting to some New England shelter for the walking wounded. It was terrible there for awhile, until I found a senator who got them to leave me alone." He was looking very thin as he told this to me, yet I could picture him working over the wounded without a wasted movement. "Let's change the subject," he said. "It still makes me mad."

"How did you meet Waddington and Hash?"

"She had the grippe and was running a dangerous fever. They called the American Hospital and I dropped in on my way home. I was living on Cherche-Midi in those days. Later, I saw Hash through the early stages of her pregnancy until they returned to the other side. Wad and I got along. As I said, I used to think I could write. For awhile, I worked pretty hard at it. Now, I know it was a waste of time." He looked up at me, trying to make a grin wipe away the pain in his words.

"*Et vous*? as the French say. And you?" he asked.

"I've been filling some notebooks, but that's about all. Wad thinks I've done more than I have simply because I never talk about what I'm doing. I try to keep him guessing. He's damned competitive."

"He said you were doing some detective work."

"Oh, he was pulling everybody's leg. I just had a theory that a man with a grudge against some woman might take advantage of a killer like Jack to settle his private score. If he imitates Jack's crimes, the authorities will add his murder to Jack's total and think no more about it."

"But when they catch Jack eventually . . ."

"Well, by then it will be too late, won't it? Nothing stays fixed on Montparnasse."

"My favourite coal-and-wood dealer is closing down to make way for another café across the street from the Select. Everything changes."

"I get the feeling — and I've had it more than once — that I've missed the best years in the Quarter. Today we have only the left-overs from a brilliant era, wondering where the parade went."

"Wad calls them 'scum,' or, in a more benevolent mood, he softens it to 'the dregs.' I think he exaggerates. I *hope* he exaggerates, considering the amount of time I waste in places like the Dingo."

"You used to know Laure Duclos very well, I hear. I knew her a little, was hoping to know her better. What do you make of her death? What was she like when she wasn't tight?"

"Hell, when you change a subject, you don't do it subtly, do you?"

"If it bothers you to talk about it . . ."

"No. Not at all. It was a long time ago. The war was just over. We lived together. Then we stopped living together. Laure was my first girl in Paris. She was quite young then and relatively unspoiled. At first we were very much in love. Then it moved away from that."

"How do you mean?"

"It was as though once she had made a base with me, she was ready to cut the wire and move on to a forward position. She was always moving to a forward position from a place of relative calm: a shell hole, or the debris from a ruined chapel."

"You're getting poetic."

"She used to bring it out in me. I was quite ambitious then, in a literary way. Saw writing as a way to escape the blood and bandages."

"And?"

"She moved on. I stopped caring. Simple as that."

Through the portholes, I could see the sun reflected in the high windows of the Petit Palais on the other side of the river. Anson turned off the gas from one of the lights. I was feeling gritty in the early light, feeling the need for a shave and bath coming on. I put down the cup near the others, some of them with dark stains, some with old coffee still in them.

"That theory of yours," Anson said. "It would have made sense, you know, if Laure was like the rest of us."

"What do you mean?"

"Laure was an opium user. She used it rather heavily. That would have put her in contact with a network that has its branches on the Right Bank. It involved her with people we would know nothing about on Montparnasse. You see what I mean?" I nodded as I saw my hypothesis fall apart and remembered La Ruche in the early dawn.

"If Laure had been like Arlette, or Biz even, your theory . . ."

"Sure, well, I should remember that I'm a journalist and not Hawkshaw the Detective, I guess."

Anson turned off another gas jet as the day poked shafts of light into all of the barge's dusty corners. I said good night and climbed through the open hatch. The sun was now shining on the river and hiding in the trees behind Notre Dame. The streets were crowded with the morning's business as I walked up the boulevard St-Germain, back to my room.

CHAPTER 15

The autumn was moving on towards winter. Paris had suffered a disastrous summer, and it was said that the winter was going to be worse. There were fewer *clochards* on the Métro gratings at night now. The door of the *estaminet* around the corner from me in the rue Gozlin was closed against the cold wind, and the patrons huddled around the high zinc bar for warmth as well as conversation. On Montparnasse, the patrons had moved off the uncovered parts of the *terrasses* to the protected insides, where a charcoal brazier gave an impression of heat if not the real thing. We watched the sign of the wood-and-coal dealer across from the Select come down: *Juglar, Chantier, bois et charbon.* This was followed by a general cleaning out of the yard. It was only a matter of time before the steam-shovels and wagons would turn the location, which went well back into the last century, into a quagmire, running muddy tracks out into the boulevard. At the Dôme, old Père Chambon joked that the new café would in the end drive him into a suicide pact, like the film actor Max Linder. If he could only find a partner, he complained. When it was suggested that he might consider Mme. Select from across the street, he admitted that there might be worse things on earth than a deteriorating Montparnasse after all.

During the day, I did my work at the agency. My command of French prepositions and irregular verbs improved to the point where I stopped worrying. I continued to play tennis with Wad and once in awhile with Hal Leopold, who always gave me a good game. In the evening, I tried to work on my notes, when I was in the mood and when I wasn't too tired from work. I have to admit that at the end of November I had no more than a slender bundle of pages. From time to time, Wad and I would walk Snick-a-Fritz in the Luxembourg. Hash never asked her "Tatie" to help out in this way, but it was obvious she was delighted to see her men going off together. On these walks, Wad tried to get me to give him some idea of what I was working on. It was my private joke, as the only would-be writer in Paris more reticent to discuss his work than Wad, to keep him stewing about my "work in progress." Mostly we talked about sports. He didn't follow team sports, had at the most a sketchy idea of the baseball standings and never talked about football. He claimed that football was something he'd missed when he didn't go to university, but I knew he was on his high school team.

Wad liked sports where one man was pitted against another force, be it man or beast. Everything was an extension of trout fishing. Even bullfighting. Sometimes he could get very sanctimonious about his bullfighting. I remember Hal Leopold once kidded him about setting up a system of points so that you could keep score of a *corrida*: so many points for the matador, so many for the bull. He didn't see the funny side of that. But, then, it came from Leopold.

He enjoyed talking about his time in Pamplona and Madrid, speaking as though he had been raised in the Pyrenees or La Mancha. It was easy to forget that Spain was fairly new to him. That's why he had to talk about it. He was trying to get it right. Wad's Spain always seemed to have more Bizet in it than it should.

One afternoon, returning from a press conference on the boulevard Diderot, I stopped with a colleague for a drink across from the Gare de Lyon. After he left, I crossed over the boulevard and the open space in front of the station. Inside, I asked to see the chief of the railway police and was directed to an office near the rear, but still under the great curved and girdered roof. When asked for my platform ticket, I explained my mission to the controller, who let me pass while shaking his head. Soon I was facing a M. La Fond in the *Commissariat Spécial de la Gare*. I told him that I was interested in discovering what information I could about the disappearance of a suitcase just prior to Christmas three years ago. He asked to see my *carte de séjour* and my press identification papers. Once he had approved these, he went at once to the bottom drawer of a wooden filing case, from which he brought a file. He placed it on his desk, while I remained on the other side of the dark-stained counter. M. La Fond took his time.

"A woman named Colbrant, who was staying with the Soeurs de St-Vincent-de-Paul, reported a theft on the 12th of December, 1922," he said unhelpfully.

"Is there anything else? Something between that date and Christmas Eve?" M. La Fond looked, then shook his head.

"Is there no record of any sort of an inquiry?"

"Monsieur may look for himself." He lifted the file, which contained a ledger and turned it around for me. He indicated the entry he'd cited. It went into some detail: ". . . *elle fut accostée par un individu qui lui offrit une consommation dans un bar, en attendant l'heure du départ du train . . .*"

I left the station, passing up the twin curved stairways that invited me to the buffet on the floor above. I was baffled. The suitcase had been stolen, but no one had reported the theft. Or, if it was reported, no record existed to prove it. I was puzzled as I waited for a bus to return me to the office.

That night I got an invitation from Sylvia Beach to present myself at the bookshop at closing time. Not knowing what to expect, I dressed well enough to be presentable at a reading by one of her favourite writers — Claudel or Valéry perhaps — but without putting on a special effort. That is to say, I wore my other suit, which was nearing retirement. As soon as I arrived, I met Sylvia, who had already rounded up Wad and Hash, and the four of us left the shop and crossed the street to pick up Adrienne Monnier at her own French bookshop. Everybody was in a holiday mood, so that even the purchase of tickets in the Métro took on a special flavour. Waddington — Sylvia on one arm and Adrienne on the other, with me and Hash bringing up the rear — announced the plan.

"We're going to take the number 4 in the direction Porte de Clignancourt and make a *correspondance* at Réaumur-Sébastopol to a number 3, the Porte des Lilas to Porte de Champerret, in the direction Porte des Lilas, and we'll get off at rue Pelleport." He said this with some satisfaction, as though he was now authorized to reveal the contents of his sealed orders.

"What's all this about?" I asked when we had settled ourselves in a second-class car and the doors banged shut behind us.

"We're going to the boxing," Adrienne said. "I thought you knew."

"Nobody tells me anything." Hash was sitting beside me, smiling to herself while idly tracing the pattern surrounding the enamelled wall panels with her grey gloves. I watched her fingers finding their way around the intricate, overlapping, interlocking square ornamentation at the corners. All the while, Wad was talking.

"This fellow Fournier is supposed to be tough, but I think that's mostly his manager talking. Batty, the other man, has a string of wins. He doesn't need to have his manager boasting. But it might be a fix. You can never tell in these small rings."

On the way up the steep stairs at rue Pelleport, Wad looked back, laughing. "You remember the last time we came, Sylvia?"

"I do indeed! Cilla was panting so hard, I thought she was about to go into labour."

"Oh, I wasn't that far along!" protested Hash.

"That was the night the crowd didn't like the referee's decision," Adrienne said. We all puffed our way to the top of the stairs.

"The policeman tried to ignore the whole disturbance," recalled Sylvia as we came to the Métro exit and then out into a small square that looked down the sloping avenue Gambetta to a church steeple.

"And, Tatie, you nearly got us all pinched when you said that, as usual, the *flic* was in the *vespasienne* answering a call of nature."

"He was trying not to get his head broken. In this part of town, a *flic* has to keep his head down."

"Well, I hope they don't repeat the performance tonight," Adrienne said.

I found the intersection we had arrived at foreign and hostile. I was reminded that I had some time ago interrupted my exploration of the streets of Paris, a recreation that had afforded me much pleasure in my early days in town.

Wad led the way through an alley to the entrance of a small auditorium, which was already filled with spectators. It was only with some difficulty that we were able to find some backless benches close to the action. "If you can't see what's happening close up, you might as well read about it in the *Echo des Sports* tomorrow morning," Wad said. Adrienne and I were seated behind Sylvia and the Waddingtons. Wad kept turning around during the preliminary bouts to tell us useful things about the fighters. I hadn't seen a fight since my friend Callaghan and I had caught one at the Mutual Arena in Toronto four months ago. Already it seemed like four years. When the main event began, Wad leaned forward and watched what was going on with a concentration that could not have been broken by an earthquake. I enjoyed the bout as well, but I never forgot where I was or with whom I was sitting. I could feel the fighters move around one another, appreciate the beauty of the way they danced in and out and be dazzled by a sudden, well-calculated play, but I could never quite get beyond the ripe smell of flesh and liniment far enough to forget myself. I envied Wad, now sitting with his knees up and his arms wrapped around them. From where I sat, Wad wasn't in his body just then; he was up there in the ring with the fighters. When it was over, he turned around and looked at us with eyes that had been well satisfied with their meal, asking questions as though sifting to see how many of the tasty dishes we had tried and enjoyed.

"Did you see how close Fournier was working to the belt? He was always close to being called for a foul, but never quite. Batty was doubling up so he'd have to reach farther. That's why they gave the fight to Batty even though he hardly threw a good punch all night. Batty didn't win the fight, Fournier lost it." He was excited and full of fun afterwards, shadow-boxing with himself as we waited for our aisle to clear and taking a few punches at the program I was still carrying.

"Tolstoi should have been there," Wad said when we were installed in a café on Ménilmontant that looked across the wide street to the Père Lachaise cemetery. "Englishmen understand about a good fight. Americans only want a scrap. There's a difference."

"At least this time there was no riot, Waddington," Adrienne said with a puckish smile. "I hope you're not disappointed."

He shot her a grin. "There'll be other fights, other riots. We'll all have to go back to the Cirque de Paris next time there's a *Grand Gala de la boxe*. We'll make sure Tolstoi comes. He used to box at Oxford, you know."

"Was he with us last time, Wad?" Sylvia wanted to know.

"No, he and Laure were having one of their battles and neither of them came."

"How long were they together?" I asked, while the women were deciding on what they were going to order. Even Adrienne was suspicious of cafés this far away from the *carrefour de l'Odéon*.

"We heard about them fighting so much, it seems like twenty years. Whenever they weren't holding hands, they were at one another's throats. She made a little money teaching and he lived on hand-outs from the manor house," Wad said, slipping an arm around Sylvia.

"Was that money to keep him out of England?" I asked.

"That's my guess, but I've never known for sure. Laure was a wonderfully beautiful woman in those days. Everybody envied Tolstoi."

"Everybody?" I echoed with a raised eyebrow.

"Everybody," he said, making sure the others were still occupied.

Later, back on Montparnasse, after we had seen Sylvia and Adrienne safely home to the rue de l'Odéon, Hash, Wad and I stopped at the Select for a nightcap. As we sat down, Wad was approached by a lanky young man in an

American army overcoat that had been stripped of all insignia and, like the young man himself, was looking a little the worse for wear. He explained that he was a writer from New York who'd heard that Wad was scouting for Burdock and his literary magazine. Hash was looking at the young writer's dirty fingernails and spotted skin. Wad heard him out, and even smiled enthusiastically as he listened. Finally, a rolled manuscript was handed over to Waddington, after its author checked to see that his name and address were attached. Wad watched the back of the writer disappear through the busy traffic of the boulevard before speaking.

"Of all the different kinds of scum that float to the surface in the Quarter, the hopeful scum of the cafés is the worst."

"'Scum'? That's a bit strong, isn't it?"

"No, it's not half strong enough. I feel like a dip in the river after talking to one of that bunch. Too late in the year for it tonight, but I'll plan to have a good wash before I go to bed."

"Weren't you a young hopeful not so long ago?" I asked.

"Yes, Tatie, you are being hard on the poor fellow. He doesn't look to be one of those talking writers you complain about, the sort that never writes a word —"

"Except home for more money!" Wad sent a cold glance into the crowded street.

"This young fellow looked serious enough to be a younger version of you when you first came to Paris." Hash's face had taken on a worried expression. She tried to mask it, but she'd gone quite pale.

"Listen, Feather P., I was here first in 1917 and I didn't parade my jottings through the Quarter as if I was selling *cacahuètes* from table to table."

"Tatie, be fair! He wasn't peddling. He asked you to add his work to the pile you're considering for Mr. Burdock, that's all. I can't see the harm in that. And as for 'scum' . . ."

"There are no office-hours at the Select, Wad," I said. Wad's heavy eyebrows were almost meeting. I'd never seen his face so dark.

"I've half a mind to do my late-night drinking at the Rotonde again. These youngsters are boycotting it because the patron called the *flics* on one of them. I'll be safer there. And if you're both on his side, I don't see why you're wasting time with a spoil-sport like me. Drunk or sober, I can find my own way home."

"Hey, Wad! Steady on. You're among friends. What the hell's eating you?"

"Every goddamned kid who can afford boat fare and a pencil is suddenly Ring Lardner or Wilson O'Donnell, for Christ's sake! Maybe I should retire and leave the field to these young Menckens and Sherwood Andersons. Maybe I'm the scum and you're too polite to tell me."

"Aw, go to hell! You don't know when you're well off! Hash, talk some sense into him."

"I think you've been working too hard, that's what I think, Tatie. Come on, kid, we're going home. You need a good night's sleep."

"Don't call me that. I don't like to be called 'kid.'"

"Tatie?"

"You go on. I'll follow in a few minutes."

Hash tried to cover the hurt and said nothing. A tram made a noisy clatter along the middle of the boulevard.

"Tatie?" Hash tried again when it was quiet.

"Goddamn it, are you going deaf? I said I'll be along in a few minutes. I've got something I want to raise with Mike, here."

"Well, don't stay up all night."

"I'll be along, Priscilla." This was the first time I'd heard Waddington use his wife's proper Christian name. I could see that he saved it for moments like this. Hash got up and left the café without looking back.

"Shouldn't you go with her?" I asked. "This is not the safest part of town with Jack around, you know."

"Hash'll be all right. It's only a couple of blocks."

"Well, if you'll excuse me. I think I'll see her home, then."

"Mike, you are a prize son of a bitch."

"These remarks must be judged in relation to their place of origin, Waddington. I don't think I'm greatly worried."

I put some notes and change on the table to cover the drinks that had been ordered but had never arrived and left the café. The night air hit me square in the face. Winter was on its way with a certainty of purpose now. There was no going back to the misty, rather balmy days.

I caught up to Hash quickly. She had just stopped at the corner waiting for the light to change. I'd called out to her, but she hadn't turned around. She was holding a handkerchief, and when I caught up to her I could see that her face was moist.

"Hash, he doesn't mean any of that. We both know that. He's just a little excited and just a little tight," I said.

"You go on back, Mike. I can see myself home."

"Don't be silly." I put my arm around her and gave her a hug. "You know he's crazy about you. He's just keyed up after the fights. Maybe he was looking for his turn in the ring."

"Well, to be frank, Mike, I'm not very content to be his sparring partner when he's in this mood."

"You said he'd been working too hard."

"Sometimes three thousand words a day. Rewriting parts of the book. Oh, his writing is going well. It's in his family life that he's having trouble. Snick didn't get out this afternoon as usual because Tatie said he had to see somebody about tonight's tickets. I was cooped up with Snick all day yesterday because of the rain. It's getting me down, and I guess it's getting him down as well."

We turned into the rue de Chevreuse, which led to her street, walking without saying anything. When we got to her door, she turned her auburn head, gave me a kiss on the cheek and squeezed my hand.

"Good night, Mike. Thank you for seeing me home. I can manage from here myself."

"Are you sure?"

Her eyes were shining in the light coming into the carpenter's yard from the street lights.

"I hope so, Mike. I really hope so."

CHAPTER 16

Y ou're a budding chump, Waddington!"

"Aw, shut up and sit down. If you don't want to do either, clear off. You're blocking the view."

"Hash loves you, you idiot! How can you be so mean to her?"

"Because I'm a son of a bitch, that's why. If I can hurt her in a big way, why not in small ways, too?"

I sat down. Wad had cleared the table of the assorted drinks that had been ordered and was now drinking a *fine à l'eau* as though he was in a contest to see who could put his chin on the table first.

"Everybody's a son of a bitch sometimes, Wad."

"Not me, by God! I'm a heel all the time. No time off for good behaviour. I'm a first-rate bastard. Oh, I'm one swell fellow, I am."

"What's eating you?"

"Don't want to talk about it."

I knew better than to press him. I waited until the waiter could be flagged down and ordered one of what Wad was drinking. I didn't say anything until it came.

"Wad, are you worried about the Spanish book?"

"Nope. Next question?"

"Aw, go to hell!"

"You stick around, kid. I've got a big bag of tricks. I've got an assortment of knives and short killing-swords for sticking between the shoulder-blades of good friends. The only safe place to be is numbered among the enemy."

"Why are you being so hard on yourself, Wad? Why not drink up and go home. Hash'll still be awake."

"It's too bad about Hash. Too bad."

"You are beginning to sound like a sentimental drunk, Wad. It's not your style. Did something happen tonight I was too thick to see? Come on, how can a guy help if he doesn't have all the cards?"

"This is a game you want to stay out of. The casualties are going to be heavy and we aren't taking prisoners."

"Okay, I'll mind my own business. But, I'll say this: you're a damned fool if you think you can improve on Hash. She's your perfect match, Wad. You both enjoy the same things and find the same things funny. She's a peach, any way you look at her."

"Yeah. I know all about that. Christ, don't you think I know all about that?"

"What are you chaps so glum and serious about?" It was Biz, wearing a man's trenchcoat over a light dress and shivering. "I say, may I have a swallow of that before I freeze to death?" She took hold of Wad's glass and drank a third of what was left in it. "Aren't you going to invite a chap to sit down?"

"Hello, Biz," Wad said. "What mischief have you been up to?"

I said hello myself and pulled up a chair for her. She sat down, still wrapped up in the trenchcoat, more as if it were a blanket than a fitted garment. "George is paying the taxi," she said, then, looking at Wad, "I haven't been up to any mischief. You sound like Harold Leopold when you talk like that, Waddington. It doesn't become you. You used to be so merry all the time."

A waiter came over and Biz ordered drinks for herself and George, whom we could see through the window conferring with the driver at the curbside.

"We've been over at the Crillon," she announced. "There's an Irishman there who wants to take me to British East with him. He says there's a fortune to be made out in British East. I told him to come back for me when he's made it. Now isn't *that* telling him? Honestly! Did he think I came with his drink, like a stale canapé? No, I take that back. The canapés at the Crillon are incomparable."

"Apart from that, how is the Crillon bar?"

"Still going around. George the bartender sends his love."

George, the bartender's namesake, came through the door and began looking among the crowded tables for a free chair. When he found one he pulled it up to our table. "Brrr! They could afford to put more peat on to the fire."

"A peat fire would be better than nothing, which is what Mme. Select is currently offering her patrons. We are warming the place with our blood. She won't install a brazier until December. Are you going out to British East as well?"

"You're well informed, old chap. Hel-lo there, Mike. No, I think I'm chary of the fires I jump into. I've also become an expert on frying pans. Where is that waiter?" George stood up and waved until he had attracted the attention of everyone in the café except the waiter. He sat down dejected. Biz tried to straighten his jacket collar, which he had turned up against the weather when he'd given his coat to her.

"We were at the fights tonight," Wad volunteered.

"How awful! Out near Père Lachaise? I'm going to spend eternity in Père Lachaise and I don't intend to go there a moment before my time."

"Père Lachaise is the best cemetery in town. Only the best people go there."

"It's too, too much the rage, my dear. I'll make my own fashions thank you very much. Would you know me if I were turned out like a *Vogue* cover? Would you recognize me in an outfit by Poiret or in a design by Lepape or Benito? I thought you loved me for myself and my old felt hat."

"Where is your old felt hat tonight?"

"I think I left it someplace. Where is that beastly waiter? Does he mean us to die of thirst like some Riff with a dead camel?"

Eventually the waiter brought the drinks Biz had ordered and we ordered the same again. For a waiter in a good café, he was of an independent turn of mind, indicating with his raised eyebrows that he might be back and, then again, he might not. Wad gave George an account of the Fournier–Batty fight with the dramatic parts illustrated from a standing position. When Wad began his reenactment of the only knock-out of the evening in one of the preliminary bouts, Biz looked over at me. Her eyes opened as though I had suddenly materialized at the table where there had been nothing before.

"Hullo, Mike," she said, leaning her cheek in her hand. "One gets awfully lonely in a crowd, don't you think?"

"That's what they're for."

"I suppose. Anyway, hullo, you." She looked up at Wad, who was finishing the knock-out punch. "No wonder you don't need a coat, Waddington, you have built-in warmth. You stay so active it's a criticism to the rest of us."

"I miss the hat."

"You must have been off at a shooting party, Waddington, I haven't seen you since you came to the studio party. You left early enough. Before the police came. That was a night to remember to forget. Of course, you chaps left with the *body*."

"Seems like weeks ago. What have you been up to?"

"Not much. Under the weather. I've got a beastly chest and it hobbles me at awkward moments. It's like a spoiled child."

"But you're better now?"

"Thriving!"

"Wad, old fellow, there's something I've been meaning to ask you," George said. "Haven't been tight enough to ask before. May not be tight enough yet. It's about that trip to Spain, actually."

"Oh, shove it along, George!"

"No, this is important. I want you to hear me out. All of you."

But a sudden cry of "Waddington, you old son of a gun!" coming from the front door of the café put a quick end to George's attempt at a serious talk. The source of the exclamation was a compact, tidy little man with wild blond hair and a pink face. "Damn it all, Jay, you haven't moved a muscle since I saw you last! Are you paying rent to Madame Select or what?"

"Don! You old son of a gun!"

Don moved through the tables easily and exchanged a bear hug with Wad, who nearly lifted the shorter man off his feet. Biz and George seemed equally happy to see the newcomer. Don shook George's hand warmly and kissed Biz on each cheek, as though this was a joke of long standing between them.

"Sit down, Donald! Oh, how we've missed you in the Quarter!"

"How was Berlin, Don? Not like fishing in Spain, I'll warrant."

Although he was a bantam of a man, he appeared to be a dynamo, slapping backs and making answers to all the questions he was asked at once. He quickly turned his energy to attracting the waiter, who actually came and then returned with drinks.

"Donald, you've been sorely missed. Sit down, damn it! When did you get back to town?"

"How was Berlin, Don? We've missed you, old chap!"

Donald Gracie Hughes, an old friend of Wad's from his days in journalism and a veteran of the, by now, nearly legendary Spanish trip that summer, tested my right hand in his as I was introduced to him. He was another literary man, I found out later, who wrote clever pieces for American magazines and now scenarios for German moving pictures. When he talked with Wad and the others, the conversation glittered with private jokes that went back to Spain and the mad happenings during the fiesta. The glitter was obscured for me, though I insisted, through growing annoyance, that they shouldn't explain things for my benefit.

"How was Berlin, Don?"

"Cold and in a ferment," he said. The others laughed. "New wine had been poured into old bottles. Or the other way around. They've got a German director after me to write English titles for his epics. Things like: 'And then the mercy for which she begged, he would not requite her.'"

"Why not 'vouchsafe'?" Wad asked. "They might go for 'vouchsafe.'"

"Not ready for it. They aren't paying me enough for 'vouchsafe.'"

"You should go into films, Waddington. I can see you have the gift for it," I said.

"You could make a big success in pictures. Look at June Mathis."

"Look at Chaplin."

"Look at me," Don added. "You know, I've been looking for you all over town. I should have come here to begin with." Don slapped George on the back, as though he had just joined the party. "How are you, George? Still undischarged?"

"Oh, it's moved along from there, old man. In the eyes of the law I'm rather naughty. My keeper threatens to cut me off and I've been borrowing money all over town."

"His keeper not only threatens, she keeps her word."

"Well, she shouldn't tie money to good behaviour. It never works. I'm living testimony, by God."

"Say, why don't we move this party to the Dingo. This place is getting crowded. Time to cross the boulevard."

"Agreed!" said Biz, finishing her drink and wrapping herself in George's coat again. "I hope we can gather a few women on the way. I feel a little conspicuous with you chaps, as if I was the only pickled onion in a jar of olives."

On the way across the boulevard, Biz caught Wad by one arm and me by the other. We waited for a number 91 tram to move along towards Port-Royal and skirted the leading edge of the Dôme as we headed up the rue Delambre. We went into the Dingo and let our eyes accustom themselves to the darkness that hung about everywhere except behind the bar.

"Oh bother!" Biz had seen Harold Leopold sitting at the bar. "Should we leave?"

"Damn his Hebrew eyes," George said. "He doesn't own the bar."

"He seems to be sitting like anyone else," I said, defending my tennis partner as well as I could.

"Isn't that Hal Leopold?" Don yelled, going up to the bar. "Hey, Leopold, shall we run with the bulls in the morning?"

Hal turned and smiled at the sight of Don. His smile faded, though, when the rest of the party moved forward. He shook hands with Don. "Hello, you people. I was wondering when you'd appear." He moved to the last stool and cleared the way for the rest of us. Wad was first to go up to him. Soon they were talking about the fight, while Hal watched Biz light her cigarette from George's unsteadily held match.

"Waddington's going to re-fight the entire card, I'll bet," said George.

"Watch him," I suggested. "He gets better."

Freddy, the barman, knew most of the party and began making conversation while he poured the drinks. The others knew him well; I'd seen him at work only a few times. He was trying to add me up through the company I was travelling in. I didn't much like it.

When I began listening to what Don was saying, he interrupted his flow to include me. "As a Canadian," he said, "you will appreciate this."

"Don's a yell of fun, Mike. Wait until you know him better."

"We're getting up capital for a great tourist enterprise," he went on. "It will make the Eiffel Tower look sick. It will rob the Alps of all but passing interest."

"You'd better tell me about it."

"Don't let George say he'll invest."

"She's right, there. I get carried away."

"The scheme is to put a gigantic fourteen-carat inlay into the cavity in the Percé Rock off Gaspé in Quebec. What do you think?"

"Quebec will be in a ferment," said George.

"Quebec? Canada, you mean! It's a capital idea, chaps. If we get in early, we should make a killing."

"For you fellows, because of all we've been through in the streets of Pamplona, I'm going to offer a special rate."

"Good!"

"Once it's known, the investment houses of the world will be in a ferment." By now Wad and Hal were listening with interest, and the scheme was explained again.

"Fourteen-carat? I should go for eighteen," Wad said.

"I don't see where your profit's going to come from. You can see Percé Rock from just about everywhere on that coast. You won't be able to control access," Leopold pointed out.

"Damn it, he's right!" Don said.

"Leopold, you *are* a spoil-sport."

"Put your money away. We'll have to think of something else."

"Oh, you are a wet blanket, Hal."

"Am I? I thought I was getting into the game. You know, taking it seriously the way you were. I've been to Gaspé and —"

"Oh, do let's shut up about it!" Biz said, with her hands over her ears. Freddy poured her another *fine*. She was looking at me again when I glanced in her direction. I let her look. It was nice to be looked at by Biz. It reminded me how long I'd been away from home, and the face of Laure Duclos flitted behind my eyes. When I smiled back at Biz, she broke off her attention and turned to Wad.

"We saw your friend Julia Lowry and her sister at the Crillon. I meant to tell you," she said brightly, "but I forgot." Wad nodded then moved closer to hear more. "I don't think I quite like her, you know."

"Why?"

"She isn't one of the chaps."

"Is she too chic for you?"

"Listen to the man! George, knock Waddington down for me! The cheek!" George got up and Biz made him sit down again.

"Well, what is it about her?" He was looking a little hurt but was smiling broadly, the way he did when he was upset.

"The sweet creature is chic enough for ten women. She has all the assurance of an Oxford don and all the vacuity of a boy sent down in his first term. She behaves as though she had studied deportment in a book published in Alabama or Arkansas or wherever she came from. She goes on and on about the moral value of the Mona Lisa. Can you imagine? She'd never heard of Picasso when I met her first. The next time she was spouting his biography and waving a tiny sketch he'd done for her on a paper tablecloth. Honestly!"

"Not jealous?"

"Waddington, I may not be Lady Diana Manners playing the Virgin in *The Miracle*, but I do have some background. I didn't step nimbly out of the gumbo next to the cotton gin in my charming silk court shoes."

"Biz, you're a snob! I never would have believed it!"

"Yes, I bloody well am, Wad. It keeps me from being taken in by that carnivorous *poseuse*. She was actually lecturing me about 'a woman's place.' *This* at the bar of the Crillon!"

"Biz, Julia is a friend of mine. She's Hash's best friend in Paris. I guess you forgot that."

"Another thing, dear Waddington. You must find another, less conspicuous restaurant for your *tête-à-têtes*. A chap doesn't quite know where to look. I wouldn't want to embarrass such a good old friend, Wad. You must see that?"

"Oh, let's close the subject, please," George said. "You promised me you weren't going to speak of that, my dear."

All of us tried to change the subject at once. The resulting outburst, scored for five parts, ended as abruptly as it began. It was George's voice that in the end prevailed.

"I think I'm tight enough now to go back to the subject I was about to broach when Don came roaring in across the street."

"Didn't mean to spoil your moment, George," Don said.

"What's the question, George?" Wad asked, with some of the heat he had not been able to expend in Biz's direction.

"Well, Wad, we all know you've been working on that book of yours. The Spanish book. Working damned hard at it, I hear."

"And?"

"Well, damn it all, we understand that you've put us all in it."

"Who do you know who's read it?" Wad's voice was even and quiet.

"Now, don't get your puttees tangled, old man. Hear me out."

"You're talking about a book that nobody has read, George. I was only reminding you. Just for the record."

"Well, good, then. We haven't *seen* the book, but all of us have a good idea that we are models for some of the characters. You've hinted as much, old man. You can't deny it. You told me yourself that you put a lot of worthless characters in it."

"Are you saying that that's how you think you recognize yourselves?" Wad threw his head back and pretended to laugh, but the effect failed. "Come on, George. You can think faster than that."

"You're not making this easy, old man. A chap gets the feeling when he's being taken down and studied. We have talked about this among ourselves and agreed that, since you're such a damned good fellow, that, well . . ."

"Come to the point, George. I want to hear the end of this."

"Well, now we hear Hal, here, has introduced you to his publisher and that they are interested in publishing the book."

"You're a little behind, George. They've already published one book of stories and sketches and I have a contract for a second and even a third book."

"You know I'm not much of a reader, Wad. The point is it would embarrass all of us to be recognized as characters in a novel. I heard that Burdock chap saying you were working on a *roman à clef*. Now we all know what that means."

"Go on, damn it!"

"You're not making this a bit easy, Waddington."

"What do you want me to do? Burn the manuscript?"

"Steady on! We're not trying to bring pressure to bear."

"What do you call this, then? A garden party? I'll be goddamned if I'm going to change a comma to please you, George, as pleasant as you are. What I write is my business and what I publish I'll stand behind!"

"This is something for lawyers to talk about!" Hal put in. "We could get an injunction. They stopped Joyce publishing *Ulysses* in the *Little Review*, you'll remember."

"And failing that, old chap, there are other ways of making a fellow see reason. Society is a very giving and forgiving institution, Wad, but one must obey the rules of the game. And when a chap crosses the line, society takes its gloves off."

"You call it society; I call it a kangaroo court."

"Try to see it our way, old man," George said.

"I don't have to justify what I've done to you, George! Christ Almighty, you don't understand about this. Mike, you tell them."

"Mike? Oh, sure thing! Mike wasn't in Spain. He doesn't even have a walking-on part in this. He didn't make a damned fool of himself with Spanish vino." There wasn't much I could say after that.

"Don, say something. You were with us. Wad's in one of his holier-than-thou moods where he is defending the integrity of the artist over chaps like us. Just look at him!

Horatius at the bridge has nothing on him." George's face appeared to be on the point of melting from drink.

"Jay, there's something in what they say, old son. I'd go through hell for you, kid, but you're playing with their lives. Hell! With my life! I was forgetting that. I'll be damned if I can see any good coming out of this for any of us, unless it's you."

"Nobody recognizes himself in fiction, Don. It's a well-known fact."

"It's other people recognizing me that I'm worried about, old man. I'll never get through the thing, to be honest." George looked to the others to see if there were arguments that hadn't been made yet.

"Wad, you know we all think of you as our friend?" Biz was trying something new. "It would be caddish of you to make public what was, after all, a private party. Even if you simply report the facts, it would demonstrate that you are no gentleman."

"You aren't giving me much credit, any of you. Do you imagine that I'm the first writer to borrow a few things from the people he knows? Where do you think a writer gets his material? Damn it all, is it news to you that Mark Twain grew up with a kid like Huck Finn and that Daniel Defoe knew of a castaway that he called Robinson Crusoe?"

"We're not talking about Robinson Crusoe or about any dead people. We're talking about us, Jay!" Don looked serious and the others were watching him. Wad had a beleaguered expression. "We are talking about the laws of libel, which has to do with damage to the reputation of a living person. You can't bring discredit on an enemy and get away with it. How do you imagine you can treat a friend that way?"

"I've been to see a lawyer, Wad. Just for clarification," said Hal.

"Leopold may have the right end of the stick in this, old man. Perhaps we should all consult counsel."

"Damn it, George, are you threatening me?"

"Take it as you see fit. The best suggestion I can make is that you forget all about this Spanish book."

"Or?"

"Be prepared to take the consequences."

"Of all the bloody cheek! I'll see one and all of you in hell first!"

"So be it! So be it! And remember, whatever happens, you brought this on yourself!"

CHAPTER 17

Freddy, the friendly barman, finally lost patience with us at I don't remember what hour. He threw us into the rue Delambre after changing his white jacket and putting on a topcoat. I was still trying to get the others to leave Waddington alone. It didn't do any good. Wad just stood there, propped against a street lamp as though he were a stag at bay. Soon his truculent silence began to pay off: Hal and Don, tired of standing around on the corner, waved that they had had enough and left; George and Biz started shouting at one another, and George stomped off in the direction that Hal and Don had taken. Wad went off into the dawn that was breaking over the rooftops along the boulevard, going in a direction that wouldn't take him back to his street. Somehow the evening ended with Biz and me in a taxi heading back to the rue Broca and Biz's studio. We were both rather tight and not responsible. We continued in that fashion up the stairs, after the concierge finally pulled the cordon, swearing loudly. I remember there was some difficulty with the key.

The studio was larger than it had appeared on the night of the party. The morning light was pouring unwanted into the room, picking out motes of dust like suspended punctuation marks in the slanted shafts. Biz dropped her coat at the foot of the stairs and walked over it towards me. I held her to me as we kissed, and then I followed her up the steps to her balcony bedroom. By the time I had loosened my necktie and removed my jacket, Biz was lying on her untidy bed, fast asleep. I looked down at her to see whether there might not still be a flicker of life, but there wasn't. I waited a few minutes, hoping that in another moment she might open her eyes, smile up at me and say, "Hello, you." But she didn't. I removed her shoes and put them neatly beside her bed, where the floor was paved with discarded clothing and accessories. On my way out, I picked up the discarded trenchcoat and hung it over the chair on the posing rostrum. There was a gentle sound of snoring coming from the loft as I let myself out. I thought about the night we'd taken Wilson O'Donnell home to the rue de Tilsitt and laughed to myself. There were more flights of stairs going down than I remembered.

I found a working-men's café, open for early starters, and ordered a shot of applejack to drink with my coffee. The stale roll needed dunking in this chicory-rich mixture before I could eat any. I was gritty around the eyes and felt like stepping into the shower-bath in my parents' house in Toronto. It was the first time I'd thought of Toronto in some weeks, I thought, and then remembered that it was only a few hours ago I was recalling an evening with Morley at the Mutual Street Arena watching some welterweights. I had to laugh.

I walked back to the rue Bonaparte. Mme. Janot was already washing down the sidewalk in front of number 56. We scarcely nodded as I hurried by her and through the door.

The morning papers brought the news of another death. The body of Madeleine Charpier had been found against the railings at the bottom of the entrance to the Edgar-Quinet station, not far from the Montparnasse cemetery. Like the others, she had been stabbed, probably with a pair of scissors. Jules Voisin, for fifteen years a veteran with the Métropolitain company, found the body when he locked the gate after the last passenger had left the last train. He was questioned at the scene of the crime and released. When asked by reporters whether this was another of Jack de Paris's unchecked series of killings, the prefect refused to comment.

Quentin Bryson was doing a story about the murder when I came into the office nursing a headache. He gave me the details, including the information that the deceased had been born in a village in the Vaucluse, near Avignon, where her family could be traced through ten generations. She had been working as a model for Poiret, the fashion designer, and, more recently, for a painter named Léger. She had a son, who had won a place at the École Normale. According to Quent's information, which was usually good, there were no additional clues found at the scene that had not been reported in the papers.

At lunch he said that his wife had been talking about inviting me to dinner in order to give me a home-cooked meal. No date was suggested, so I filed the invitation with all the others before it. Quent stated at lunch that what I needed in my life was a motor-car and a place in the country. That, he thought, would give me an outlet from the pressure of work, a chance to rekindle the resources depleted during the day, and would present vistas of fields and forest that rest the eyes and hurt not. I told him I thought I needed to find a girl. I suggested that we take a walk along the rue du Faubourg-St-Denis after we finished our luncheon. There we could find a solution to my problems for a few francs and hardly any risk. Quent held his match in the air above the pipe he was about to light and said that there was no use talking to me when I refused to be serious.

Wad stood me up on the red clay courts off the boulevard Arago. He'd never done that before, and so, after waiting around for another half hour and watching a couple of newcomers slam the ball around, I set out walking in the direction of Notre-Dame-des-Champs. As I walked, I started going over in my head the final box score of the night before. I remembered the prizefight clearly, and even Wad's quarrel with Hash. After that things began to get tangled. There were too many faces and they were all of them drunk and shouting at one another. If Wad had packed all of them into his damned book, he couldn't have left much room for plot, I thought. Still, when Wad wandered away from the rue Delambre, he and I were still on speaking terms. There was no explanation of his failure to appear on the boulevard Arago to be found in the events of last night. Unless it was a headache.

The sight of Don Hughes sitting at a table in the Closerie des Lilas pulled me back to the reality of the cold wind blowing across the wide boulevard St-Michel and into my bones.

"Hello there, Mike!" Don called, having sighted me about the same moment I'd seen him. He waved me to take the yellow wicker chair opposite him. "Did all of that really happen last night or was it a nightmare for general admission, no reserved seating?"

"You remember it all?" I asked.

"It needed editing. I cut it short before the voices were raised and the threats began."

"Don, you're the only person in the world I can ask this. What the hell happened down in Spain to cause all of this? I feel like an outsider, the only man in town who doesn't know what went on. Can you give me a short version, or will I have to wait until that book comes out?"

"I can't see a pal writhing in pain. Puts me in mind of Berlin, which is still in —"

"A ferment. I heard," I said, beating Don to his joke.

"The very word for it, Mike." The waiter hovered near. Service was always good at the Lilas. As soon as drinks arrived, Don began.

"Wad had arranged to go down to the fiesta in Pamplona. He's been going every summer since '23. Last year he invited me along, and we went up to Burguete first for the fishing. Had a wonderful time. This year we did the same, but it was terrible. Logging had spoiled the river. So, he was in a black mood when we got to Pamplona. Then things got worse. Biz and George had invited themselves to the fiesta while we were still in Paris, when it was almost too late to get tickets. Hal Leopold was going to be there too."

"An unwieldy party at mealtimes," I said.

"That's not all. You see, before we left Paris, Biz had run off with Leopold to San Sebastian."

"Hal with *Biz*? I don't believe it!"

"Biz confessed to Wad, who tried to warn Hal that Biz was coming to Spain with George. Hal refused to change his plans."

"How embarrassing for everybody."

"Hal wouldn't recognize that the nuptial flight was over, that he'd been a momentary whim of the lady. You know how stubborn and long-suffering he can be."

"Jesus!" I said.

"As usual, Mike, you understate the case. Can you imagine us in the same hotel for a week of drinking, dancing and bull fighting? Of course, Waddington tried to be protective of Biz and had a conniption fit whenever Hal came near her. Wad knocked him down one night."

"He repeated that scene recently at the Dingo."

"Glad I missed it. Wad was either crazy in love with Biz himself or demented with alcohol poisoning."

"Well, if he was in love with her, why didn't he do something about it?"

"He couldn't with Hash sitting there, in the role of the adoring wife who'd put her inheritance on the table to support both of them. Besides, it was all too public. No place to hide."

"What happened then?"

"George ran out of money at the end of the fiesta. Everybody went away mad."

"Biz didn't dance on any tables or run away with a picador?"

"Not while I was around."

"That's not much to fill a book. I guess he could describe a bullfight or two."

"Don't forget that we were all tight for the week and Biz can hold her liquor with the best. Still, I'm not anxious to see all of it between the pages of a book. Wad will change our names, of course, but I'll know I'm the American lug without the Jewish mother."

"I thought they were all down on Hal because he was Jewish."

"It didn't help. But mainly it's because he didn't know when to go away. He kept hoping he could find a little of what went on in San Sebastian and fan it up again."

"Well, well, well."

"Couldn't have said it more brilliantly myself."

We drank our drinks and talked of other things for a few minutes. I told him that Wad had stood me up on the red clay courts and that I was on my way to see what had happened. Don told me to give the gang his love. "I'm catching the slow afternoon train back to Berlin. I got a wire this morning. They found my last draft of the script cold and they're in a ferment about it, and I won't see you again until I get back after Christmas." I put some money on the table to cover my drink, against Don's protests, and we shook hands.

The high whirring of the buzzsaw in the courtyard distracted me from my speculations about what Waddington

had done after the *débâcle* at the Dingo. The concierge recognized me and let me go up to the flat above the carpenter's yard. Hash opened the door quickly when I knocked.

"Oh, Mike! I'm glad you've come. Have you seen my
husband anywhere?" She was carrying young Snick in her
arms. He held his mother tighter as I followed Hash's invitation to come into the front room. Snick was examining
me closely.

"You not Papa. Ward notta Papa."

"He didn't keep our date for tennis," I said. "That's
why I came here."

"You know he didn't come home last night?" She was
wearing an old shirtwaist; her nose was looking pink, as
were her large eyes. "I hope you don't want a drink, Mike.
There isn't a drop in the apartment."

"No thanks. Have you any idea where he is?"

"I'm not allowing myself to think in that direction. He
promised to take Snick for a walk in the Luxembourg after
meeting you for your match. He didn't go near the Closerie
this morning. They haven't seen him since yesterday.
That's what they said."

I sat down in a worn blue-velvet chair with a nice
French shape to it and watched Hash with the boy. She kept
looking out the window, and I saw how her short auburn
hair moved with her head when she turned. After awhile
she closed the window, and the noise from outside was cut
in half.

"Has this ever happened before, Hash?"

"Not for a few months. Not after a quarrel. Sometimes
he just forgets to come home and it has nothing to do with
me. He just gets involved and forgets. But last night . . ."

"Hash, after you left, the crowd from the Dingo caught
up to him." I told her about their threats and his brooding
anger and how he had stomped off.

"Oh, poor Tatie!"

"Everybody'd had quite a lot to drink."

"He has no sense of humour about himself, you know. So he wouldn't think of trying to show how silly they were being. I can just see him, getting deeper and deeper into that stolid cocoon he wraps himself in. Oh, Mike, why wasn't I there?"

"Now don't start blaming yourself, Hash. He was damned mean to you after the fights, remember?"

"This is a lot more serious. I should have been with him."

"If it will make you feel any better, I don't think any of the worthless characters he was with could have done him any harm. We were all too tight."

"Oh, Mike, it's not them. It's where he went when he should have come to me." Hash began opening drawers around the room until she found what she was looking for, a handkerchief.

"Is there anything I can do, Hash? I hate to see you unhappy."

"You're a good friend, Mike. No, I don't suppose there is anything either of us can do. We'll have to sweat it out, as Tatie says." Hash blew her nose and rubbed her eyes before looking back at me. I was sure that the same name was in both of our heads, but neither of us said anything. "Of course, it may be that he woke up some crony here in the Quarter."

"Sure."

"Sometimes he just forgets to come home," she said again. "He gets involved and forgets he has a wife and family sometimes, but I'm getting good at recognizing those episodes before they happen."

"You aren't really worried?"

"Heavens no! Tatie's just forgotten where he lives for the moment, that's all. I don't think Jack's got him, if that's what you mean."

"He's probably got talking to some people in a café. You know what retired newspapermen are."

"I was going around the corner to get a recipe from Alice Toklas when you knocked. I hate sitting and waiting. It would have given the Piddler an airing, too."

"If you still want to go, I'll carry Snick. It's on my way home." She handed me her bundle and ran to find her coat, hat and gloves. She put a sweater over her shirtwaist, but she still looked chilly. The concierge chucked Snick under his chin as we passed her on the stairs. Snick looked around at the carpenters as we walked through the yard, demanding in French to know their names. Hash told me he liked playing in the curled shavings near the planing table. "That's where he is learning his French," she said.

It wasn't a long walk to 27, rue de Fleurus, which was a substantial building. To me it looked as close to a Right Bank place to live as one could find on the Left. Being so close to the park, it was a fashionable address.

As we walked along the passage to the *garçonnière* in the rear, I was wondering about Wad and Hash. Had he made the final break, or was this a superficial slash of the razor with the lethal cut still to come? I couldn't seriously believe that Wad had come to harm through that gang from the Dingo. They couldn't organize a packet of cigarettes among them most of the time. I couldn't see them planning and executing some plot against Waddington, especially when it had to be put into operation so quickly. And could the Spanish book be so great a threat to any of them? Wasn't it drink talking at the Dingo, egging George on?

Coming around the corner of the *bis* portion of 27, rue de Fleurus, we nearly collided into a small woman with short-cropped brown hair and bangs. She was wearing a blue apron and carrying some green herbs in her hand. Something about her dark, leathery face was familiar.

"Oh, Alice!" Hash said.

"Priscilla! How nice to see you! I was just cutting the last of the basil and some chives. How is Goddy?" she asked, examining Snick more closely. She addressed him in baby-talk which would have been more appropriate for a child half Snick's age and which I will not attempt to reproduce. She reached out to Snick, but the child dug deeper into my arms. Snick had been born in Toronto; we fellow Canadians stick together. Meanwhile, I was trying to place Alice's face. It was obscured in my memory, but I knew light would shine before long if I didn't play with the wick.

"He's a bashful little man, isn't he?" She said this to me, seeming to notice me for the first time. Hash introduced us and appeared to be at ease in spite of everything.

"'Fraid o' nothin'," said Snick.

From the sidelong glances I saw Alice giving me, I suspected that she, too, was trying to place my face. We were both of us far from the original context of our earlier meeting. Was it at the American Club? At the embassy? What was it about that dark face? Did it come from a bad dream? While Hash explained the reason for her visit, Snick began to play peek-a-boo with Alice, looking into her large brown eyes, first over one of my shoulders and then over the other. As soon as he was feeling safe and friendly, I handed him to Miss Toklas, who by now had put her herbs in a wicker basket. Snick liked being bounced up and down, and Alice gave him a fair measure. While this was going on, Hash explained that Gertrude and Alice called the boy "Goddy" because Gertrude was his godmother.

Soon the women were discussing *boeuf en daube*, while Hash made a memorandum with a bridge pencil on a folded piece of paper whenever Alice happened to mention one of the ingredients.

"*Daube* is one of the masterpieces of Provençal cookery," Alice said, clapping her small hands together, as though she could smell the dish steaming on the stove of her imagination. "Reboul, I think it's Reboul, says that much Provençal cooking comes from the Romans. Imagine that! I always thought of the Romans stuffing themselves with coarsely ground grain and badly cured pork."

Just at that moment, a white poodle came leaping at me from around the corner, and as he clung to my trousers I knew where I'd met both dog and mistress before.

"Down, Basket!" I said. "Down, boy!"

"You know one another?" asked Alice with raised eyebrows. She was pulling the beast from me while Snick laughed and grabbed at the dog. "Of course! You were the rude man in the park!"

I explained to Hash how we had met some time ago in the Luxembourg Gardens. "Basket and I are old friends," I said, watching Miss Toklas's face. I rubbed the poodle's ears and he moaned his approval, which I hoped might break the ice with Alice. It only served to stiffen her already straight back. While this was going on, Hash was trying to explain that, while Wad and Gertrude Stein were talking about literature, she and Alice had passed many useful evenings talking about good things to eat.

"Are you, by any chance, a writer too, Mr. Ward?"

"I am a journalist, Miss Toklas, with a news service. Anything more is ambition and speculation. I suspect that I have as much chance of becoming a good writer as I have of becoming a great chef." This seemed to amuse her. She hadn't expected to be amused and didn't know how to proceed. I saved her the trouble by beginning to make signs of withdrawing.

"Will you be able to get back all right?" I asked Hash.

"I'm a big, husky prairie girl, Mike. I can do almost anything."

"Well, if you're sure . . ." I smiled again at Miss Toklas and turned to find my way back to the street, thinking of the famous paintings inside the house that I should now probably never see.

CHAPTER 18

I walked home, skirting the park and up past St-Sulpice with its twin rounded towers. A priest in a long cassock was tucking it into a broad belt prior to mounting a bicycle as I came into the rue Bonaparte. Like a lot of priests, he was wearing a *béret basque*. I stopped at the corner of the rue du Four to buy a fresh packet of cigarettes, cursing the high price of tobacco. I was lighting the first of the cigarettes from the flame at the counter when I got a surprise. As I turned to the doorway, Wad was filling it.

"Come outside, you pinch-gutted bastard!" he said, almost hissing.

"Wad! What's going on?"

He removed his bulk from the doorway and we both came out into the sunshine. He was red in the face and sweating. It was the suit he'd been wearing the night before. His necktie was crooked and his jacket looked shabbier than ever.

"I followed you here," he said. "They just turned me loose and there you are, walking up rue Bonaparte."

"I live on rue Bonaparte, remember?"

"Haven't spent the thirty pieces of silver yet, have you? I'll be glad to lend you something to buy a rope with if you have."

"Go to hell, Wad! What's this all about? Stop talking rot."

"Don't play the innocent. You knew they brought me in. You told them about me and Laure. Some friend I've got!

Some friend!" With that, he threw a punch that hit the side of my head. I nearly fell over, but, in fact, it was Waddington who dropped. I hadn't raised my hands. He was on the sidewalk and people were staring at him, sprawled in front of the kiosk and under the tobacconist's orange carrot sign.

"Are you able to get up?" I asked.

"Judas!" he shouted. I hadn't missed the reference.

"Oh, for goodness sakes, Wad, get up and take off the crown of thorns. What the hell happened to you and why do you think I'm to blame?"

"I'll be damned if I'll get up," he said.

"Then sit there," I said and turned back into my street, feeling angrier now than when he hit me. I tried to piece together what had happened from what he'd said. "They" and "them" could only be the authorities.

"Hey, Mike!" It was Wad, of course, but I didn't turn around. I had almost come to the window of the antique dealer next to my building. Chinese furniture had been added to the window since I'd last noticed. Through the glass I could see the woman crocheting tea cosies with great vigour. It was plain that the old camel, her employer, was not on the premises.

"Mike, I'm sorry." I turned to see Wad, a pathetic sight, standing behind me. "I take it all back," he said. "You're the one true friend I've got."

I looked back at the store window, but I could still see him in the glass and hear his heavy breathing behind me.

"The *flics* took you in?"

He nodded. "I was walking towards the Closerie. They grabbed me and took me to the commissariat opposite St-Sulpice."

"Did they hurt you? I hear they beat up on Malcolm Cowley two years ago."

"One of them was rough, but the others made him stop."

"You want to come up? I've got some brandy."

He didn't answer, he simply followed me up the stairs and along the twisting corridor to my room. With the two of us sitting in it, one on the single chair and the other on the bed, the room looked as small as a railway signalman's hut, but with a red-tile floor.

"You still think I told the *flics* about you?" I said, handing him some brandy in my tooth glass. He took it and drank it all down fast.

"I don't know what the hell to think. You were asking me questions about Laure. You know about the piece of manuscript and her asking for money."

"Blackmail, Wad. Call it by its right name. She was trying to blackmail you."

"How could it be blackmail? If she had those manuscripts, I want them back. She wasn't threatening to do anything with them."

"She could threaten to destroy them. That might get your attention. Did she say anything like that?"

"Damn it, Mike. Don't you start. At least they don't know about the manuscripts. They think they know that I saw her recently but they can't identify me as the man with her in the Dôme that night."

"They'd heard about earlier meetings? Is that right?"

"Laure and I were attracted to one another, Mike. You know how it is. We met a few times. It was wonderful while it lasted."

"Did she ever threaten to tell Hash?"

"Sure. But I was able to handle that."

"What did you do?"

"I got her to fall out of love with me. It's an old trick. You tell them you're going to be so happy together. You tell her that she'll get a job and support both of you while you're writing stories, hoping that the *Saturday Evening*

Post will buy one. You say that you'll be wonderfully happy in a one-room flat above a *boucherie chevaline*. Stuff like that."

"So that's how you got rid of her?"

"The end came when I asked her for money to tide me over while I made the break with Hash. Then I didn't see her for weeks."

"Interesting technique. I must remember that."

Wad took the bottle and poured himself another drink. He drank this one more slowly.

"What do the police know for sure, Wad? Why did they bring you in?"

"Somebody told them that I had known Laure and that we had — you know — and then broken it off."

"I think I can guess who might have reported that. And then?"

"They tried to get me to tell them where I was on some dates going back to the spring. I couldn't account for some of the dates, because I don't keep track of such things. But I told them that my passport would show that I was in Spain all of last July. I showed it to them and they began to lose interest."

"There were two Jack killings in July. They were trying to get you for all of the murders."

"That's crazy! I'll get on to the American Embassy. They can't walk all over people. I'm an American citizen and they'll bloody well hear about it."

"But Wad, you see, if you were away in July, you're home free. They'll have to find a suspect who was here in July. You're in the clear. You won't hear from them again."

"You think so, Mike? Damn it, I'd like to believe you."

"As long as they think that Laure was killed by Jack."

"Well, wasn't she? Oh, yes, I was forgetting your theory."

"Hell, I don't know. But a lot of people aren't too sad now that she's dead. She had a lot of people she depended on for money. And blackmailers get murdered all the time. At least they do in books."

"Sorry I hit you, Wardo. I've got one hell of a temper. I had to hit somebody."

"That's okay, Wad."

"Once you've fought professionally, your hands are considered weapons. In the States, I could have got into a lot of trouble."

This wasn't the moment to dispute his career in the professional fight ring, so I let that pass.

"Where'd you go last night?"

"Go? Oh, after the Dingo you mean." He was playing for time to think. I prepared myself for a free sample of prime Waddington fiction. "I flopped at a cheap hotel near the Gare de Lyon."

"That's a long way from anywhere."

"Well, Mike, I just wanted to walk until my head cleared."

"I thought you might have gone over to the rue Picot."

"That's where Julia Lowry lives. Why'd you think that?"

"Thought I might have done the same thing in your shoes."

"Julia's one very Catholic lady, Mike. She'd be the last to open her door to a half-drunken Chicagoan on the loose after four in the morning. How'd you know where Julia lives, anyway? I didn't tell you."

"Looked her up in the *Bottin*. Is that a criminal act, Wad? I'm single; she's single. A fellow has to think about the future."

"You know how to pick them; her family is rolling in money."

"So is mine, or did I forget to mention it? We well-to-do families get together, nuptial mergers as we call them, Wad."

"Oh, go to hell, Wardo. I half believed you for a minute."

We finished the last two drinks in the bottle, then Waddington got up and stretched.

"Well, I should be getting back home. Hash might worry what's become of me."

"Yes, that's right." When I thought of what he'd put Hash through, I nearly threw him down the stairs.

"I'll let myself out, Mike. I think I know the way."

CHAPTER 19

It was a Saturday morning. Not having a thing in the world to do, I took a handful of unanswered letters with me to the Café Voltaire, across from the Théâtre de France in the Place de l'Odéon. It was a quiet, well-lighted spot with back tables where nobody bothered you. I filled my Parker pen from a newly purchased bottle of ink and began writing in earnest, but the letter to my parents in Toronto as well as one to a friend from school both had the same melancholy note. I didn't know I was unhappy until I reread the letters. From the details I gave them, it was clear that I thought I had come too late to Paris — a feeling I'd been having more and more lately — that I had not made any contacts that were worth having, and that my return to Canada, whenever it occurred, would not be unwelcome.

I thought about the friends I'd made . . . probably the Waddingtons were the most interesting. At least through Wad I had met most of the others. I remembered how he had helped me find my room. As a former journalist, he was sometimes condescending to my present status at the agency. He had done all that just after the war, as he never tired of telling me. Hash was all right. I liked her and felt close to her. I could even imagine her life in Toronto, with Wad off in Timmins or New York on an assignment. It must be hell to be married to a newspaper bum. I filed that thought for a nightmare.

Lady Biz Leighton's eyes across the table at the Select the other night, or the memory of them, should have cheered me up, but they didn't. She was doomed to a short, fast trip on an express train to oblivion. She wasn't interested in the company she kept; we were merely fellow passengers. It was the speed and the hoped-for end to pain that held her attention. Still, I was enough of a snob to be touched by her infrequent glances in my direction. Otherwise, why did I find myself writing about her to my parents? Did I think that her title would impress them? Surely not. There were titles enough in their address book. No, I think I mentioned Biz's title to suggest that I was keeping my feet on the ground, meeting the right people and not making a great fool of myself.

After a visit to the *bureau de poste* in the rue Tournon with my letters, I struck out for a walk in the Luxembourg Gardens. I admired the tiny Statue of Liberty, so much friendlier here, amid the falling gold leaves and scruffy palms, with children playing with their hoops nearby, than the colossus of the New York harbour. I was still not quite settled on the French idea of a garden; my training led me to favour the less orderly colonial variety, where one could sit until the cows came home without a pinched-looking drab charging a few *centimes* for the use of a metal folding chair.

I had been moving in the direction of the gate on the rue Guynemer when I saw the woman with the dark, prunish face again: Miss Toklas. She was walking the white poodle, Basket. I tipped my hat to her and congratulated her on the weather. She became anxious when Basket began to show an unnatural interest in my trousers again. To foil him, she took in the slack of the dog's lead like a good sailor tightening the sheets on his sails.

"Are you enjoying the sun, Miss Toklas?"

"Oh, we enjoy weather, Mr. Ward, in all of its moods and whims. If we did not, we might as well have remained in California."

"Surely California has other charms. I've heard good things about the San Francisco art gallery. Many Canadians have gone there to study, in fact."

"Ah, yes! Priscilla told me you are a Canadian."

"Yes, I come from Toronto."

"I have always believed that we settlers of the west coast, whether Canadian or American, are brothers under the skin." I didn't correct her impression that Toronto was on the Pacific coast. Perhaps she has been getting geography lessons from Cyril Burdock, who was always placing me in Vancouver.

"Gertrude Stein says that it is from the west that the energy of the New World comes."

"A land of promise, certainly. Most of its history is still to be written."

"Gertrude Stein says that the geniuses of the next generation will come from there."

"Europeans, I think, are often intimidated by the sheer size and health of North Americans. We are like prize cattle, and we come wearing our blue ribbons into French salons, often breaking the figurines." Miss Toklas allowed herself a short, stifled laugh at that.

"You must call on us some Saturday evening, Mr. Ward. I'd like you to meet my friend, Miss Stein."

"I should be greatly honoured and more than pleased," I said, almost hearing my mother's voice as I repeated one of her pet phrases. How curious to discover that the friend of the Great Innovator was so old-fashioned in her manners.

"My friend might be amused to meet a young man who thinks it is as difficult to become a good writer as to become a great chef."

"You have a good memory, Miss Toklas," I said.

There were a few more pleasantries exchanged and we finally went our separate ways. As I walked out of the park, I remembered that this was Saturday. It was too late to run back to remind Miss Toklas, although, I must say, I was tempted.

I bought a cheap lunch at an artists' restaurant on the rue de la Grande-Chaumière. It was small, crowded and self-absorbed. There was sawdust on the floor. The faces above the soup bowls belonged for the most part to solitary diners. Most of the noise came from the waiters carrying on a conversation about Jack Dempsey, who had visited Paris earlier in the year. One waiter said that Dempsey and Georges Carpentier had fought a private bout for some well-to-do sportsmen. The other said that this was just a story. He went on to tell another story about Carpentier that he knew to be untrue and presented it as evidence that his fellow waiter's story was equally false. None of the diners pointed out the fallacy. My steak was served with Béarnaise sauce, bled freely when cut and did not remind me while I was eating it that it had once worn a bit in its mouth and iron shoes. The *café-filtre* device on my cup failed to function, which I was beginning to discover was a common occurrence. I was just getting up, after settling the *addition* scrawled on the paper tablecloth, when I thought I saw a familiar figure walking down the street on the far side. I pocketed my change and set out in pursuit.

Arlette La Motte had nearly reached the boulevard when I caught up to her.

"Oh, it's you," she said. "I didn't recognize you in the daylight. Most of the people I know sleep all day. *Comme les vampires.*"

I led her to a small café that was lost among the three great cafés at this end of the boulevard. It had no terrace and only half a dozen tables, but the patron was serving a very handsome-looking omelette to one of his customers. We ordered coffee.

"Mike, what have you heard about our friend Waddington? I heard that he has left his wife and that the police detained him for questioning?"

"You're very well informed, Arlette." She smiled at that, as though I had intended it as a pure compliment without irony. In the light of day, Arlette was still an impressive-looking woman: tall, with fine teeth and a good figure. She moved her coat from her shoulders to her chair, a practical gesture informed with pleasing sensual overtones. I remembered thinking on our first meeting that she looked complicated. Today she seemed simpler, as though there were nothing on her mind but the hot coffee in front of her. Her face, heavily made-up at that time of day, aged her and distanced her.

"Wad was questioned because he, like so many of us, knew Laure Duclos. As for him leaving Hash, I don't know anything about that," I lied. Had she heard about the argument after the boxing match or was her news better than mine? I know that when he left me, Wad said that he was going home. "I hope it isn't true," I added. "They seem so right for one another."

"They get on well enough together, but we all know that Waddington is not going to be made into a comfortable bourgeois, is he?"

"Is that the direction Hash is pulling him? I thought they planned to keep on working and living simply here in France."

"With Waddington it is always the career that counts first. The career demands that he find a richer woman. Julia Lowry *évidemment*."

"Julia is Hash's best friend here in France, Arlette. She has gone out of her way to help both of them. She may have more money, but she isn't half the woman Hash is. She hasn't had the chance to be."

As I spoke, I got the impression that Arlette thought this defence was commendable, transparent and, somehow, rather Canadian.

"Oh, men! You have no eyes to see what the women do around you. You are all like that."

"So you think that Wad is about to change partners?"

"But of course. Isn't it obvious?"

"Not to me, damn it!" I was getting warm and uncomfortable. I didn't like thinking in this direction. "What about their child?"

Arlette shrugged as though that altered nothing. She sipped her coffee, studying my reddening face over her cup. Something was going on, something she was not saying.

"Are you usually so acute at divining these things? Do you read palms as well?"

"Oh, Mike! Now you are being angry with me." She opened my cigarette case, which was lying on the table, frowned at the contents and closed it with a snap. She took a pink, oval cigarette from her own case. I watched her eyes as I lighted it for her. They were green, lustrous and clear. I could easily see why Anson Tyler escorted her everywhere. I was growing envious. As I allowed myself to speculate on their relationship, one thing was very clear: Dr. Anson Tyler was not keeping Arlette on his barge on the river. Arlette needed the elbow-room of the *grands boulevards*. She liked clothes, followed the fashions. She didn't sit down to play bridge in an old sweater and skirt. Arlette was expensive.

Thinking that, I began to wonder what led her to spend so much time with these American and British expatriates. That night in the Dingo, she had labelled them all "tourists" and claimed to despise our likes. Was she fleecing them in these bridge games of hers? Or did I have the wrong end of the stick about her completely? Perhaps, like so many Parisians, she lived in a small flat, squalid, without water or light, and spent her life in cafés and public gatherings.

She was looking at me again, and I tried to remember what we had been talking about. Then I remembered my flash of anger. I told her I was sorry for that. She smiled, reached across to take my hand, and soon we were talking about the village where she was born.

"Someplace you've never heard of. It's near Le Puy, south of St-Étienne in the Cévennes. I still go back there to see the old people and my cousins. My brother, of course, lives here. Most of the family was wiped out in the war: the men were killed, the women moved to the factory towns. Nothing ever happens there. Once, in the spring, the river changed colour. When I was a little girl. It was never explained."

She continued smiling and I wasn't angry any more. I asked her about Anson. Perhaps that was a mistake. She began by telling me things I already knew. I asked about his writing.

"Oh, he's given all that up. He lets things go when he is unable to achieve what he wants."

"I know the feeling."

"He's after more than competence in most things. When he can't master something, he loses interest. I would very much like to live with Anson, but he is content to see me now and again." There was a blush now under her smile. "I am being quite frank with you, Mike. You have a purging effect on people."

"Yes, I work like a laxative. What happens when I say Warren Pease?"

"Tolstoi? Oh, Warren is still a boy. He is like a boy who has always looked through keyholes. He is well-known to the perverse in life, without knowing very much about the ordinary run of things. He is naïve about sex. Completely. I used to think he was one of those youth lovers. Like these abandoned young men of the Quarter, who strike poses and misunderstand women."

"Does he take drugs? I heard that from someone."

"How would I know about that?" The question made her nervous.

"I was just asking. There are lots of people taking drugs. We know some of them. You knew, for instance, that Laure smoked opium, of course?"

"Of course. But she did not die from opium."

"But her habitual use of the drug linked her to another world, where such things are available. That's why that theory of mine doesn't work. Laure was connected beyond Montparnasse. The drugs had to come from somewhere. If Tolstoi is taking them, then he too needs to have a supply. Arlette, do you know where one can buy drugs?"

"Mike, why are you asking me? Do you think I smoke opium or use cocaine?"

"Arlette, I'm asking everybody. You are not under suspicion." But even as I said that, she fell under the shadow of doubt. Something was marring her usual assurance.

"Why don't you let the police find out who killed Laure? You shouldn't get involved in these things. Especially as a foreigner. As an outsider, you lack the sensitivity to see what you are walking into. You could get hurt."

"Are you warning me, Arlette? I just want to be sure."

"Mike, I am beginning to be very fond of you. I would not like you to come to harm. What I say, anyone who knows this town would tell you. You must be careful, *chéri*. It could save you a great deal of pain."

"What if you were talking to an extraordinarily obtuse Canadian, who has failed to understand you?"

"Such a one should not go abroad without having his insurance in good order."

"It's as bad as that, is it? Okay, Arlette, I can take a hint. I won't pursue this particular angle. I'll continue to translate the police reports that come into the office and collect my pay at the end of the month. Apart from the occasional night when I'll drink too much, I'll keep my nose to the grindstone. Okay?"

"Okay, Mike. I think that way you will have a wonderful memory of your life in France to tell your grandchildren."

"Here's to my grandchildren."

CHAPTER 20

When I got home, the concierge was waiting for me. Her arms were folded and in her hand was a *petit-bleu*, an express letter, addressed to me.

"*Voici un pneu pour Monsieur Ward,*" she said. Already there was a note of respect in her voice. *Pneus* don't arrive for people of no consequence. I took it upstairs with me, wondering what it could be. Nothing was expected of me this weekend from the agency, so it had to be of a personal nature. I tore it open.

> Mike,
> Join us for dinner before going on to see the Picassos at Gertrude Stein's. Regards, Wad.

"*Monsieur Ward? Voulez-vouz que je vous fasse couler un bain?*" I told Mme. Janot that a bath would be in order. I could see that should I ever run short of rent money, a self-addressed *petit-bleu* would earn me more time. I'd seen her reading articles in magazines about the Prince of Wales. I might have to exploit that before I was finished.

In the meantime, I took my bath, dressed as well as I could and arrived at the Waddingtons' primed for an adventure. Both of them answered my knock at the door.

"Wardo, come in. Have a beaker or two!"

"Hello, Mike. Wonderful to see you."

Dinner was a mixture of French and Italian: fresh oysters followed by spaghetti in a clam sauce. "The seafood is so cheap at the market, we have it almost every day. I couldn't get the correct pasta to do it right, but I've almost given up trying to find things that aren't French here. Just try to buy sauerkraut on Montparnasse!"

For dessert, Hash had made a real American deep apple pie, which we finished among the three of us. Before we left, Wad exchanged an old sweater for his jacket, Hash put on a hat and we were off. I had so recently walked over the same streets with Hash and young Snick that I couldn't help noticing the happy couple sharing the sidewalk with me. Their spirits were high, with Hash holding close to Wad, who left her side only to kick a chestnut ahead of him three or four times, until a bad connection sent it bouncing onto the road.

"You're in for a treat, Michaeleen. You can't find modern pictures like these anywhere else in town."

"I'm not afraid of the pictures, Wad, it's their owner I'm worried about."

"Aw, Gertrude's not as black as she's painted. We're like brothers, she and I. Just remember not to mention James Joyce. If you mention him twice, you'll never be invited back."

"Oh, go on, Tatie. She says Joyce is a genius. I've heard her."

"Joyce is one genius too many when Gertrude is talking. You see, Mike, she thinks she invented the twentieth century. If you give her that, she's a pet."

"I suppose we can talk about early American history."

"That can be tricky too. She has an interest there. I'd stick to a neutral subject."

"Does she hold strong views on geology?" I asked.

"Safe as far as I know. Quite safe. Leads directly to Cubism."

"Oh, stop it, you two! You'd think we're off to see the

witch in her cave to hear you talk! You're going to love Gertrude, Mike. Tatie's only trying to scare you."

We walked down the rue de Fleurus. It was dark, with the trunks of large trees casting shadows and dead leaves blowing across the street.

"By the way, Wad, I saw Arlette La Motte today. She's the only one of the gang I've seen since that memorable night."

"I always said they were worthless characters. No loyalty."

"Does Arlette have a brother working here?"

"I think he's a bartender over on the other side. Why?"

"I was asking her about taking drugs and she began warning me to stop asking questions. I assumed it was because she had somebody close in the business."

"Jean-Paul La Motte's name is well-known in a few sordid holes. There's one on the rue des Italiens. He's been there. It has a back way out that leads through the sewers to the catacombs. So they say. I paid a visit to the sewers once, just to see where Jean Valjean carried his wounded friend, but I saw no arrows pointing the way to the catacombs. I guess they want you to pay another admission. One thing about the famed sewers of Paris, you don't need to show your *droit d'entrée* to prove you've been there. People will tell *you* where you've been."

"I sympathize completely. In fact, as we get closer to Miss Stein's, I begin to feel as though I'd passed the day exploring the lower depths myself."

"Calm yourself, old man. Alice came around to the flat herself. She was most insistent that we bring our young Canadian friend. You don't think I send *pneus* around town on a whim, do you?"

The door was opened by Hélène, the cook, who greeted Hash warmly. Hats and coats were passed over and we

followed her through a passage into the atelier, where
Gertrude Stein and Alice Toklas were enthroned in a large,
square room surrounded by glorious pictures. Gertrude was
enormous. She seemed part of the architecture, and yet she
was perfectly balanced by the diminutive frame of Alice on
the other side of the room. They smiled at us without getting up. I had been expecting a roomful of people. We must
have arrived early. Since I was taking my cues from Wad, I
took no responsibility.

"Waddington," Gertrude said, after introductions had
been attended to, "I was thinking about you this morning.
About the matter we discussed." She was trying out a
frown on Wad, who answered it with his dark smile. "You
should think again about that Anderson matter. He's been a
friend to both of us and it's unfriendly to turn on a friend.
Besides, you both are very close to me and I don't like family quarrels."

"I see."

"Waddington, whenever you disagree with me, you
say 'I see.' Does that mean you intend to pursue this?"

"It was just a thought, Gertrude. Can't act on them all.
Never enough time."

"Yes, I know all about time. Why can't the summer
pass like the minutes in a doctor's waiting room?" She now
turned her attention to me, the newcomer. "Alice tells me
that you are a great favorite of our dear Basket."

"We only look to become better acquainted."

"What do you think of Waddington pouncing upon poor
Sherwood Anderson and making fun of *Dark Laughter*?"

"I didn't know anything about it, but *Dark Laughter*
was such a self-parody, I don't see what more Wad could
do to it. It wasn't a good book."

"Yes," said Alice, "but to do that to a friend! Someone
who has helped you so much, Waddington. You are

naughty even to think of such a thing." Hélène had arrived with a tray of drinks and offered them first to Hash. "It's an infusion of thyme in a cordial that I made in Belley this summer. Oh, how I long to have the run of a real kitchen down there! As it is, I have to do everything in a hotel room." She said this in a lower voice to Hash and me, leaving her stinging comment to Wad still floating about in the golden glow of the pictures. It looked to be a trick of illumination, but even under the artificial electric bulbs, the paintings seemed to send out their own light.

"In writing as in everything else, Gertrude, you know you have to kill your father. I've been trying to break away from influences for years now. First it was Ring Lardner, then it was Anderson. He's been wonderful to me, but, damn it all, I have to start walking on my own soon or I'll never learn." This conversation was interrupted by the arrival of more guests, painters, I was told unnecessarily: their wide-brimmed hats and overcoats worn as capes over their shoulders did not suggest stockbrokers. Some of them brought their wives or "companions," as they were described. They were often beautiful women whose faces, if not more, were already familiar to art connoisseurs. They appeared to be cowed by the present company and began looking at the pictures as soon as they had been presented.

I failed to catch all of their names, but the ailing Juan Gris put in an appearance, as did Marie Laurencin, who, bravest of her sex, went up to both of our hostesses and embraced them warmly. The sculptor Jacques Lipchitz was soon telling jokes about Picasso, who, he said, had grown so grand nowadays.

Soon the first batch of newcomers was augmented by a second wave. Maurice Denis was among them. He quickly scanned the walls for something he had painted, as though that would make him more comfortable.

The sound of talk and laughter filled the room. Alice and Gertrude were no longer enthroned: their high-backed Renaissance chairs now looked more than empty, as their former occupants circulated among the company. One picked up scraps of conversations, no more:

" . . . He said to Radiguet and me, let's go to Marseilles . . ."

" . . . Roché knows everybody; that's his trouble . . ."

" . . . Auric and Honegger and, of course, Darius were there . . ."

" . . . Man Ray didn't retouch the picture. He swears that's the way she is . . ."

"Are you enjoying yourself, Mr. Ward?" It was Gertrude Stein, and the question was meant for me.

"Of course," I said, "but the painters do get in the way of the paintings."

"You must see them by daylight. Why don't you come and we can drink in the pictures and have a real talk."

"I would be greatly honoured," I said.

She moved her magnificent head closer. "You can talk the language of convention very well, and you do it very often, but can you talk, really talk, Mr. Ward? That's what I want to find out. Because, once you learn to talk, and learn to hear yourself talking, you will soon be ready to write."

"Waddington has been talking too much, it would seem."

"Oh, come now, Mr. Ward. We all have our egos. They crave a dance in the sun. Let yours romp in the sun too. And bring me something you have written. Pussy has taken quite a shine to you, and I want to see what is under the shine."

"How do I say I'm deeply flattered in an acceptable way?"

"You've made a beginning. Now go talk to Marie Laurencin. She was Apollinaire's mistress, you know. Go, learn something."

While Marie Laurencin was very charming, she really had very little to say to a young Canadian who neither painted nor collected. She passed me on to Jules Pascin, a painter I had often seen at the Dôme and the Select. His eyes were heavy-lidded and his face was tragic in a public way, as though his troubles were the subject of a play and he were the chief actor. For awhile, he was telling me about how he painted a portrait from the inside out. We looked at the Picassos together. He agreed with everybody else that Picasso had become rather grand these last few years. "You cut off your friends — it's like cutting your roots," he said. "He has broken with all his old friends: Derain, Braque, Gromaire, Utrillo, Miró, Soutine, Léger. He owes them all drinks, so he avoids them."

Later, I was standing near Hash, who asked if I was enjoying myself. I told her that it was all nearly over-whelming. I hadn't expected Gertrude Stein to be so friend-ly. I described to her my imagined version: the probing questions, the icy look that penetrated the emptiness within me, the failed examination, the summary dismissal.

"Oh, she's not a bit like that," Hash said, taking a clean handkerchief out of her bag and catching a sneeze just in time. "I'll grant you, she can turn on the crystalline gaze if she wants to. She doesn't suffer fools. But she couldn't help liking you, Mike. You're so nice. Damn it! I'm getting a cold."

"Are you well enough to stay, or would you like to go home?"

"I'm fine, Mike. You're so good to look after me. I'm thinking of the other day, too. I don't know how . . ."

"Let's not even talk about it. I'm glad things have worked out."

"Whenever I fall out of a window, some nice man saves me. Did I tell you I fell out of a window when I was little? I was rescued from the bushes by the gardener. My Tatie came along to rescue me later from being an old-maid piano teacher. Then, when Tatie was away in Switzerland and I caught that terrible influenza, Anson Tyler was at my bedside every day until I was well again. I never would have been able to get up out of bed to join Tatie in Lausanne if it hadn't been for Anson. And now you, dear Michael. You're my guardian angel."

"Archangel, actually. But don't let it get around."

"You're very sweet."

"You're pretty swell yourself, Hash. It's good to see you smiling again."

I next talked to a dapper little man who ran a bookstore and art gallery and was married to Helena Rubenstein, the cosmetician. He told me that he was also getting into publishing some things in a small way on the side. I liked the way he examined what was happening in the room over my shoulder.

Marie Laurencin returned to me. I was surprised by that. She was carrying two glasses of wine. She moved beautifully. I had seen the group portrait she had painted with Apollinaire and Picasso. At first, I'd taken the large head of the poet for that of Miss Stein. Apart from what my hostess had told me about her, I knew little else. I tried to recall what I could of Apollinaire's tragic death just at the Armistice. Up close, there were lines around her eyes, but the electric light was not altogether unkind to her. She had a way of holding her head first on one side and then on the other. I confessed my near-ignorance of most things and she laughed over her glass at me. She began telling me about Apollinaire.

"That was a long time ago, you know. When you were a little boy cutting up worms with your jack-knife. Even to me, it is like a story in a storybook I read a long time ago. Some think I was his mistress when he died. I let them think that sometimes, when I'm in the mood, when I feel like it. The others I tell that I threw the great bear out of the studio in 1912, before the war. I couldn't have him tupping every ewe in sight, the old ram, now, could I? I was twenty-five, remember. I threw him out; I gave him his *congé*, his dishonourable discharge from my studio. He may have been a great poet, but I was just a kid. What did I know? Twenty-five!"

As I was leaving the gathering with Marie, who had by this time asked me to call her "Coco," we passed a compact, quiet figure in a dark suit. Coco nodded at him and received a deep and formal acknowledgement. "You find policemen everywhere these days," she whispered to me after we had moved closer to the front door.

I put her into a taxi on the rue Guynemer. The parting left me with the impression that I had just kissed the hand of a gallant and beautiful woman. I walked home along the edges of the Luxembourg Gardens. Before going to sleep, I put together a few of the blue notebooks which I thought I might show Gertrude Stein when we met again.

CHAPTER 21

Bright and early on Monday morning, I was waited on by a police officer, who asked me to accompany him to the *préfecture*. When I asked if the request was of such urgency that I could not call my office, he shrugged. I took that to mean there was no great urgency, so I called Bryson at the agency and made an excuse. Perhaps I should have told my lie out of the hearing of the sergeant, but I didn't think of that. I had not yet had breakfast and was a little hung over from Saturday night. I wondered whether the officer would be submitting a report along with my arrested body: "tells lies at the slightest opportunity."

A motor-car was waiting for us with a driver already in place. We were whisked down the rue Bonaparte to the river, along the quay, where I got a glimpse of the Institute, and then across Pont Neuf to the Quai des Orfèvres. We went into the Palais de Justice through a guarded portal marked "36" over the impressive entrance. With the sergeant at my side, I was conducted — yes, conducted is the right word — through high, narrow passages built within the walls of the old building. Occasionally, through a high window, I caught a glimpse of green roofing, or once, I thought, of the steeple of Sainte-Chapelle. We climbed a narrow staircase that opened up, though a closet, into a wide, carpeted corridor. Here I was asked to take a seat. Across from me, a thin young man was in close conversation with his well-nourished *avocat*.

"Mr. Ward?" It was a compact but well-built man of about fifty who addressed me. I stood and followed him into an office. Immediately, my eyes went to the walls. He had as many modern paintings hanging as did Gertrude Stein. I couldn't believe it. I recognized Utrillo, Modigliani, Kisling and Soutine. When I looked back at the man now standing behind his desk, he was obviously enjoying my surprise. With a gesture, he told me to take a chair. This I did, and pulled it close to the clutter of papers, surmounted by a black hat.

"Mr. Ward, my name is Léon Zamaron, I am a commissioner of police. In recent years — I've been here since Picasso was in his 'blue period,' 1906 — I have had a rather fancy title, but what it boils down to is the fact that my colleagues have put me in charge of foreigners. They throw up their hands and say, Léon, you deal with them: you understand them, or pretend to." I smiled to show that his act to disarm me was at least putting me more at ease than I otherwise would be in the office of the Sûreté.

"How may I assist you?" I said. This would save him from explaining to me how he was the benefactor of all these painters on the other side of the river. I wonder how many of the pictures on his walls were bribes. Apollinaire was arrested when the *Mona Lisa* was taken from the Louvre before the war, but Picasso was only questioned, although he had had some dealings with primitive sculptures taken from the Louvre's collections. Had the amiable man across from me, with the hair coming down over his forehead and the neat moustache, been bought off with the pictures I saw behind him? I was taking no chances. The police were a breed apart. They often pretended to be a part of society, but, in fact, they were not. They owed a loyalty only to themselves and were more closely linked to the criminal classes than they were to respectable people. Was not the great detective Vidocq a reformed thief?

Zamaron was examining me even as I was sitting in judgment of him. "You were acquainted with the woman Laure Duclos?"

"I knew her. Yes. I suspect you know that already."

"Yes, we do. We also know that you have an interesting theory about the reason for her death."

"Theory rather puts a gilt frame on what may be a half-baked notion."

"You don't see her death as one of the series of murders that has been ascribed to the so-called Jack de Paris?"

"M. Zamaron, with all due respect, will you please come to the point? You keep telling me what is known. Could you get down to what you want to talk to me about?"

"Saturday evening, you were in less of a hurry. You had time to enjoy the pictures."

"Saturday evening? Oh, at Miss Stein's. How do you know I was there? Am I being watched? If I am, I shall consult my embassy as soon as I leave here."

"Please, Mr. Ward, please!" He got up and came around his desk to sit on the edge. "My dear fellow, I saw you myself. I was there as well, looking at the pictures. Miss Stein and I are old friends." That took me aback. Then I remembered the quiet man in the dark suit and Coco Laurencin's comment about policemen. I felt my back unstiffening. My collar was growing uncomfortable.

"I'm sorry," I said. "I have spoken too hastily, sir." I was still very stiff and formal, and probably right to remain so. Zamaron stayed perched on the edge of his desk.

"I know you enjoy looking at pictures, Mr. Ward. I know that you knew Mlle. Duclos. I know exactly how well you knew her. I know you had argued. I know that you are a foreigner, working under the usual arrangements for your news agency. Everything is all in order and I am not questioning any of that this morning. Do you understand?" I nodded and he went on. "I, too, believe that Mlle. Duclos was killed for private reasons and not by our random killer. How do I know this? I have a feeling in my bones. A presentiment; what can I call it? I don't know the life expectancy of a presentiment in a Canadian court, Mr. Ward, but I can assure you that such a will o' the wisp would not live as long as a canary under a bell jar with the air removed in the courtrooms next door. Of this I am sure." He got up and walked back and forth in front of his private gallery.

"In order to discover the murderer of Mlle. Duclos, whom, incidentally, I knew somewhat better than you did, it is necessary to build a pyramid of proof."

"You have talked to Jason Waddington? You have his testimony."

"Oh, yes. He made a statement. We know all about his intrigue with her. That may be beside the point. We also know that he talked with her on the evening she died."

"Did he tell you that, or did that information come from an informant?"

Zamaron laughed and then blew his nose as he walked over to the window, where he examined the view I couldn't see from where I was sitting.

"The information of his — shall I call it, dalliance with the deceased? — came to us anonymously. He, himself, told us of his meeting with the woman on the night in question."

"And I can confirm that," I said. It struck me as typical of Wad that he should have been less than truthful to me about what he had told the police. "I saw them talking at the Dôme from across the boulevard. She left Waddington sitting at the table alone when she got up to leave."

"Mr. Ward, were you, by any chance, our anonymous caller? Did you telephone about Mr. Waddington's affair with the Duclos woman?"

"Mr. Waddington is my friend. But he has recently acquired a group of enemies, who might have informed on him."

"This becomes more interesting. Were these people also acquainted with the deceased?"

"Yes, they were. And some of them may have had a reason to kill her."

"I think I have a pretty good idea who they might be. I don't think I will ask for names."

"You're the first policeman I've met who didn't want names."

"I'm not your average policeman, Mr. Ward. I tell myself that every day and my wife reminds me, for a different reason, every night."

"There is a corner of this case that you may not have thought of: Laure smoked opium. That may, perhaps certainly, have put her in contact with another group of people, the drug procurers. They may have had motives of their own."

"Thank you for that information, Mr. Ward."

"Did you know that she was blackmailing a number of people in the Quarter?"

"Yes, we knew this all along. Mlle. Duclos once tried to see if a commissioner of police was susceptible. He was not."

"*Monsieur le Commissaire*, you are being very frank with someone you have just met."

"My dear Ward — if I may? — it's the well-kept secret that gets a fellow into trouble. If you have a secret, share it with the world. It's the only defence. Try to see it as a master chess opening, such as our beloved Philidor would have employed." He put his hands in his pockets and returned to his side of the desk.

"By the way, Mr. Ward, I haven't thanked you for returning Mlle. Duclos's handbag to the commissariat across from St-Sulpice. I should not make assumptions, but I believe you came across the purse in an innocent way?"

"I was following Waddington who was following Laure. I lost both of them, but I found the purse near where the body was discovered. I saw no other sign of her. Was she found in a doorway? Was she hidden in some way?"

"Exactly that. Why were you so interested in Mr. Waddington's movements, if I may ask?"

"I had just had a drink with Laure. She wasn't interested in prolonging our conversation after a certain point. She was obviously expecting to meet someone. I was curious to see who that might be, so I moved across the street to watch from the Rotonde."

"Good!" he said, getting up and returning to the window, where the light washed over his face. He showed few lines for a man in his profession. I was surprised.

"Now, Mr. Ward," he said, turning back to me, "I must officially warn you that these things that you have been looking into are police matters. I formally ask you to leave off this private investigation of yours and to report anything germane to the matter to this office at once."

I had always been aware that there was a mail fist under the fine grey glove: I was surprised to see that he had an iron gauntlet to put on over the glove. Yet there was something about the way he said *officially* and *formally* that left me wondering whether he was not telling me to keep up my good work and to count on him as a friend. I may have misread him, and I'm sure he would deny that he had implied any such thing, but I walked out of his office confused. Did I have an ally in Commissioner Léon Zamaron or not? It was a curious question, and I argued it back and forth in my head as I walked down the broad, curved staircase that led into the formal rotunda of the Palais de Justice. I came out into the Cour du Mai to see a group of tourists standing by the high, gold-tipped, wrought-iron fence consulting their Baedekers.

CHAPTER 22

The only face I recognized on the *terrasse* of the Dôme belonged to Warren Pease, "Tolstoi" to the chaps at the Dingo. I had not seen any of them for some time. It was as though they had, of a sudden, changed the Quarter, as they say, carried the party with them to a new location. He greeted me warmly and we both huddled as far away from the cold as we could get while losing nothing of the view. He said that he had seen me coming along from the direction of rue Vavin. I explained that I had just delivered a package — my few stories, in fact — on the rue de Fleurus. Earlier I had been working at the news agency.

"Ah, work," he said, as though it were an obscure reference he had stumbled across. "My mother's favourite theme. She says that there is much to recommend it. I concede that society as a whole has great regard for it. I was never able to see anything very ennobling about it, myself. I tend to agree with old Oscar Wilde. Work is a curse. It possesses no values I respect. Just look at someone who has lost his job. Work is the basis of his self-respect. *Merde*! It hasn't given him a philosophy to beat back the gloom. Work offers nothing of value and takes in return all of one's time and energy." The way Tolstoi was waving his arms about, I could see that he had been sitting in the Dôme for some time. The pile of saucers confirmed my observation.

"I'll tell you something, old man."

"What?"

"I think the Puritans elevated the wrong golden calf when they chose work. As for me, I'll have none of it."

We ordered drinks: he another whisky and I an aperitif. I disputed the question with him for a few minutes, in a playful way, but I was dealing with a mule on the subject. Hadn't he seen the soup kitchens and breadlines in England just after the war? Hadn't he read Gissing? Hadn't he talked with people of his own class, the men he was up at Oxford with? I finally had to say that I thought he was a thoroughly bad lot, with which he solemnly agreed.

"Have you seen Waddington?" he asked, after we had been watching the pedestrians for a few minutes.

"Not for a couple of days," I said. "He was questioned by the police about Laure's murder, you know."

"Fancy that! I can't really imagine Wad running up dark alleys in a dark cloak looking for strange women to stab, can you? Like a character out of Gaston Leroux? No, Waddington's the open, above-board sort. Killer of the afternoon, or perhaps as the dawn creeps into the village square. I see him as the officer in charge of a firing squad, the pistol already drawn for administering the *coup de grâce*, a neat ball in the head, behind the ear, about here," he said, showing where the bullet should enter.

"You're very morbid this afternoon," I observed. "Is it anything special?"

"Oh, no. It's just the way I am." He quickly drank off his whisky and began scouting over my shoulder for the waiter. "I don't suppose there's anything that drives you to drink?"

"Well, I didn't think so. But now that I've heard your views on honest work, I'll have to give it a try. What I need is some dark mystery in my life, something I'm trying to forget."

"You're describing the Foreign Legion, old man, not Montparnasse."

"I always thought of you as a man with a secret, a secret serious enough for serious drinking," I said.

"And you would like to know what that secret is, I suppose?"

"Tolstoi, I was talking to a policeman today who told me that the best way to protect oneself from a secret is to share it around. It's the buried secret that comes back to haunt one."

"By 'one' you mean me. I'll be damned if I'll tell you for nothing. I've paid out good money to keep that secret."

"I'm not asking. That was Laure's line of country, not mine."

"Nature abhors a vacuum, Ward. Perhaps you are thinking of taking up her . . . interrupted . . . work?"

"I'm afraid I would make a poor replacement for Laure. I lack her burning desire for money. You and she must have had some curious conversations about money. She thought it was so very important and you have no respect for it at all."

"I didn't say that! I have a healthy respect for money, old man. It's work as a method for acquiring it that I object to. I wasn't brought up for it. No, money is a very important commodity. May we both live to roll in it." Here he raised his empty glass in an empty toast. When he discovered that there was nothing left to drink, he stood on his unsteady legs and waved his arms about as though he were an adept at semaphore. I assumed the waiter saw him, because he soon sat down again and rolled the empty glass between his hands, as though to warm the imagined cognac within.

"Laure was a curious sort," he said at length. "She tried to get me organized, to get me on my feet. It was for her own selfish purpose, of course — so she could bleed more money out of my family — but putting that aside, she was the only one who gave a damn about me."

"You're not getting sentimental, are you?"

"Of course I am. I've earned it. It complements my drunken state."

"You know, I knew Laure as well. I was really quite fond of her."

"Yes, I think we all saw that coming. Laure has — had — a way of slipping into an early intimacy with people, then becoming more formal with them once the ring was firmly placed in their noses. All of us wear one. I wouldn't carry on about yours if I were you."

"I knew her well enough to know that her habit for opium was perhaps more serious than your own."

"Oh, you know that too, do you?" He took advantage of the waiter's arrival to put his response in order. After sipping his fresh whisky, he looked me in the eye. "We all pass the word to Freddy behind the bar at the Dingo. He gets it from Arlette's brother, Jean-Paul. Freddy's a good scout. There's not much he won't do for a good customer." I kept quiet, hoping that he would go on. He did.

"Freddy used to work across the river in 'the Hole in the Wall,' Le Trou dans le Mur. Boulevard des Capucines, or maybe further up on the boulevard des Italiens. It's on the odd side of the street. *Côté impair*. Freddy used to work for Jean-Paul. Did I tell you that?"

"And Laure was blackmailing you?"

"That's where my patrimony went and went and went. What is it George calls his mother? His 'keeper,' that's it. At least my governor pays me directly, not through a lawyer or bank. That takes courage, wouldn't you say? I get my allowance for staying out of England, you know."

"Tolstoi, everybody in the Quarter knows that much. What they don't know is why."

"Do you think it's because I killed somebody or because I was buggered at school? George thinks I pinched another boy's five-shilling postal order, like that Archer-Shee chap who was killed in the war."

"I think George was rather naughty in reporting Waddington to the French police," I said, to see what his reaction might be.

"I tried to talk him out of it, old man, but they pay informers very well over here. George is broke, you know."

"You're not as worried as the others are about Wad's book, then?"

"I skipped Spain this summer. But I was there last year. He has me in the setting if he wants me. He could have me running down those narrow streets in my under-shirt pursued by those damned bulls he is forever talking about. Or he could put me at the Quat'z Arts Ball doing a strip-tease. I couldn't stop him. And my reputation, as it is, is stretched as tight as Kiki's dress over her hips."

"You're not as excited by the book as Hal Leopold is?"

"The book will finish Hal, Ward. I have a sketchy notion of what went on down there and, if you ask me, Hal is beside himself with frustration. I wouldn't be surprised at anything he did. If I were Jason Waddington, and thank God I'm not, I would get out of town before the book is printed. If I were Wad, I'd deliver my head to that Dr. Freud in Vienna. For all that bluff, hail-fellow-well-met front of his, I think he's deeply cross-grained and troubled. He's all knotted and gnarled inside. He's got a secret bigger than mine to hide. Maybe he only learned the first half of the alphabet. Maybe he has never read a word of all these writers he keeps slamming. Like Anderson. I met Anderson, and he thought the world of Wad. Now Wad never misses a chance to slam his old mentor. And he's started slamming Bob McAlmon as well."

"McAlmon was Wad's first publisher over here! I don't get it."

"Wad is always moving on. He can't record his progress if he doesn't leave old friends behind. I mean, is the train moving if you don't leave people standing on the station platform?"

"What do you think of this cabal of friends leagued against him?" Tolstoi's head was wavering now. I couldn't even be sure he heard me. He was lost in the aptness of his latest similitude and half smiling to himself.

"When I think of Wad's character," he said at last, "I begin to feel better. Ward, if you were trying to cheer me up, you've succeeded. Damn it, now I suppose I'll have to do something purposeful with the remainder of the day."

"I thought you were looking better. But I wouldn't become a changed character, Tolstoi. Remember, you have an investment to protect. You wouldn't want to abandon a character you've worked on for years after one quiet chat. You think more of yourself than that, I hope?"

Tolstoi was smiling when I put down enough money to cover my drinks. His own stack of saucers was his problem. I caught sight of old Père Chambon, the proprietor of the Dôme, shaking his head at Tolstoi as I got up to leave. Tolstoi's head was now close to the edge of the table. In another moment, they would come together, but by then I was back in the bustle of pedestrian traffic along the boulevard.

CHAPTER 23

Freddy Briggs had been an assistant bartender at Le Trou dans le Mur before he earned the running of the place. There, his pleasant Liverpool accent and the right note of servility won him hundreds of friends among the English-speaking colony. When he crossed the river to the Dingo, he took many of those customers with him. A shortish, rosy-faced fellow with slicked-back hair, he had the knack of remembering names and drink preferences. He was the still point in this whirling world of sodden characters. His bar was solid and dependable. Freddy had the manner of a corporal who had not only survived life in the British Army, but who had learned to live like a king without any of it showing on his bland countenance.

He always greeted me now by name and with some remark that linked me to the band of drinkers who sustained the establishment. It was still too early for Biz, George or the others to be found, so I took a seat at the bar and made conversation with Freddy, while drinking some Scotch that he recommended.

"That's good stuff, Freddy. Best I've had in years."

"Ought to be, Mr. Ward. Twelve years in the cask. It's hard to come by a Highland malt over here. When I see you come in, I says to myself, 'There's a man with a taste for a fine malt.' There aren't many, I'll tell you. Most people don't really taste whisky. But this is so good you don't want to put a siphon on the table. In the old days, Mr.

Stearns liked a good malt, but he's beyond that now by a long stroke, poor chap. It's a serious problem with him and some of the others. Don't think I don't notice. I try to keep things reasonable, like, not let things happen because somebody's got a drop taken, sir, if you know what I mean?"

"From your side of the bar, Freddy, it must seem a three-ring circus."

"Cor, a few days ago, would you believe it, Mr. Leopold comes in, sober as a judge, askin' for Mr. Waddington. I'm glad Mr. Waddington didn't come in, because I'm sure Mr. Leopold was armed."

"You mean he was carrying a gun?"

"Yes, sir. You could tell by the way his jacket didn't hang right and the way he kept putting his hand in his pocket."

"Does Mr. Waddington know this?"

"I mean to tell him when I see him, but he's made himself a stranger these last few days. Probably off at some peace conference for a paper. But I'll tell him when I see him, Mr. Ward. You can count on that."

"Swell." I made a mental note to let Wad into this story as soon as possible. I wondered about the others; were they as serious as Hal? "Mr. Leopold packing a weapon is serious, Freddy. I'll tell him about it when I leave here."

"We don't want any more bad luck at the Dingo, do we, sir? After what happened to Miss Duclos." I sipped my whisky neat, as they say, shoving the siphon away from me with my elbow.

"Tell me, Freddy, on the night she died, did Miss Duclos look in for a short time?"

"Since it's you asking, there's no harm in telling you that she did."

"But she didn't usually come to you, did she?"

"How do you mean, sir?"

"Didn't she usually get what she needed at the Hole in the Wall?"

"I didn't know you knew about that, Mr. Ward." He gave me a slight smile, as though he were welcoming me into the select fraternity. "I first met her when I worked in the Hole."

"What's this fellow Jean-Paul like? I hear he's a hard man."

"Greedy, that's what Jean-Paul is nowadays. Plain greedy. The Hole is only a front for under-the-counter stuff. He used to be a reasonable bloke, like, but not lately." He poured another measure of Scotch for me and moved it in my direction. "The only thing he cares about is his sister, Arlette. He's glad she's only smoking a little hashish now and again. Nothing serious."

"Was she smoking the night Laure was killed?"

"She was always very discreet about it. She'd always trot off to the lavatory. I was on good terms with her, until she wanted a favour. Then I told her to piss up a rope, if you'll excuse the French, Mr. Ward."

Freddy did some cleaning up behind the bar and I watched him. I always enjoyed the precision of people working in confined quarters. In another minute, he was back with a question of his own.

"Mr. Ward, may I ask why you're so interested in Miss Duclos's death, sir? Not that I haven't been asked all sorts of questions since it happened."

"I think that there are those who would like to see Mr. Waddington arrested for her murder, Freddy." He whistled, and then looked around at the faces that had turned in his direction. He returned their good-natured grins.

"But I thought that it was this Jack fellow what done it? I mean, that's what I read in the papers."

"That's probably what did happen, Freddy, but it

hasn't stopped some people from trying to implicate our friend."

"Cor! If there's anything I can do to help, Mr. Ward, you let me know."

"Thanks, Freddy. I knew I could count on one of Mr. Waddington's oldest friends over here."

"I remember when he used to come into the Hole, you know. In those days, he came in with his newspaper friends. I forget most of their names, but we had a lot of good talk over a bottle, believe you me. Never understood half of what they were saying, them being educated men, you understand."

When I was half-way to the door, Dr. Anson Tyler came into the Dingo with Lady Biz on his arm. They both appeared glad to see me; I accepted their invitation to join them at a table. Biz cut a fine figure in a new coat and what looked like a milliner's recreation of her old felt hat. She lit up the room when she sat down. Anson was wearing an English suit and carrying an umbrella and bowler hat. He might have just alighted from the London Underground. He managed to wear the clothes and make them take orders from him in a way that poor Wilson O'Donnell never quite managed to do.

"You've been making yourself very scarce, Mike!" Biz said, "What have you been up to? Tell us something to make us laugh, that's a good chap."

"I've been giving my liver a rest. Where have you been?"

"Same old watering-holes. Disgusting, isn't it? Oh, I know! Some money came! And then it went. I'm wearing most of it. I think I'm all foolish virgins rolled into one. And, don't be facetious, either of you. It's perfectly easy to be facetious after a remark like that."

"You *are* well turned out, Biz. You look wonderful."

"How's your detective work going? Have you caught Jack at it yet?" Anson leaned the crook of his umbrella against the table's edge and placed his hat on an empty chair.

"Mainly I've been running up to the Gare St-Lazare with dispatches and trying to stay out of trouble," I said.

"Freddy!" Biz called in a loud voice. "Will you save me from these two boring men? Neither of them is in the least amusing today." Freddy smiled from the bar and hurried to our table. Meanwhile, Biz continued scolding. "I don't think you two deserve to have a well-turned-out chap sitting between you." She pretended to pout. Freddy wore an expression that was poised to go along with the joke, if it was one, or to discourage any real aspersions cast upon her character. We placed an order for drinks and he retreated behind the bar.

"Coward!" Biz said. "Men always let you down in the end."

"Biz, you may despise us," Anson said, "but you'll have to own that you've never cared much for the company of other women. Perhaps it's because we are the best of a thoroughly bad lot. What do you think?"

"Women stifle me, Anson. I'll have to give you that. Men bring me out in colour like a rotogravure Sunday magazine."

"You're like Waddingstein," Anson said, "a perfect romantic."

"I'm a romantic, Anson, but I'm not a bit like Waddington. Why do you say he's a romantic? I thought he was always pulling the wings off life as though it was a butterfly that got caught in his hair."

"His new book will have familiar wings in it," I said.

"Is that your cue to blame it all on me again? I do wish we could shut up about Pamplona. I did rather spoil everyone's fun. But I wasn't myself. If I was a writing sort of chap, I shouldn't think I'd get two hard, hopeless lines out of all our shenanigans."

"Oh, I don't know," Anson protested. "I've read some of his stories about northern Michigan. He talks about the deep woods, the trout streams and Indians with primitive passions. I know that country. It's potato-growing country. He never says that. But when you know it's being farmed by the locals, you can see that it's only primitive to a city boy, to a kid from Oak Park. Old Waddingstein's a bit of a magician."

"I don't see the crime in leaving things out, Anson. Maybe that makes the stories stronger. You can't put in everything anyway. So, writing is always selecting. Isn't that right? That's the way it is at the news service."

"I count three empty glasses on this table, chaps. That's bad luck where I come from."

"Where exactly do you come from, Biz?"

"I left the Ritz bar less than half an hour ago. Anson saw me coming up the rue Delambre and rescued me from the taxi driver, who was holding me for ransom."

"Not quite ransom, Lady Biz. Simply his just and honourable reward."

"You're so literal, Anson. Waddington would never mention a thing like that."

"He wouldn't have paid the driver. I know that!" said Anson.

"I thought you chaps were off Waddington? Have you decided to let him publish and be damned?" I asked.

"If he publishes, we'll certainly be damned. Waddington's not to be trusted. He gets everything wrong. He can no more see into the heart of a woman than he can walk through a doorway without banging his head. That's why George — you remember George, Mike? — George has been speaking to the family solicitor. The family takes its name very seriously."

"So, there will be legal action?"

"Among other things. I hear Waddington's had a brush with the police."

"Yes," I said. "Extraordinary how the news of his infatuation with Laure Duclos was brought to their attention." Anson looked at Biz, who was examining the weave of her skirt. Freddy sent a boy over to the table with a tray of drinks. When he had finished, I asked:

"Did you know that Hal Leopold has been going about armed in case he sees Wad? That could get him into trouble. The French don't take firearms as lightly as you Americans do, Anson. French jails are no summer camps."

"For once, I think Harold has the right end of the stick."

"Come on, Biz! You can't be serious!"

"As serious as a beak in a black cap about to pronounce sentence: an eye for an eye, a scalp for a scalp and the devil take the hindmost. Come on, Mike, be honest! How would you like it if a chap started making notes about your private affairs?"

"From what I've heard, none of the affairs Wad has written about were very private. What do you say to that?"

Biz squirmed and shifted her coat from her shoulders to the chair. "There may have been a circle of friends who knew what was happening, but Waddington means to broadcast these seeds far beyond our little thistle-strewn garden. Don't you see that, Mike? This is to be a *real* book, now, not a published-in-Paris pretend book. My dear old mother will read about it and, worse, George's mother will read about it."

"Is that very likely? Come on, both of you. How many American novels do they read in a year? You're assuming that this book is going to set the world on fire. What is more likely to happen is that the book will not even be reviewed in the big papers. Wad's just one of dozens of writers returned from the war. People are getting sick of books about the walking wounded who survived into this decade. At best he'll get a pat on the head and be told to try again. Really, Anson, aren't you flattering yourselves a little when you think that the outside world gives a damn about who did or did not make an ass of himself on the far side of the Pyrenees?"

"You're forgetting that I wasn't among that happy few, Mike. I was cutting and stitching in Neuilly. But maybe it's important to let Waddingstein know that you can't kidnap whomever you please into a goddamned book just to be a hell of a fellow on the literary scene. And, as for the book not causing a stir, you're forgetting that Wilson O'Donnell has been writing to a lot of influential people about that foul book. Wad might be a nobody, but O'Donnell isn't. When he talks, people listen."

"You're talking figuratively, Anson. Nobody ever listens to Wilson, even when he is sober enough to be presentable."

The argument raged through three more rounds of drinks. At one point George was in the fray. The arguments got stormier, but the logic crumbled into the wet rings on the marble-topped table. It need only be said that it was a very late hour when I pressed a few bills on Anson, who was taking the others home in our shared horse-cab. Even the clop-clop of the horses' hooves didn't stop the talk. I think we had a late supper somewhere near Les Halles, but I'm uncertain. As I wound my way up to my room, I wondered whether talk dissipates action. Are talkers doers? Did this evening of blather help Wad in the end? I hoped so, I hoped so.

CHAPTER 24

Waddington met me after I finished work the next day, and we walked to the inside courts at the American Club. I never much liked an inside game; it made me feel large and clumsy. This showed, of course, in the final score, which delighted Wad. I took his crowing with a patient spirit until he began to demonstrate where my game went awry. By the time he'd finished, I was in an uncharitable mood.

"What do you say to a beer, Michaeleen? I'll explain more what I mean about your backhand."

"I don't know. I've got things —"

"Oh, come on! You can't let a man drink alone. It's unchristian. Leads to unprofitable ruminations. Take pity, Wardo."

"Alright, I'll have a *demi* if you know a good place nearby."

"Hey, you *are* in a mood! Can you tell a fellow?"

"Will it end up in print?" I could see I'd hit him below the belt. He said nothing. We walked along in silence. The boulevard Raspail is not one of my favourite streets. It is like a stuffy London street that wandered across the Channel in the fog. There were few places that invited us to sit down and have a drink. In the end, we found a stand-up zinc bar on the rue du Montparnasse. Each of us ordered a shot of *marc*, which we could see behind the bar. There was no draught beer or foreign spirits. The *marc* was sharp and hard and we had another two.

"That was a mean thing you said, Mike. If you weren't a friend, I'd resent it. You know you can talk to me. I thought we were pals?"

"Sure, we're pals, Wad, but have you any idea how the people around you are stewing about your book? They feel violated. They think you took advantage of them, that it was an unfriendly act."

"That's too bad about them! Good night, nurse, who do they think they are that they can try to get me to suppress the best thing I've done so far? I didn't use anybody's real name, so if they tell people that they are so-and-so, they'll only have themselves to blame. You know yourself, Mike, a novelist is many people, if he's any good."

"I've heard Wilson say something like that. Still, one of those people is the friend who was part of whatever went on down in Pamplona."

"Aw, Mike, I've seen it a hundred times. They're all saying 'Stop it, I love it!' That's what they're saying."

"Hal Leopold is carrying a gun. I don't think he's loving it. Do you?"

"How do you know that? Carrying a gun? Is he looking for me?"

"That's what I understood from what Freddy at the Dingo told me."

"I've got to talk to him. I haven't seen anybody for days."

"I'm sure he does the rounds of your old haunts. You can see him any night you want."

After I'd settled with the bartender, we left the bar and walked up the rue du Montparnasse towards the boulevard. Wad said he'd catch the next one. He told me that he had a couple of things he had to do and that if I liked I could tag along. I had nothing pressing in my diary, so I went along with him to Lavenue, the restaurant, which was his first stop.

"I've got some stuff I have to leave for Burdock," he said. "Burdock's trying to set up some guaranteed memorable dinners for a dozen of his friends. Being sensitive souls, they all like to drink deep at the Pierian spring and anywhere else that has licensed hours. I think he's pre-sold the series on the strength that Joyce will be there. I don't know if he's told Joyce that he's to be fêted in this way. At least they'll get a good dinner, whether Joyce arrives or not. That's what literary lions care about."

"Who are these literary lions?"

"Oh, McAlmon, Natalie Barney, Djuna Barnes, Tzara, if he's in town. Burdock told me that McAlmon wanted to have Josephine Baker on the grounds that she's turned hootchee-cootchee into high art. But Burdock wouldn't have it, said it was too accessible, not high enough. He went on to say that Walter Pater would never have appreciated Josephine Baker. McAlmon argued that Pater was a hell of a guide to the twentieth century. Who the hell is this Walter Pater anyway, Mike? Is he somebody I should know about?"

"Great prose stylist. Oscar Wilde took a ride on his back. He wrote *Marius the Epicurean*."

"Sounds pretty dry. No jokes, right?"

"That's Walter. He was never the life of the party."

"We should introduce him to Georgia O'Donnell. She'd loosen his necktie and have him running for her drinks in no time."

"Alas, Walter has been collected to his ancestors. All in all, that's more his idea of a good time." We had reached the corner and crossed the boulevard. It was harder to cross at the busy Place de Rennes. Wad took a package from his gym duffel and I stayed outside reading the menu, while he went into the Lavenue.

There was a great deal of activity in the triangular *place* in front of the station. At first, I thought this was the normal bustle of a large railway terminus, but at second glance I could see that a large number of the motor-cars had police insignia on the doors. There were even two horse-drawn Black Marias with narrow, barred windows. Altogether, there were quite a few of the navy-blue uniforms in the square. I hadn't seen so many in one place since I went to cover a *manifestation* near the Mutualité on one of my earliest assignments.

As I looked through the glass into the restaurant, Wad was still busy talking to the manager. I took advantage of the delay to ask the nearest *flic* what was going on.

"*Circulez! Circulez, monsieur! Ce ne sont pois vos affaires.*" I explained to him that I was a journalist and he pointed out a senior officer to whom I should address myself. I did that.

"We think we have Jack penned up in the station, monsieur," he said. For a moment I thought he'd said "in the oven," the way the assistant headsman had, but what the policeman said was "*enfermer*," not "*enfourner*." My ear sometimes lets me down. But the difference between being penned up in Gare Montparnasse and put in the oven was not all that great, if you allow for an oven of that size.

"What's going on?" Wad asked, when he saw me coming back towards the restaurant.

"They think they've got Jack run to ground in the station."

"That's like trying to catch water in a sieve. If he knows the terrain at all, he'll run for the freight sheds south of here."

"I suppose he could have bought a ticket for Versailles. He's probably miles away by now." We watched the police moving about in front of the station. Waddington wore a superior smile: so much wasted effort.

"The old bugger in there didn't want to take responsibility

for the stuff I wanted to leave," he said at last, turning his back contemptuously on the scene we'd been watching. "I'll have to come back tonight."

"You might even get to meet the great man."

"Oh, Mike, I met Joyce years ago. You're the only man in town who hasn't kissed the hem of his garment."

"Yes, because I've seen those worn hems from fairly close. It could be that his life is poorer for not having met me. Try to think of it that way. Is he as daft on the subject of Gertrude Stein as she is on him?"

"Never heard him mention her. Most of the time he talks about the tenors he has heard and those he'd like to hear again before he dies. He's very musical. Plays the gramophone."

"Where to next?"

"I've got some money for Miró, the painter, to give to his dealer. I bought a picture from him for Hash as a peace-offering."

"He's the Catalan I've been hearing about. They say he's good."

"He's too shy to hang out around the cafés. He's the real thing, Michaeleen. Not like Pascin, who's always talk-ing and never at work. Miró holds the time clock when I go boxing. You sure you don't want to put on the gloves again, Mike? I think I could take you."

"I'm sure you could. That's why you're not going to get the chance. You may think I'm hiding a champion under these tweeds; I know I'm not." While we were talking, I fol-lowed Wad down the rue du Départ. At number 26, he turned into a cobblestone courtyard with an outside tap marked *eau non potable*. Wad led the way into a stairway on the left side and we began the inevitable climb up the steps.

"Miró is meeting me at the Dutchman's studio. He says André Breton has taken over his place. An actor named Artaud is turning his studio upside-down. So he's begged a corner at the Dutchman's."

The climb was not as high as I expected it to be. I was beginning to be impressed by the Dutchman. He could afford the higher rent of a third-floor space.

It was, in fact, the Dutchman who opened the door. He was a large man wearing a cook's apron over his street clothes. Wad spoke to him in English and soon Miró was pointed out, asleep on a couch with a fur rug pulled up to his chin. The Dutchman explained in a whisper that they had shared some wine at luncheon and offered the remainder of the bottle to us. Wad at first refused politely, then accepted a glass, as did I, when it was handed around. Waddington addressed the Dutchman as "Pete," or, more correctly, "Piet." Both of us admired the paintings on the wall, which to me looked more like designs for wallpaper than fine art. But I was not *au courant* with much of what the new people were doing. Judging by the discarded pieces of cardboard on the floor, Piet first designed his pieces on the insides of cigarette packages torn open and then transferred the drawings to canvas. Miró slept on.

When he awoke, about twenty minutes after we'd arrived, Miró was immediately happy to see Waddington. They talked in Spanish or Catalan — *"Qué tal, hombre?"* or something on that order. Wad tried to give the painter a handful of French banknotes, which the little Catalan at first declined. I could see that this, like the invitation to share the last of the wine, was a ritual, where one declined in the first exchange and accepted a few innings later. Miró was made very happy by the money. I think that an arrangement was made for the painting to be delivered on the following day. Miró was sorry I couldn't see the picture, which was of a farm, but it was, sadly, back in that madhouse of a studio on the rue Blomet. He protested that, like his Dutch friend, he loved the quiet life. He hated noise, discord and arguments. And noise, discord and arguments had been his lot since he had first become associated with the Surrealists.

"Tristan Tzara may be the maddest of them all, but at least he isn't noisy," he said to me in French.

A knock at the door introduced a smart young policeman, clicking his heels and saluting tidily. The Dutchman invited him into the studio.

"Sirs, we are searching this whole block of apartments. We have reason to believe that a fugitive may be hiding here. Have you observed anything out of the ordinary in the neighbourhood? Are there strangers lurking about?"

"Is this the same operation as we saw in front of the Gare Montparnasse?" Wad asked. The policeman shook his head, either in ignorance or a professional dislike of giving out information. "If it is the same job, your net's too big. How do they know it's Jack, anyway?"

"Monsieur will understand that information is in short supply just now. But I believe the suspect attempted to attack a woman going into one of the studios above the Café de Versailles. He ran off in this direction."

"How can they be sure it's him?" I asked.

"The woman was hurt, monsieur, stabbed superficially. She was taken to Val de Grâce to be treated. The woman was a model, like the others." He then shrugged to indicate that this was not his idea, whatever we thought.

After the policeman left, we heard him hammering on the doors along the corridor. We had a drink of schnapps that the Dutchman kept for special occasions, and then, in another few minutes, the tall painter and the short one walked us to the head of the stairs and waved goodbye. With me I carried away a memory of the designs on the torn cigarette packages, the pure, clean colours corralled between black vertical and horizontal lines. I remember the white space in the pictures, the round table set with a clean-ish cloth and large, northern coffee bowls. Last of all, I realized that the arrangement of the wicker furniture was also along geometric lines.

We crossed the Place du Maine and began walking south. "You'll like Miró when you get to know him," Wad said, as I puffed along trying to keep up. "I've been learning Catalan from him. It makes Valéry Larbaud sore when I use it. He talks Spanish like a native. Learned it from Argentinians when he was at school."

"Larbaud? I thought you didn't know Larbaud."

"Whatever gave you that idea? Met him at Sylvia's years ago."

"Couple of weeks ago you'd never heard of him." Wad kept going, but he shot me a glance that told me to be careful. Funny, being careful when we were alone, I thought. I was wondering what other messages he had on his mind. I was also getting weary of walking. "Where are we going now?" I asked. I think some of my anxiety showed in my voice, because he answered:

"Break your gun, kid. Don't shoot till we get across the fence."

"There's nothing down here but freight sheds and a roundhouse."

"I know. It's only half a roundhouse. But there's a hobo jungle down here I've been trying to remember. I tried making it up. That works most of the time, but I haven't got it right. It doesn't smell right, so I want to take a squint at it. Do you mind?"

"Lead on. Into the jaws of death."

"Speaking of those particular jaws, Mike, Gertrude Stein wants to talk to you. She's read your stuff and, as they say in the British Army, 'You're for it.'"

"Why do you talk about her like that? I thought you were like brothers?"

"Yeah, we are, kiddo, but she's beginning to get my goat. The way she summons and dismisses you. You don't meet and talk with Gertrude, you have a bloody audience. And Alice has been sniping at me again. Thinks I want to break up their happy home. Gertrude — I'll say this much for her — is always up front and straight with me, but her friend! That Alice is wise in the ways of low cunning."

We had left the apartment buildings behind us. The cement wall that marked the line of the right-of-way was on our right as we went down.

"What about that beer we were going to have? I'm getting —"

"Shut up!"

"What?"

"There's somebody out there." I looked at Wad, and then in the direction he was looking. We had reached a break in the wall where a set of tracks led off to a line of warehouses, teamways and loading bays. Wad was watching something through the gap. I couldn't see anything but tracks and signal levers. A brick signal tower stood out against the sky, dark and abandoned. The structure that had replaced it was higher and closer to the station. To the north, the tracks converged and entered the open rear of the station. Most of the quays continued south towards us, covered from the weather by slanted roofs that reached about a hundred yards beyond the end of the station. The quays went on not much further. The quay that led to the old signal tower lay at the far side of the tracks. It didn't look as though it got much use.

"He's in that old tower now, Mike. I saw him go up the steps."

"You think it's Jack?"

Half a dozen policemen came out of the station and walked along one of the middle quays. They kept coming until they reached the end, where they stopped. They turned and looked around and lit cigarettes, which they cupped in their hands as they faced one another. Nobody climbed down to the ballast.

"They think the tower's been searched already, I'll bet," I said.

"Sure. It's the first place they'd look. That's why it's safe now," Wad said.

"Should we go over to tell the policemen?"

"That'll be his cue to make tracks. Then they'll never get him. And there isn't time to go back the long way and report him at the front of the station." After three or four minutes, the policemen went back inside the station.

"I haven't seen anything moving in the tower," I said.

"That makes it more likely that it's Jack. A signalman would have waved or shown himself."

"Why did the police disappear?"

"Because they know the yard back of the station was searched earlier. Let's get back so the wall covers us."

"Wad, you don't mean to try to take him, do you?"

"Sure. We'll surprise him if he heads this way through this gap. Just keep your head down and don't let him get his hand on those scissors of his."

"It's probably just a *clochard*."

"That's what the odds say. But what if it is Jack, Mike?"

"Wad, you're as crazy as he is!"

"You want me to take him alone, Mike? Just stand clear."

"Oh, go to hell. I'm with you, damn it. But we're both crazy."

Wad took a look around the gap. When he pulled his

head back, he shook it. "He's going to stay in there for a while. It's a mistake. He should run for it."

"Hell, Wad, it's his head."

"He knows they're doing a sector-by-sector search. He knows that they'll get to the tower again before long. If he heads out the back, he'll think he can be seen. But he'd be wrong; the tower would mask him from the station as long as he kept it between them." Wad peeked around the corner again. "He's coming," he said.

We were both standing on the north side of the break in the wall. Wad's back was close to the white cement. I took a similar position and tried to remember when I'd done anything so hare-brained before. At the same time, it was exhilarating. I checked my breathing and found that Wad was trying to control his as well. Beads of sweat stood out on his forehead. I wanted to feel mine, too, but I didn't want to move.

It wasn't long before we heard him, his shoes scuffing over the rails. He was making a wheezing noise, as though he was talking to himself aloud in a whisper. Suddenly the noise stopped. We could see nothing, of course, and the sound had been our sole guide. Then the whispy, whispering breathing started again. Perhaps he had turned around to see if he had been seen. From his point of view, it didn't matter now. He had only a short block to walk or run before he could lose himself on boulevard de Vaugirard. He was almost out of the box.

Then he came through the gap and Wad was on him. I went for his feet, got him off balance. He fell to the ground before we heard him cry out. The man was kicking up rough, but I soon was sitting on his legs. I slid my belt free of the loops in my trousers and fastened his legs together at the calf. Where his corduroy trousers had been hitched up during the struggle, his skin looked mouldy. I still hadn't seen his face, which was hidden by Waddington's shoulders. From what I could see, Wad was busy keeping the man's arms pinned on the ground on either side of his head. At one moment, the man freed one of his arms and immediately made a move, which Wad was obliged to discourage with a move of his own. It was a punch; I couldn't see where it landed, but I heard the scream. From then on, he behaved. As Wad shifted off the body, I could see that the man's hand was caught in his trousers, as though he had been reaching to protect his groin. Wad put his knee down on his arm at the elbow. He did it firmly, but not with violence. The whole assault had lasted perhaps a minute. All three of us were breathing heavily.

Jack's face, if indeed it was Jack, was long, red and heavily lined. He wore a skimpy moustache that lacked enough bristle to do a credible job of it. His brown hair looked matted, greasy and long. With some caution, Wad pulled the man's hand out of his trousers. There was blood on his fingers. Shifting his knees, he pinioned the arms and extracted a long-bladed pair of scissors from the man's groin. There was blood on the scissors as well. We hadn't heard the sound of running up the railway tracks, but suddenly there were other faces looking down at us. The first faces were followed by others. Soon the place was full of caps and capes and uniforms with brass buttons. Wad looked over at me, grinning like a damned fool.

CHAPTER 25

T he worst fighting I saw was with the Arditi on the Asiago Plateau behind Mount Pasubio."

"They were fine troops, the Arditi," said Commissioner Léon Zamaron, nodding. "How did an American with the Red Cross happen to be fighting with them?"

We were sitting around a mahogany table across from the bar in the main room of the Closerie des Lilas. Wad and I had our backs against the banquettes, while the policeman sat with his back to the rows of bottles that lined the bar. It was about an hour after the police had taken charge of our prisoner. The commissioner, who'd made an appearance at the office of the railway police at the Gare Montparnasse, had expedited matters so that we were now able to take some light refreshment after our adventure. It was easy to see that the policeman was fascinated by Waddington's stories. He mentioned all of his favourite themes: the hobo jungles, boxing on Chicago's North Side, as well as his exposure to fire during the war.

"That's a long story, M. Zamaron, and I don't think I can tell it yet without getting some very fine Italians into trouble for cutting through a lot of red tape."

"I see," Zamaron said, not looking as though he either believed or disbelieved what Wad was saying. Perhaps a policeman learns to listen without judging these things. "Our dossier says only that you carried chocolate to the trenches. But, then, the war records are in a great tangle, are they not? There is so much that has been omitted."

"You have a file on me?" Wad asked.

"Of course. You were an accredited journalist in 1922. You were one of the people in the files on my desk. I get all the foreigners, as I have recently explained to M. Ward." He smiled in my direction with such simplicity that I postponed asking him about the dossier on me.

The room was high-ceilinged with shiny yellow paint coming down to the top of the banquettes, except when intercepted by mirrors. Brass rails, which followed the banquettes, were used as a temporary repository for our coats. The Closerie was actually warm inside, unlike the places further along the boulevard. We were drinking the best cognac the Lilas could provide. It looked a little curious in our dirty hands. Wad's jacket was dirty on one side and my trousers were split at the knee. Apart from that, and the bruises that would not announce themselves for another twenty-four hours, we had survived the ambush without casualties. Even Jack was found to have been hurt only superficially: the blades did minor damage to his own upper thigh.

Waddington had been right to a degree about Jack. He was a man who rarely had had his picture in the paper, but he wasn't a complete unknown. He had been the coach of a six-day bicycle-racer of the third rank until the man was killed in the Alps during an ill-advised attempt to break out of velodrome confinement. Since then, Jack had been working as an assistant to a tailor who made football uniforms. He was from Lille originally and had been living on the fringes of the sporting world since his cyclist's death. Christian Caron was hard-up, thirty-five, unmarried and living with a former champion weight-lifter. He made no statement upon being arrested and charged except to insist that the papers get his name spelled correctly.

"The Arditi were the finest and toughest shock troops on any side of the wire," Zamaron said with conviction. I was slowly getting angry at both of them for so casually not discussing the chief event of the day.

"Were you in the army, *Monsieur le Commissaire*?" Wad asked.

"Ah, no. I was considered to be irreplaceable here. I appealed the decision, but to no avail. Instead of finding a marshal's baton in my knapsack, I found saboteurs at the Rotonde."

"We were told that Caron had been up to his old tricks across from the Gare Montparnasse at the Café de Versailles," I said, hoping to shunt the conversation back to a track that held more interest for me.

"When M. Caron attempted to accost Mme. Camille Maure, he found more than a match for him and his pair of scissors. Camille was a dancer up in Montmartre as well as a model in the studio across from the *gare*. She told me that she has even scrubbed floors to help make ends meet. Naturally, a dancer of this description is a better physical antagonist than our sewing-machine operator bargained for. According to a witness who came on the scene and saw the struggle, he was almost convinced that it was Caron who was being attacked. But, *messieurs*, let that in no way abridge the value of your contribution when you ambushed this murderer behind the station. I am not directly connected with this investigation any longer, but I should be surprised if you didn't both receive citations from the highest civil authorities for taking this criminal."

"Let's drink to that!" Waddington said.

Later, when I'd had a chance to clean up, medicate my few scratches and change my clothes, I walked across the park to 27, rue de Fleurus and knocked.

"Oh, it's you," said Hélène, the cook. "We were expecting M. Picasso."

"Perhaps I'll come another time," I suggested. "Please give your mistresses my compliments." I turned and was about to leave when I heard Gertrude's booming voice.

"Mr. Ward? Is that you?" She followed her inquiry into the hall, and before I could get away, she had me by the arm and was pulling me into the apartment.

"I understand that you are expecting company. I'll come back another time."

"Pablo never comes when he says he's coming, Mr. Ward. He has a Surrealist's sense of time. So do come in. I've been hoping that we could have a chat about your work." I was soon in the large studio room being regarded by the surrounding paintings. Pushed into a chair, I found myself in a moment literally sitting at the feet of Gertrude Stein.

"Hélène is bringing you a cup of tea. She brews excellent tea. Alice has taken Basket out. She is anxious not to see Pablo."

"May I ask why?"

"Oh, she fancies that he is unfair to Matisse. Matisse is devoted to Pablo, so Pablo should be devoted to Matisse. It's probably fair, but not fair in the way of the world. Pablo is a genius and his genius is made the goat for a deal of incivility."

"Not having met either of them —"

"Pablo wants to live forever. There never was such a man for squeezing the juice out of every moment. That is why he will not come today."

She was wearing a huge corduroy skirt which came within inches of her ample ankles. Her feet, encased in sandals, looked red and troublesome; her hair was newly trimmed and her face was intimidating. She seemed like an animated version of the life-sized sculpture that Jo Davidson had made of her.

"Now, to business," she said, placing my manuscript on her lap. "I think that you are not reading enough of the right people, Mr. Ward. I hear echoes in your prose, echoes that run back to stuffy English drawing rooms and American universities. Is that what Canadians aspire to sound like?" She had taken a cigarette without appearing to watch what she was doing, and lighted it from a box of kitchen matches. I needed a cigarette myself, but I was too wrapped up in what was being said to me to attempt to smoke. Gertrude blew a large smoke ring across the gap between us and watched it drift towards the ceiling. As we talked, her ample bosom collected her ashes.

"Writing is always a matter of voice and sound, Mr. Ward. Yours is yet unformed. I detect familiar accents here and there. You have humour, which is good, and good because rare. You are beginning to see things in the new way. Like our friend Waddington, you often make your sentences experience the thing you are talking about rather than let them simply describe what is going on from a distance. Your narrator is close to the story, but you must not leave him a cipher. Make him opinionated, smother him in the action. Dump ashes before his feet." At this moment, Hélène brought in a tray with tea and bread and butter. Gertrude didn't look up. She went on telling me how my work had failed to impress her. I could hardly keep my cup still in its saucer as she told me that I must abandon what I had already written.

"You must start again, Mr. Ward," she said, sipping from her cup, "only this time you must concentrate."

Half an hour later, I was back in the street with my manuscript, full of tea and bread and butter, trying to remember every suggestion she had made. I took the manuscript back to my room and opened it. I sat there for some time staring at it without reading a word. I was not a born writer, she had implied; I showed no special talent. I was not working in the spirit of the modern writers that she cared about. The only word of hope was to try again. I still don't know what she meant by "concentrate." Had she imagined that I had written my stories in a haze or a dope-inspired dream?

I was now thoroughly out of spirits. Not only had I been condemned as a mediocre writer, but I hadn't even met Picasso. For a day that had started well, it was now sagging in the most unattractive places. In an attempt to defy the foul fiend of depression, I decided to bury my troubles in an excellent dinner.

I went to Dagorno's for a steak. Near the slaughter-house, it boasted that it served the best broiled meat in town. I've always enjoyed this place, from the picture on the menu of semi-nude female chefs holding up platters of sturgeon and grills of suckling pigs, all mounted on the back of a prize and garlanded steer, to the reality of the truffled *foie gras* and a variety of fine wines. Because of its location next door to the Cochon d'Or in La Villette, I never expected to run into people I knew there. On this occasion, I was surprised. I was sipping the last of my coffee when Wilson and Georgia O'Donnell came into the restaurant in a company of what looked like well-to-do Americans with the odd monocled Englishman thrown in to make the scene cosmopolitan. They didn't see me at first, but as I was settling my bill, Wilson clapped me on the shoulder and asked me to join them for a drink. I tried to beg off, but he insisted.

"Mike! How nice to see you!" Georgia said, leaning across the table to take my hand. She was looking dreadful. With dark lines under her eyes, she seemed haunted, un-healthy. Her smile was warm and her grip was cold without being clammy. I sat across from her in the chair provided from the empty end of the table. I was introduced around the table and quickly forgot most of the names.

"Georgia's been under the weather, Mike. Thought I was going to lose her for a few days."

"Nonsense, Goofo, it was just the *grippe*. You thought I had peritonitis again. That's because you don't know anything at all, at all, at all, as the French so charmingly say. French women say that, not the men. The French have two languages: one for the women, one for the men. I don't know either. Mike, do you think that Valentino is cute? Seriously, though? Is he the ideal of masculine beauty, Mike?"

"Georgia, what are you talking such rubbish for? Mike would like to hear our good news, I'll bet. We are at last getting out of town. I can't work worth a damn here, so we're moving down to Juan-les-Pins for the winter. There are too many people here," he said, with a glance at the row of animated faces at the other end of the table, "for me to get back in the groove. I can't write with an ice pack on my head, can I, precious?"

"You could write standing on your head, Goofo, if you wanted to."

"Did you hear that Wad captured Jack de Paris this afternoon? Almost singlehanded."

"Waddington did *what*?" I repeated what I'd said and added a few details. "That's amazing," Georgia said. "I never took him for a real he-man at all. I thought he was bluff from head to toe. Well, Goofo, I'd better get my opinions dry-cleaned."

If Georgia let the matter drop there, Wilson wanted to hear about it all over again. He became as excited as a racing fan at the track with a wad on the dark horse.

"We've got to get over there and congratulate him! Come on, Georgia. Drink up and put your hat back on."

Wilson made his excuses to the others at the table and settled with the waiter for his share of the expected bill. The women at the table scarcely interrupted their conversation. Perhaps they had never heard of Jack de Paris. It was certain the name Waddington was unknown to them. Wilson sent a waiter out into the avenue Jean Jaurès to flag down a taxi. He returned after three minutes, smiling.

Twenty minutes later, Wilson, Georgia and I were coming down the stairs from the Waddington apartment on rue Notre-Dame-des-Champs. Mme. Rohrbach was there minding Snick. She had no idea where the Waddingtons might be. Discouraged, we looked along both sides of boulevard Montparnasse into the bright interiors of the cafés. No sign of the Waddingtons. But we did meet with some of his old gang: Lady Biz and George Gordon were sitting at the Rotonde. They had heard the news and decided to join us in running down the hero of the hour, or at least one of the heroes of several hours ago. When I think about it now, I might have made a better case for my share of the victory, but I was perhaps depending on Wad to share the laurels with me.

We found him, as you might well have expected, at the Dingo, telling his story while Hash and Julia looked up at him from each side. Youpi, the wife of the owner, herself brought the drinks. Freddy left the bar for a moment and slipped into a chair near Anson and Tolstoi to hear better. Arlette La Motte looked equally rapt by the story. Julia was looking up at her god and Wad was playing the scene to her. Hash was quiet and tense. At our appearance, Wad interrupted his tale.

"And here's the man himself!" he said. "If Mike, here, hadn't been there, I would never have thought of tackling the fellow. Michaeleen gave me the moral support that was needed. He even lent his belt for tying up the man's legs, so that when the police finally came, we had a neatly trussed bundle for them. If there wasn't the formality of a trial to go through, they could have taken him to the boulevard Arago just as he was: properly pinioned for the national barber."

There was a little fuss as we arranged the seating. Biz sat near Anson, who gave her a friendly peck on the cheek. George demanded his favourite Scotch from Freddy, who got up to see if there was any. For the moment, the resentment and bitter feeling between Wad and his gang was forgotten.

From his perch on the edge of the table, Wad was certainly enjoying himself. For the benefit of the newcomers, he went back on his track to first of all discover what they knew and then to paint the picture for them again, beginning with the mobs of police in the Place de Rennes in front of the station. He was a wonderful storyteller. At times he seemed to be inside the consciousness of the fugitive. He contrasted him with a charging bull during a *corrida*. He seemed to favour the dumb charging of the animal over the devious movements of the killer. Certainly he didn't miss a possibility in telling the story. I found that he made it more exciting to hear about than to have actually been present at. All eyes were on him as he spoke. Nobody saw Harold Leopold slip into the Dingo and come up to the table. Nobody saw that he was holding a gun in his hand until he'd fired off a round into the floor.

CHAPTER 26

Now hold on, Hal! Let's talk this over, damn it!"

"What's the point, Wad? You've done what you pleased with our lives. Why should I care about yours?"

Freddy had been making slow movements, trying to move as far as possible away from the centre of Hal's focus. Then the gun went off again and everybody sat dead still.

"I'm not joking, everybody! Nobody's going to get hurt if he sits still. My quarrel is with Waddington, nobody else. But I don't want anybody to move until I'm finished. Sorry, Freddy. I didn't mean to frighten you. Just stay seated and we'll all get along just fine." He leaned his back against one of the tables, then ordered Youpi to get him a drink with no "funny business." She complied, making slow movements as she reached for the glass and bottle. There was a sound of glass clinking against glass as she poured.

"This is a damned lousy way to act, Hal. Why don't you and I settle this between ourselves? You don't need to hold all of these people." Wad was sounding like his version of the taking of Jack de Paris. There was more Douglas Fairbanks than Waddington in his manner.

"You're very glib for a dead man, Waddington."

A highlight of sweat had appeared above Wad's eyebrows. When he spoke, he kept hitching the right side of his mouth up into that boyish smile of his. His moustache seemed to quiver as he talked.

"I hope you're not still angry about that book of mine, Hal, because I've had second thoughts about that."

"Keep talking. Not that I'm going to believe you, Wad. A rat will try to lie his way out of a tight corner."

"Well, you can decide whether I'm lying or not. Look, I've had nothing but abuse from you people since I wrote that damned book. At first I thought I could ride it out, that the wind would change, but I was wrong. Then I started seeing it from your side. You have to give me credit for that, George. I tried to see how I would like it if Jason Waddington exposed me as a drunken bankrupt."

"Steady on, old man. There are friendlier ways of saying that."

"And I was worried about the ethics of showing Biz going off with you, Hal, and then going off with a bullfighter."

"Bullfighter?" Biz looked open-eyed with surprise.

"Yes. I didn't tell you about that part. You see, I am a bloody writer of fiction. I do have to make up some of it. That's why you run off with a bullfighter. You would have liked him, Biz. Only the best for you."

"Get back to the point, Wad. You're drifting."

"Right. Well, you know the next step, Hal, because I have you to thank for it. You set me up with your publisher in New York. That excited me. After all, being published in Paris is one thing, but New York means the best-seller lists and money and financial independence. If you've got a minute, I could say a word or two about what I think about the life we've been leading for the last five years. Poverty stinks, Hal. You'll never know that. Even George, here, with all his problems, won't ever know what it's like to sleep on the floor and eat the way Hash and I have since we got married. You don't know what it's like to save centimes and cadge drinks."

"What's this got to do with me? Keep talking, but make sense."

"It'll just take another minute, Hal. You see, with your publisher in New York, I could have been set up for life. Never have to worry again about who was going to redeem the pile of saucers on the table at the Dôme, never have to avoid the look in Mme. Select's eye."

"You're wasting time again," Hal said, raising the muzzle of the gun.

"Boni and Liveright brought out my first book in the States. All thanks to you, Hal. The contract was for three books. If I sent them the Spanish book you're all so set against, it would probably come out in the spring. But you didn't want that. After a lot of thought, I put together a book that Boni and Liveright will reject. A different book."

"Reject? How the hell do you know that?"

"Put a lot of rough stuff in it, did you, old man? Lots of bums and —" Biz grabbed George's arm and he shut up.

"What I put in the book was a satirical description of their top writer. They can't publish that, and that voids the contract. Sherwood Anderson is their ace writer of the moment, now into the tenth printing of his last book. Are they going to let some upstart from Oak Park spoil that, Hal? You give me the answer."

"Why are you doing this for us?"

"I could say it's because of friendship, but you wouldn't believe that. So maybe you'll believe me when I say it's for business reasons. I don't want to become known as a writer who kidnaps his friends into his novels. I'd be isolated. Nobody'd ever talk to me again. Mike, you reminded me about that, and it made me think."

"So, you want us to believe that you purposely scuttled your book because of us?"

"I didn't say that, Hal. What I said was that I didn't want to get a bad name in the business. Damn it, I don't want to earn my reputation in the law courts. I don't want to be the best-known writer ever to be convicted of criminal libel. I want my stuff to be judged as a book, not as a slice of your life or anybody else's."

"So the Spanish novel is not going to be published?"

"I can guarantee that Boni and Liveright will wash their hands of me. My satire on Anderson's a contract-breaker, Hal. You know what that is."

"They're not the only American publishers, old man," said George.

"They are the only ones who've ever heard of me. *You've* got as much chance of being taken on by one of the others as I have. Do you think that I'd pass up a sure thing hoping to make a better deal elsewhere, George? You're a gambling man. Are they odds you'd like to play?"

Hal had steadily been lowering his gun. At last it was no longer pointing at Waddington's liver. He looked as though he was beginning to believe Wad's account of his motives. The rest of the group looked convinced as well. There was a moment when the room seemed to draw a collective breath. And then suddenly a hand reached out and took the gun out of Hal Leopold's hand. It was Léon Zamaron. Nobody had seen him come into the room. Nobody knew how long he had been standing behind Hal or how much of what had passed he had witnessed. He removed the ammunition and returned the gun to its owner.

"My friends, may I suggest that we all sit down," he said. I could make out the shape of a plainclothes policeman standing near the door. He wasn't as obvious as his Toronto counterpart might have been, but he was not hard for any journalist, even a neophyte, to spot.

"M. Briggs," Zamaron said to Freddy. "Why don't you pour for each of us a drink?" Zamaron nodded to several of us, and to me as well. Slowly, he manoeuvered a chair so that it joined the group at the table. If this were just a matter of laying a firearms charge against Hal, why didn't he get on with it? I wondered.

"By now, no doubt, you know of the great success of Messieurs Ward and Waddington. Of course, they are to be congratulated for the capture of this desperate wanted man, whom we now know to be called Christian Caron. We are slowly putting together a picture of the man's life and the workings of his mind. This, happily, is none of my concern. It is in the excellent hands of my police colleagues." Zamaron was leaning back in his chair, speaking in a brand of French he reserved for foreigners. His idioms were clear and focused, his selection of words and constructions perfectly clear, even to George, who often had difficulty expressing himself in what he called "that objectionable jargon." Freddy brought drinks to the table.

"Are we all under arrest, M. Zamaron? Why is that man standing at the door?" Arlette demanded in a staccato voice that sounded like fingernails on slate. This was the first time she had spoken in some time.

"Mlle La Motte, please try to understand my position. I have for many years carried responsibility for the good behaviour of foreigners. The Prefect of the Seine appointed me himself. On the whole, since the war, you have made my job easy. Once in a while, however, I must stop looking at my beloved paintings and become a policeman again. *Au fond*, I am an *agent*, a *sergent de ville*, a *gardien de la paix*, a *flic*, no? We may be as common as the sparrows on the boulevards, but we all have our jobs to do. Mine is to try to find out what I can about the murder of Laure Duclos, whom you all knew."

"But you have Jack locked up at the commissariat. Isn't that enough?"

"Unfortunately, M. Pease, it would appear that the brutal murder of Mlle Duclos was not the work of Christian Caron."

"And may a chap ask how you know this?"

"Lady Leighton, in the Paris police we have produced no geniuses, unless you count Vidocq, the first thief-taker known to French history, but we are not all stupid, either. Rather, we muddle along. Sometimes we are lucky, as in the killing of Laure Duclos, whose death was superficially made to look like the work of M. Jack. The killer of Mlle Duclos, fortunately for us, did not know all of the details that we have found at the scenes of the other killings. Details — I will not mention them in appreciation of the fact that there are ladies present — that group all of the murders together as the work of one madman. Perhaps we will prove that madman was M. Caron. But, one of those crimes was not the work of this madman, whomever he proves to be! Because the same details were not present. These details constitute the fingerprints of our killer. When they do not appear . . ." Here Zamaron shrugged, letting us finish the sentence for ourselves. Anson and Arlette sipped their drinks. Biz whispered with George. Julia looked frightened, not for herself, but on behalf of Waddington, judging from the object she most often regarded.

"Tell me, M. Ward," the Commissioner continued, "how is it that without our special knowledge you too began to believe that Jack was not the killer of Mlle Duclos?"

I was surprised that he brought me into it. I cleared my throat and began trying to sort through the ideas I'd had at the time.

"I had no proof, *Monsieur le Commissaire*. I had what we call 'a hunch.'"

"Entirely respectable as a tool of the mind, Monsieur."

"It seemed odd to me that someone who was a known blackmailer should so handily turn up as the random victim of a crazed murderer. It was too pat."

"I sympathize with your hunch. But one must remember

that in all detective work, the most obvious thing is very often what has happened. It is not very helpful to writers of novels or to playwrights, but that is the banal truth of police work." He nodded at both Waddington and Wilson O'Donnell when he mentioned writers. The O'Donnells had not spoken since Hal Leopold began waving his gun around. Georgia's eyes were bright with excitement; Wilson looked as if he were losing blood rapidly through an unseen wound.

"Thank you, Monsieur. I'll remember that. I also remember what Dr. Tyler told me the night we carried Mr. O'Donnell home from a party. He said that Laure was an opium user. That connected her with a much bigger world than the tight little colony here in the Quarter. The drug business is centred on the Right Bank. The dealers that Laure knew might have killed her for any of a dozen reasons: she might have owed them money, she might have threatened them with blackmail."

"So, you discarded your theory about the murder having been committed by one of her Montparnasse friends?"

"How well informed you are, M. Zamaron!"

"Alas, the paid informer is not a well-respected part of Anglo-Saxon culture, M. Ward. But since at least the days of Pépin the Short, the world here in France revolves around them. I make no apologies for French traditions, Monsieur. Did you replace your dead hypothesis with a more lively one?"

"Not exactly. I revived the dead one when I discovered that Arlette, our charming friend here, was related to Jean-Paul La Motte, the chief source of drugs, who works at Le Trou dans le Mur on the boulevard des Capucines." Everybody looked at Arlette, who opened her mouth as though she were about to speak and then changed her mind. She began looking at her well-lacquered fingernails and avoiding all attempts to exchange glances.

"You see, Arlette joined the two worlds together again. There was no longer a Left Bank and a Right Bank focus to the crime. It was the same focus. The part of the story that involved drugs was simply part of whatever happened on Montparnasse among the people Laure was blackmailing."

"We know that she was blackmailing M. Waddington," Zamaron said, trying to be helpful.

"Now, look!" Wad cut in, "I don't have to listen to my private life being dissected in public!" He was on his feet and looking very much like an outraged Rotarian, pinched for drinking after licensed hours in a strange town. "If you want to arrest me, go ahead! But I don't have to sit here and take this!"

"M. Waddington, would you care to spend time with us at the commissariat? The questions will be the same — I promise you that — but the setting will be less agreeable." Wad exhaled loudly, crossed his arms over his massive chest and at last sat down without saying another word.

"Continue, M. Ward."

"It's not my wish to get any of you into more trouble than you're already in. Please believe me," I said. "M. Zamaron?"

"*Oui, Monsieur?*"

"You are looking for a murderer, is that not correct?" Zamaron nodded. "Then we are not at all interested in smaller things: the smoking of opium, the reasons for blackmail and so on?"

"That is correct. What we say in this pleasant room will stay in this room. Only the murderer needs to be wary. But, I assure him, or *her*," he said significantly, "that we will find you out whatever the cost. A little lost privacy is a small thing, a bagatelle, as you say in English."

"If that is clear, Arlette," I continued, "let's begin with you. We are talking about murder and nothing but murder, you understand? Does your brother deal in drugs at Le Trou dans le Mur?"

"I don't have to answer that."

"Your family loyalty is admirable, Arlette. I'm sure we are all touched by it, but it isn't helping us find our killer."

"Try to think of me, Mademoiselle, not as a policeman, whose ears prick up at every breach of the *Code Napoléon*. Think of me as a specialist in murder. It is only facts about murder that interest me."

"All right, Jean-Paul does have some dealings of the kind you mention." Arlette continued to examine her nails as she spoke.

"Do you know either directly or indirectly whether Laure was a regular user of opium or any other drug supplied by Jean-Paul?" I asked.

"Laure Duclos had a problem. Yes. She was addicted. That's the only word for it."

"Can you tell us how you know this?"

There was hate in her eyes as she looked up at me. She directed her answer to Zamaron. "Laure and I have smoked a pipe together on several occasions going back five years or so. I don't do that any more, Monsieur, but she was always telling me when the boys brought in a new supply. Some of it came from the big steamboats docking at Le Havre and Cherbourg."

"Thank you, Arlette. So, now we know that she took drugs habitually. Was there any difficulty getting drugs during the last few months?"

"The supplies have been limited. There have been fewer boats, and the boys in the band have not been carrying as much as usual."

"So, you weren't surprised to see Laure a little more desperate than usual?" I asked.

"M. Ward, this is no court of law, but please try to let

the young lady tell the story herself." He smiled at Arlette. I think Zamaron was trying to build a sympathetic bridge between himself and Arlette, who was still speaking in a guarded way.

"What was Laure's manner when you saw her last?"

"She was desperate to see Jean-Paul, even though I told her he could do nothing for her. Then she went to see Freddy."

The face of Freddy Briggs dropped. His usual amiable smile and knowing ways gave place to confusion. "What's this? I don't know what she's going on about! Honest I don't!"

"Freddy, let's have the minimum of guile. You heard what the Commissioner said. He's only interested in murder tonight. We all understand that a bartender is often put into a difficult position by his regular customers. People want all sorts of things after hours, under the counter. So, let's try to be frank."

"Damn it, I didn't want to get mixed up in that stuff, but I've had dukes and young milords asking me to get it for them. So, what could I do? It was just part of the job. Not a pleasant part, but it was part of being 'Freddy on the spot,' 'Freddy'll get it for you.' 'Good old Freddy.'"

"And Laure, did she approach you?" I asked.

"She did when she was hard up. She was hard up when I saw her last. That was the night she was killed."

"Did you sell her anything that night?"

"I didn't have nothing to sell or give away. And that's the truth, so help me."

"And there might have been some inconvenience later on once you'd helped her out the first time?"

"She'd have been at me night and day if I gave in."

"Where did you talk to her?"

He threw his head in the direction of the door near the

end of the bar. "Back there. No sense talking to her when she was upset with the shop full of customers, like."

"So, if somebody came in looking for her, she'd have been out of sight for several minutes?"

"That would be about right, sir."

"I looked in myself that night. Dr. Tyler was here with Mlle La Motte."

"That's correct, sir. I remember."

"M. Ward, you are doing very well. I congratulate you. But where are you going to take us from here?"

"*Monsieur le Commissaire*, I wish I knew. We know that Laure was desperate to renew her supply of opium. We know that she tried to blackmail Mr. Waddington on the *terrasse* of the Dôme." Waddington gave me a warning look. I closed my mouth so that he might say something. Soon we were all looking at him.

"In spite of what you might think about Laure and me, she wasn't blackmailing me about anything that had been between us in the past. Hash has known all about that from the beginning. I'm not keeping any secrets from her."

"It would be more useful, Mr. Waddington, if you would tell us what she *was* holding over you. We are not interested — I speak for myself, naturally — in what she was *not* threatening you with."

"Threatening me with? Hell, I've yet to meet a woman who could threaten me! Laure was simply testing me to see if I would go along with a proposition she outlined to me. In the end, I decided I didn't want to have any part of it."

"This had to do with a manuscript of yours that had disappeared some years ago? Isn't that right, Wad?" I said interrupting.

"No secret there. She showed me a bit of it and asked me what it would be worth to have the whole thing returned to me, no questions asked." Hash looked at her husband with surprise showing on her face. He had not been keeping her fully informed. From her expression, the tale of the missing manuscript was still a painful one.

"And?" I said, prompting.

"And she mentioned a price that was out of the question. It was the kind of money that we haven't seen for months and months. And she wanted it right away. I thought I might try to sell a picture I'd been buying on installments. But that wasn't the solution, since I neither owned nor had possession of the picture. We were scrimping to buy it from that Catalan fellow you met at the Dutchman's."

"What did she threaten you with if you didn't buy the manuscript?"

"There wasn't much she could do, Mike. It wasn't stuff I didn't want the world to see; I was proud of most of it. It wasn't pornography, if that's what you're driving at."

"So, her only move was to threaten to destroy it? Is that what she said?"

"She said get the money or else. That's what she meant, all right. I tried to borrow some money from Julie, here, but Laure went missing before I could collect it." Hash glanced at Julia, who was still watching Wad.

"Had you arranged to meet Laure the following day?"

"That's right. She didn't show up. Naturally, I never heard from her again."

"M. Zamaron," I said, "there are others in this room who had reason to dislike Laure Duclos. She had something on several of them. Something disreputable, something that they would not want others to find out about. Thus, we are surrounded by people who at the very least were not terribly saddened by news of her death."

"But, strangely, it is only about Mr. Waddington that we at the *préfecture* have been favoured with information, anonymous information."

"That's because some of these people have been trying to put me out of business!" Wad explained about the Spanish book to Zamaron. "Nobody here has read it, but they'd be happy to see it buried at Père Lachaise, along with its author."

"I see, so some of your erstwhile friends would not be unhappy to see you charged with the murder of Laure Duclos?"

"If it would stop publication of the book, sure. But I've just explained to these good people how I've arranged to stop the book from coming out."

"If I may say so, that's an unusual sacrifice for a writer, Mr. Waddington."

"If it will stop them climbing up my back, it'll be worth it. I don't like the idea of Hal, here, waiting for me with a gun in his pocket."

"Very sensible. I see. And Mr. Leopold, I suggest that you dispose of that weapon in the river when we leave the Dingo tonight. Firearms are taken very seriously in France, I assure you."

"All of this talk may be of great interest to you people, but I'm beginning to find a need to get to the last act." Georgia had not so far been heard from. "Americans are not supposed to be very good at writing second acts, so why not jump to the third? That'll be much tidier than a French play with God only knows how many acts before the curtain comes down."

"I am glad that Mme. O'Donnell is able to discover dramatic structure in these outpourings. You are very flattering, Madame, even if you find the plot less than absorbing. At least it concerns yourself as well as your friends."

"Don't be silly, Commissioner. How does any of this touch me or my husband?" Georgia looked to Zamaron for an answer. The Commissioner smiled nervously, then he brightened.

"Was not the deceased a tenant of yours at 14, rue de Tilsitt, Madame?" Zamaron did not seem to be aware of the hornet's nest he was testing with his foot.

"Oh!" Georgia sounded genuinely surprised. It was a notion that hadn't occurred to her. Wilson, who had grown quite white, managed a smile in the direction of the policeman. With it went a silent prayer. Zamaron acknowledged that something had passed between them with a movement of the eye that could never be taken for a wink.

Georgia laughed nervously. "But Laure was with us for such a short time . . . when we were down south."

"She needed a place to stay," Wilson added. "It was sort of an emergency for her. And as we were going to be away . . ."

"Nevertheless, *Madame et Monsieur*, you knew the woman. She was not a stranger. You are, in this, then, in the same vessel as your friends."

In order to take the pressure off the O'Donnells, I turned back to Arlette. "Did you see Laure on the night she died?" She was not expecting a question.

"You mean here?" I nodded. "No, I didn't see her. I must have been in the WC."

"But she was here for quite a few minutes talking to Freddy?"

"Yes, but he says in the back room."

"But you didn't see her come in or leave? Isn't that odd?"

"Perhaps I was in the WC for some time."

"For other than the usual reasons?"

Arlette paused before answering. "I may have been smoking one of my funny cigarettes. I don't remember."

"Something you picked up at Le Trou dans le Mur, I expect. So you missed both her going out and her coming in." I was suddenly sounding quite biblical to myself. "Did you see her, Dr. Tyler? Laure, I mean."

"I may have, Mike. I'd been celebrating a modest win at the races. Auteuil had been pretty good to me, thanks to a tip I got from Harold Stearns, a Harvard man of my acquaintance. I was pretty potted. Ask Freddy."

We all looked to Freddy, who was only too happy to help out now the subject of drugs had been dropped.

"You were rather jolly as I remember, sir. You were having trouble making your umbrella stand up when you crooked it over the table, sir. It kept falling on the floor."

"Sorry. It's all gone," he said, waving his open hand around his head. "Thanks anyway, Freddy."

"Was Anson a little drunk, Arlette?"

"He seemed just a little *gris* to me, but what kind of judge am I about that night? I had my own celebration. But at least until you went out for cigarettes, you were a perfect gentleman. Afterwards, *qui sait*?"

"That's right, sir. You didn't want the brands I had back of the bar. I remember you trying to muster your dignity as you said you didn't use any of the packets I had. You weren't half stiff when you went out in a huff!" Freddy's cheeks were getting quite rosy as he recalled the event. "Remember, Miss? He went through the tables so straight and tall with the umbrella, Miss, tipping his hat down over his eyes? It was like a turn on the music halls. Like watching 'Little Tich' at the Shepherd's Bush *Empire*, where I first saw Mr. Burdock, must be twenty years ago."

"What's Burdock got to do with this?" Wad asked, and not without reason. Zamaron shrugged and looked at me. I returned an English-Canadian's version of the Gallic gesture. It was a moment for Freddy to collect the empty glasses and bring fresh drinks. For a moment, I thought that Arlette had brought out one of her "funny cigarettes," but there was no trace of hashish in the air after Tolstoi leaned over to light it. I found my own case and offered its contents to O'Donnell and his wife, who were sitting nearby. Suddenly it occurred to me. What a ridiculous place to hold an interrogation. We were under no compulsion to sit here. We were not under arrest. Still, we were held by that same base desire that makes us read half the night just to see how a cheap mystery novel works out at the end. It was human nature at work. There was nothing that anyone could do about that. Just now, waiting for my drink, it felt like the pause in a baseball game at Maple Leaf Stadium before the last, crucial innings. When the drinks arrived, they were very welcome.

CHAPTER 27

It was a few minutes later; the women, and then the men, had visited the WC and Zamaron was looking at me to continue this possibly fatuous exercise. The Commissioner may have been looking for a dramatic mistral, but I feared that a mild breeze was all I could muster. And, of course, he had never heard of a chinook.

"If I may," I said at last, "I'd like to go back a few years, back indeed to 1922. At that time, many of the people here in this room were already here. Wilson and Georgia were still in the States, as was Julia. I was on the other side as well. But Freddy was here, working as an assistant barman at Le Trou dans le Mur with Arlette's brother, Jean-Paul La Motte, and doing favours for special customers. Hash and Wad were here. He was working for a Canadian paper then, the Toronto *Star*, where we both still have mutual friends. He'd also been working hard at his writing, encouraged by Sherwood Anderson, Bob McAlmon and Gertrude Stein. He'd written some short stories, a few stark, dramatic sketches based on his Eastern travels and the war, and possibly the fragment of a novel. (When he was in Toronto, he boasted that he was writing one about his boss, Harry Hindmarsh, who married the publisher's daughter. He was going to call it *The Son-in-Law*. But we don't know about that, do we Wad?) The *Star* wanted Wad to cover the Lausanne peace conference, which began in late November of that year. The

Waddingtons planned to turn it into a working pre-Christmas holiday before finding a place in Switzerland to ski and eat well. Only it didn't work out like that, did it, Wad?"

"I don't know where you're going with all this, Michaeleen, but, yes, you're right. Hash was sick with a hell of a cold, so I had to go on by myself. The plan was for Hash to join me as soon as Anson got her feeling well enough to travel."

"Ah, yes. I was forgetting. You had met Dr. Tyler here in Paris. You told me it was a house call, didn't you, Anson?"

"That's right, Mike. It was nothing special. A bad cold, just as Wad describes it."

"But by the time Wad was in Lausanne, you were more than just the family doctor, isn't that right?"

"Well, I'd treated them both on several occasions. Both Wad and I had been in the war. Sure, we became friends. Wad is a hell of a fellow, as you know, and everybody loves Hash."

"Were you ever in love with Hash, Anson?"

"That's a damned funny question! As I said, everybody was a little in love with Hash. She's one damned fine woman. But we were all friends, the three of us. I would never have done anything to spoil that."

"And, of course, in those days you were writing, weren't you?"

"Sure. I was working away at a couple of stories. Waddington took an interest. We talked a good deal about writing and what we'd been reading in those days."

"Were you ever jealous of Wad's success as a writer?"

"What success? He worked damn hard for his Toronto *Star* money. He had to make a deal to sell the same stuff to two Hearst agencies before he sent it, rewritten, to the *Star*."

"Didn't the *Star* pay for 'exclusive services,' Wad?"

"A man has to make a living, kid. You'll come to understand that."

"So you were counting on the ice-bound Canadians not reading the Hearst papers. And back in Paris, Anson was applying his healing arts to making Hash well enough to travel. Can you pick up the story there, Hash?"

"Oh dear, I'd just as soon listen, or rather *not* listen to this story. It was the most painful time in my life. I'd hate to go through it again." Hash was looking uncomfortable. It was partly because she never did say very much and partly because, except for Georgia and Arlette, the women had been silent.

"In the interests of getting to the bottom of what happened once and for all, Hash, would you help us?"

"Well, as everybody knows by now, I was sick in bed with a cold. Anson had given me a few things, but I was still feeling weak, and it was getting closer and closer to Christmas and the break in the conference. I know Tatie — I mean Jason — wanted to get away into the mountains, so, as soon as I was feeling better, a little better, I started to get ready to go. Anson came over with a prescription and helped me pack. I was as weak as a kitten."

"That was when you packed up Wad's manuscripts?"

"Yes, I put the stories and the carbons in separate manilla envelopes, and I put in the rough drafts, too. I just cleaned out the drawer that he kept his things in and put them into a small suitcase."

"You saw her do this, Anson?"

"I saw her packing, yes. I didn't particularly note the packing of the suitcase with Wad's work in it."

"And so you took the suitcases downstairs, with Anson's help — I'm guessing here — and put everything into a taxi?"

"That's right. Anson came along to see me off. He helped me find a porter and then went on in the taxi. I got the porter to put everything in my compartment and then went out to see that the trunk with our winter things went into the baggage car. When I got back, the suitcase was missing. The one with the papers in it, I mean." Hash was crying again as she retold the story of this episode. Wad looked as though he still felt the knife turn in his chest, the way he had when she'd first told him, when he met her train, one terrible night later.

"Is there any point in putting her through this?"

"I'm sorry, Wad. I think it might be important. You'll see in a minute."

"Tatie thinks I went out to buy a magazine or a sandwich from the buffet, but it was the trunk I was watching. It *was*, Tatie. I know you don't believe me." Wad looked as if he were going to say something to her but then thought better of it. I remembered what he had said to me about breaking a gun before going over a fence: the loss of the manuscripts was like a hunting accident to Wad. A gun going off that wasn't supposed to be loaded.

"Anson, where did you go in the taxi after dropping Hash at the Gare de Lyon?"

"Mike, you're talking about 1922. That's three years ago! I suppose I went to the hospital in Neuilly. I honestly don't remember."

"Are you sure you didn't follow Hash into the station, buy a platform ticket and remove the suitcase with the manuscripts from Hash's empty compartment?" There was no change in Anson Tyler's face when I made that accusation, but the rest of the people sitting around him suddenly became animated. Especially Julia Lowry, the quietest of the group.

"Anson! I don't believe it!"

"He'll have you for slander, Mike!"

"How could he?"

"I'm sure you're just making up stories, as Waddington is always doing. What an odd thing to say about a chap like Anson."

"That's quite an accusation, M. Ward," the policeman said. "You know our laws well enough to know that it is a serious business to make grave charges against someone in front of witnesses."

"Yes, I know. And I want all of you to know that I'm sorry that I have to ask Anson such questions. You may say they are accusations, M. Zamaron; I say I am asking questions, just requesting information. He needn't answer. But I do have a few more questions, if you don't mind."

"Mike, I have nothing to hide," Anson said, showing a little colour. "Fire away!"

"You knew how important these manuscripts were to Wad?"

"Of course. Even an amateur writer like myself would understand. I did what I could to help. When Wad wired me from Switzerland, I went to the station police and made an inquiry. They had nothing to show me. They shrugged and said that suitcases are stolen all the time."

"Where are the railway police located in the Gare de Lyon?"

"Why, I'm not sure I remember. Somewhere in the back, I think."

"At that time you were living with Laure, is that not right?"

Anson forced a smile. "You're always changing the subject on me, Mike. Laure and I had been living quite openly here in the Quarter. As I remember, I was very much in love with her at the time you mention."

"Was she smoking opium in those days? Was she hard up for money?"

"I think perhaps we both may have had a pipe or two — just as a lark, you understand. Neither of us was addicted. As for money, I paid for all of our expenses while we were together. Laure earned a little through teaching and translating. Both, as you know, are not well paid."

"Anson, we all know that in later years Laure took up the hazardous practice of blackmailing some of her friends in order to support her increasing need for drugs. And I wonder if you would agree that Laure had grown more desperate recently, her demands more ambitious, the interval between demands shorter." I looked around the room, hoping that someone would volunteer to back me up or suggest something. Finally, it was Wad who came to my rescue.

"Michaeleen, I don't know where you're leading us, but, for what it's worth, Laure was getting to be quite a pest. She was always after me with her hand out. I told her she had exaggerated ideas about the size of my writing income. She thought I could get money from Hash, but that's all gone now. She even suggested that I borrow it from a rich friend. She wanted more cash than I've seen in a year to get that manuscript back again. And if I'd had the money — and I tried to get it — I would have paid her." Wad looked over at Julia, who was examining the stem of her glass. Lady Biz gave her a cross-eyed look that was borrowed from Josephine Baker. It wasn't meant to be kind.

"Wad's right in what he says," Tolstoi said. "She was quite ready to tell all of you that my father rented a young fellow named Richard Ross to take my place in the British Army. I never met him; he was killed before the white feathers started arriving at home. Someplace on the Somme. That's why I'm here in Paris instead of doing something in the City, with my father."

"I thought it might be a white-feather story," said George. "A lot of chaps can't show their faces nowadays."

"Shut up, George," said Biz, pulling him towards her.

"I didn't know about it until the chap was dead, of course. Kept wondering why I didn't get my papers. I should have made it my business to find out. Don't know how Laure got on to it. Suspect she read my mother's letters." Arlette took Tolstoi's hand. He didn't look up at her.

"Anson," I said, "now that these two have confessed, can you tell us why Laure was blackmailing you? I suspect that you were the major source of money for her opium. What was it she knew about your past?"

"Let me say something before you speak, Doctor," Zamaron said quietly. "We have ways of finding out the truth about the spending of money. It is not very difficult to discover the financial pattern of a salaried employee of a hospital, for instance. We have the power to subpoena records and documents, you know."

"Yes, Laure was blackmailing me, along with some of the rest of you. And I agree that she was becoming desperate. I have never been short of money — as she very well knew — so I was not having difficulty in acquiescing to her needs. I told her time and time again that she should let me try to arrange a cure for her. I told her I'd pay for it, but she wouldn't listen, or — and this was worse — she would pretend to agree, only to get her hands on more money."

"I think we can all sympathize with that, even those of us who gave in to her demands. Tell me, Anson, why was she blackmailing you?"

"I say, old man, that's a bit thick, isn't it?" George said. "I don't think I'd much relish telling you about what she had on me, if she did have her hooks into my hide. One good thing about being known as an undischarged bankrupt is that no one ever bothers you for money. Funny thing, isn't it? You get to know who your friends are, I'll tell you. Nobody flatters a pauper." Biz patted his knee.

"Anson, in spite of what George says, I'd still like to know your secret. Remember, the Commissioner is only concerned with murder, nothing else. Why was Laure blackmailing you?" I was beginning to sound like a cracked phonograph record even to myself, but I had to keep trying. "Could it have had something to do with the missing manuscripts?"

"That is a suppositon I heartily deny in front of all of you!"

"Indulge me for a moment, Anson. For the sake of argument, let's suppose that Wad's early stories had fallen into your hands. Somehow. Then it would be likely that Laure knew about them. She wouldn't have to look further for something to blackmail you with."

While I was talking, another idea struck me. I interrupted the course of my argument to insert the notion. "Of course, Laure now would have had the manuscripts in her own hands, wouldn't she? She could hardly extort money from you if you still had the power to destroy or dispose of the contents of that suitcase. Laure was living with you in 1922. She was clever enough to have taken them with her when she left. I suspect, M. Zamaron, that at the time of her death Laure had possession of these papers. You searched her room, did you not?"

"I know nothing of the manuscripts you allude to, M. Ward, but it is quite clear that the murderer went through Mlle Duclos's apartment on the night of the murder. How did you know that, M. Ward? Have you other friends on the Quai des Orfèvres besides myself?"

"You're forgetting her handbag. Remember, I found it in the gutter. There were no keys inside. The murderer must have taken them. The rest was a logical inference."

Zamaron bowed in my direction. It was too deep a bow to be totally serious. "What can I say?" he said at last. "But where does this lead us?"

"If Laure had the manuscripts for the last three years, she had been collecting a regular allowance from Anson for all that time. The amount never presented a great problem. You were, in Laure's terms, well off. Now, what changed? Why would you suddenly decide to stop paying? What changes had occurred that made Laure a nuisance who could no longer be tolerated?

"One thing," I said, beginning to answer my own question, "Wad had become less obscure as a writer. He wasn't simply appearing in the little magazines. Two books had appeared here, one had come out in the States. So there was at least a possibility that our Jason Waddington was on the brink of a major career. I know, it's hard to imagine my tennis friend becoming a household word . . ." Here the group exchanged smiles with one another. "But don't forget that Wilson O'Donnell was unknown five years ago. Who among us can say that Wad won't be almost as well known in another few years?"

"Mike, I've been beating the drum for Wad in New York," Wilson said. "I've written to a lot of influential people. His name is, as you say, becoming known."

"Goofo, I'm anxious to hear how this ends and I'm not going to hear it from you."

"Quiet, precious." He patted her hand, but she pulled it away. "Wad's going to be a great writer. I'm sure of it. He's going to give me a run for my money. You can bet upon it."

"Well," I said, "that being so, it gave Laure a greater hold over whoever had taken those early manuscripts. An insignificant act of spite or jealousy had now been altered into something approaching an art theft of some magnitude."

"I see that you are still looking at me, Mike. I don't much like it, old man. The humour escapes me. I'm not a dunce. I can see where all of this fiction is pointing. And it is fiction, Mike. You haven't a shred of evidence to hang any of this theorizing on, now have you?" Anson was speaking calmly and without much animation. He went on. "Commissioner, I have some very good friends at the Quai des Orfèvres. My information is that they are quite happy to lump Laure's death in with the total claimed by Jack de Paris. So, I'm happy that you people are having all this fun at my expense — I can take a joke — but I'm beginning to find it a little stale, like a croissant left too long in the sun."

"You're right, Anson. I have been long-winded."

"*Monsieur le Commissaire*, if there is no reason why I am not free to go, I think I'll wish you all good night. Biz was quite right about the effect of this kind of talk on good liquor." Anson's chair squeaked as he got to his feet.

"Pray sit down, Dr. Tyler," Zamaron said. "I *suggest* you sit down and continue to help us in these inquiries. As far as my colleagues on the Quai des Orfèvres are concerned, like the Bourbons, *ils n'ont rien appris, ni rien oublié*; they have learned nothing and have forgotten nothing. For instance, they have not learned that Jack used a weapon that made a wound of approximately twenty-one centimeters in depth. Laure, on the other hand, was killed by a pair of blades that were at least fourteen and a half centimeters in length. A difference of six and a half centimeters; almost, as you would say, three inches!"

"That may be very interesting to you, Monsieur. As for me, I am going home."

"Back to your barge on the river, Doctor?"

"Why, yes. That is where I live. Is there anything wrong with that?"

"Such a charming location, Doctor. I must congratulate you on finding it." Zamaron put his hand to the flap of his briefcase and tugged at the straps until they came free. "It was in that charming setting that my men discovered this pair of scissors." Here he held up a pair of very ordinary-looking scissors. He held them in a handkerchief with the open blades pointing up to the ceiling of the Dingo.

"You've been to the barge! Sir, you had no right —"

"Monsieur, when I heard about your telephone call to the Prefect of Police, I became interested in your sudden interest in the capture of Jack de Paris. A friendly judge supplied me with the proper papers and a thorough search was made less than two hours ago. We were assisted in this work by M. Georges Sim, your Belgian tenant. He told my men that the scissors are his. Do you recognize them?"

"They look like any pair of scissors, Commissioner. What are they to me?"

"What indeed! The blades measure fourteen and a half centimeters, Monsieur. I have taken them apart and have seen stains that could be bloodstains at the point where the blades are held together by a screw. As a doctor, Monsieur, perhaps you have heard of the Uhlenhuth test for human blood. It's a very simple test, but most instructive. Such a test has been ordered for these scissors."

"I hope Georges has a good lawyer," Anson said, still maintaining a calm exterior.

"Luckily for M. Sim, he has an excellent alibi for the night of the Duclos murder. He was in the company of a woman, the writer Colette, and two other well-respected men of letters. It is you, Dr. Anson Tyler, who should be looking for an *avocat* to defend you from the grave charges that will undoubtedly be laid before the day is out." Léon Zamaron did not raise his voice, but the effect was such that we sat stunned, as though he had shouted these words at the top of his voice.

"I see, M. Ward, that you are perhaps not as surprised as your friends at this turn of events," the policeman said, while urging Anson to be seated again. "Did your amateur sleuthing uncover the same result that we hope the Uhlenhuth test will confirm, Monsieur?"

I took a deep drink of the whisky Freddy had brought me. He'd been smart enough to recognize that a single malt would be wasted on my palate at the moment: this was no time for sampling rare pleasures.

"There are two things that occur to me," I began. "The first is that when I visited the Gare de Lyon, I saw the record book for December 1922 that is kept by the railway police. All reported incidents are recorded, some in considerable detail. There was no mention of a theft of a suitcase on the day that Hash left for Switzerland."

"Mike, old boy, that's because Hash was on the train when she made the discovery," Wad said, taking a cigarette from George.

"Granted, she might not have had time to make a report before the departure, but you wired someone to do that before you returned from Lausanne, didn't you?"

"Damn it, Mike, Anson just told you that! He told me that he talked to the railway police and got nowhere."

"Then why wasn't there any record of Anson's report in the ledger, Wad? He told you he went to the station. If he went to the station and talked to the police, there would have been a record. Go to the station, look it up yourself. There was no report of your stolen suitcase made either on the date Hash left or later that month."

"Well . . ."

"There's only one explanation I can think of," I said. "Anson knew that it would be a waste of time going to the station, since he had the suitcase himself. Why ask a question when you already know the answer? Anson *told* you he'd spoken to the police because he knew that you would believe him."

"I searched everywhere except at the Gare de Lyon. I

believed Anson. Why wouldn't I have believed him? He was a good family friend." Wad called Anson's name, but the Doctor refused to turn in Waddington's direction.

"That brings me to the second observation, M. Zamaron." The policeman made a gesture which I translated as leave to continue. "Wad, do you remember your last meeting with Laure at the Dôme?"

"How could I forget?"

"You might recall that she'd been scattered with flecks of gold."

"Yes. She said something about Beaux-Arts students. Sure, I remember."

"It was hard to get off. I was combing it out of my hair for days afterwards. I was sitting with her when they fired the gold at us," I explained. "Well, I saw that gold-dust again. It was on the lapels of a jacket I saw hanging on Anson's barge. How could he have got the gold flecks on him without having come in close contact with one of the people who were dusted before Père Chambon threw the students out? I'm sure that there are other possible explanations, but one of them surely is that Laure and Anson met and stood very close to one another that night. It would have to have been after you saw her, Wad, and before I stumbled across the handbag in the street."

Wad whistled through his teeth, trying not to look at Anson.

"That's not much time," I said. "Hardly half an hour."

"*C'est bizarre*," Arlette said, almost to herself.

"What, my dear?" asked Tolstoi.

"That gold-dust you spoke about. I seem to remember seeing it someplace. Yes, it was on Anson's coat. Just as you say. I had to help Freddy with him. He was very drunk, you know. It took the two of us."

"And which of you brought the unfortunate man's

umbrella, may I ask?" said Zamaron, looking first at Arlette and Freddy and then, triumphantly, at me. The other two regarded one another but neither spoke. "So, the umbrella that refused to hang properly at the side of the table and that made the doctor look so droll when he went out for cigarettes was found on the floor by the cleaners in the morning. Is that so, M. Briggs?"

"Sorry, sir, I don't know anything about no umbrella. I don't think he left it here, sir. I would have heard about that, him being a regular customer and all."

"So, we have the case of the missing umbrella," Zamaron said, looking around the room with an amused expression on his face. "M. Briggs saw him leave with the umbrella when he went to buy cigarettes, but it was not with him when he was assisted to leave the second time."

"I suspect that you have a clever theory to cover that, Commissioner?"

"You are quite right, Lady Biz, I have," he said, at the same time making a motion to his man at the door. "But I imagine that our friend, M. Ward, will have already guessed the answer to that question. Am I correct, M. Ward?" At this moment, the plainclothesman handed a furled umbrella to Zamaron, who inspected it before passing it on to me.

"Are you showing off again, Ward?" It was Hal. He had, by the look of him, forgotten all about his own melodramatic entrance that evening. I found the catch on the stem of the umbrella and released it. Quickly I pushed the ring of wires to the top, expanding the umbrella against Hal's chest.

"Anson stabbed Laure through here so that he wouldn't get any blood on his clothes. He was a surgeon, remember. He knew exactly how much blood to expect. When she fell, he ditched the umbrella in the gutter further down the street and hurried back here."

At that moment, Anson got to his feet. His face was white with agony and tension. In a second he had knocked Hal out of his way. Zamaron himself was sent sprawling as a chair fell on top of him. The man in plain clothes made a dash after him, but Tyler was through the door and out in the rue Delambre before any of us fully realized that he had made a dash for it. It was so sudden and dramatic that I was reduced to uselessness itself, and I saw the others standing equally impotent. Wad, especially, was still sitting, his mouth half fallen open. Not exactly the picture of the man who had singlehandedly taken Jack de Paris just a few hours earlier.

I extended a hand to Zamaron, who clambered to his feet. Hal kicked the ownerless umbrella out of his way as he got up himself. The plainclothesman went out the door at last, almost, it seemed, as an afterthought.

"I have men in the street," Zamaron said. "He will not get far, I assure you." The policeman dusted off his dark trousers. There was a short pause, then, from somewhere in the room, Hash was speaking.

"Come on, Tatie, it's getting late." She tugged at the heavy arm in its tweed sleeve. He shifted his weight and slowly got to his feet. There was a question on his face when he turned to me.

"Before we go, Mike, there's one thing I have to know." Wad sounded winded, as though we had just played a set on the red clay courts back of the boulevard Arago, or maybe under the trees in the Luxembourg. "Why did he take my manuscripts?"

"Because he hated your writing, Wad. He loved you like a brother, but he was so jealous of your apparent ease with words that he had to try to destroy your work. Don't look for a rational explanation. You won't find it. Anson saw you as an unworthy competitor, getting ahead of him and apparently not even aware of the effort that he had expended. He was angry, Wad, because you're so damned good at what you do. He doesn't know the blood it's cost you; he only sees the sentences one after another put down with precision and simplicity. I guess it was his way of tearing your talent out of you. To him, with your talent for friendship, your sloppy manner around the Quarter — maybe he thought you were unworthy of your genius. A genius has to be humble, he thought — I'm really only guessing — and Wad, you're a lot of things, but humble isn't one of them. You weren't his idea of a serious artist."

"The poor son of a bitch," O'Donnell said, quoting himself. "I hope he gets away."

"Come on, Goofo, let's get out of here. Have you ever thought of jumping the fence and climbing up the Eiffel Tower at night?"

CHAPTER 28

Of course they caught him. He was crossing the railway lines behind the Gare Montparnasse, not far from where Wad and I had put an end to another murderous career, and he very narrowly missed being killed when a train bound for Versailles cut off his escape. They say he put up a damned decent fight before they overpowered him. *Rien ne va plus. Les jeux sont faits.*

This information would be carried in the afternoon papers, but it was still the small hours of the morning when we slouched out into the rue Delambre. The air hit us like an alpine blast. I could see our breath riding on it as Freddy closed the Dingo's door behind us. The shutters were up on the shops across the way; only a glint of light from the bar shone on the brass discs above the doorway of a *Hussier de Justice* an *avocat*, a *notaire* and a *Commissaire Priseur*. Lawyers. There was going to be a need for lawyers.

We broke up into groups of two or three as we turned towards the boulevard. Wad caught up to me, with Hash and Julia coming in behind us. Wad shook his head. "We used to talk about writing. Quite a lot. He was serious. He didn't like it the way I didn't like talking about particular effects. Damn it, I hate talking about it. Never could get that through to him. It's like making love and calling everything by the names in *Gray's Anatomy*. I don't want to spook the Muses. But he could never get enough of dissecting things; always doing a post mortem on my stuff. I got so I could smell the formaldehyde."

When we got to the corner, the group came together again before parting. Zamaron shook hands with all of us. When he came to Hash, he asked her, "Mme. Waddington, do you remember the date of your unfortunate departure from the Gare de Lyon? I assure you I'm not trying to stir up the unpleasant memory for a frivolous reason."

"I'm cursed with a good memory, *Monsieur le Commissaire*. I'll never forget that date. It's engraved on my heart. It was Friday, the fifteenth of December."

"Good," he said. "*Merci beaucoup*, Madame. You have rendered a great service." Hash explored Zamaron's face for a moment, as though trying to discover more, but it was clear that at the moment he was unwilling to speak further to her, or to Wad and Julia, who were hovering close to us. A few minutes later, when the others were trying to scare up taxis from the rank in front of the Dôme, Zamaron passed an envelope to me. Opening it, I found a small piece of card, which at first looked like a bus ticket. It was a platform ticket marked "*Gare de Lyon*." Under a street lamp I was able to make out some numerals on the back. With difficulty, I was able to read "15:XII:22," the fifteenth day of the twelfth month, 1922. I read it aloud. Zamaron smiled and took the ticket from me; he replaced it in the envelope and put that in his breast pocket.

"It's amusing, is it not?" Zamaron said. "This little ticket confirms something to me, but it will mean nothing at a trial. I knew that you would like to see it."

"You found it on the barge?"

"Among some other things of interest. In a suitcase." He looked at me significantly. "I will examine it all in the morning. My young assistant tells me that he found stories with Jason Waddington's name on them."

"Congratulations!" I said. He smiled.

"I will naturally return the manuscripts to their rightful owner when we have no further use for them. They may be needed to prepare the case against Dr. Tyler. In all events, I shall inform M. Waddington about the recovery of his property in the morning. I see no reason why he may not make copies of the writing for his own purposes in the meantime. It will give me a chance to show off my paintings."

"I think your news will cheer up my friend enormously."

"You think so? I hope you are right. I will see him just as soon as I have confirmed to my own satisfaction that the contents of the suitcase are indeed what we suspect they are. I would speak to him now, but there are too many people with him for a private conversation. And tomorrow, he will already be 'yesterday's hero.' No, I will speak to him tomorrow."

"You are very considerate, Monsieur."

"And what will you do now, M. Ward? Will you be able to return to your work happily?"

"I have no choice, Monsieur. I must work to eat," I said.

"Ah, you are no true artist, I see. Somehow the proposition presents itself differently here on Montparnasse. I can see that you do not paint."

"Nor do I collect, Monsieur. But, following your example, I might begin."

"Excellent!" he said.

"And what will you do now that you have one Jack behind bars and another giving your men a merry chase?"

"I shall continue to collect paintings. I have a feeling, my young Canadian friend, for two things: painting and playing cards. Gambling is my other passion. When I win, I buy more pictures; when I lose, an Utrillo leaves my happy home."

"You will speak to Waddington tomorrow?"

"I assure you, M. Ward," he said. "And, before I say good night, may I say thank you for your assistance. It was quite irregular, but it was welcome all the same. Will your stay in Paris be a long one?"

"I hope so, M. Zamaron."

"Then I will only say *au revoir*. Good night."

I continued walking down boulevard Montparnasse after Zamaron had been picked up by a police motor-car. He was lucky to be out of the weather. Gusts were coming along the wide boulevard, bending the empty branches of the trees and cutting through the defences of my coat. Paper and leaves had been pressed against the wall. I read *DÉFENSE D'AFFICHER* on the wall as I passed. The year of the law was stencilled just underneath.

Some of the others were still in view: the O'Donnells and the Waddingtons, with Julia holding onto Hash's arm; Arlette and Tolstoi had disappeared, as had Hal Leopold. Perhaps he'd gone to drop his pistol into the river as he'd been instructed. I could imagine him standing on Pont Neuf, leaning over the dark water.

I felt an arm hook through mine. It was Biz, and she was leaning close to me. For a few moments we walked in silence. Our feet were in step. "Poor Anson," she said at length. I agreed with her. We walked around a pile of stacked chairs and under the yellow light of a brasserie. There were no customers. "Why couldn't he be happy being a good doctor?" I didn't answer. "Poor lamb, he wanted more from life than life gives to a chap."

"Poor lamb": that had been Laure's pet expression. I'd forgotten.

We walked past the closed front, where the new café showed little sign of progressing. It was still a wood-and-coal yard, but now without the wood and coal. The sign stood on its end, leaning against a wall. There were no signs of builders.

"He made one mistake, Biz, and he just slipped in deeper and deeper," I said. "Then he took a chance."

"Pretending to be Jack."

"If it had worked, he would have been free of Laure, blackmail and the rash act of taking Wad's manuscripts once and for all. Some people can't bear to have anyone have a hold over them. Anson couldn't live like that any longer."

"I'm a bit like that, you know, Mike," she said, turning her face up to look at me. "I hate giving in to George and his life. But what's a chap to do? I can't go on living the life of a reprobate. I hate these hole-and-corner affairs. Maybe I should become a nun and say the world's well lost and spend the rest of my days in contemplation. What do you think?"

"They won't let you wear your old felt hat, Biz. But I can't imagine a lovelier nun than you'd make."

"You're very sweet, Mike. It's always easy to talk to you. You must have some idea of how much I hate this life. Always telling lies, making fantastic stories to cover things up. I'm sick of all that. I'd just like a moment to rest, to catch my breath, then maybe I can go on." Again we walked silently as we passed the church of Notre-Dame-des-Champs across the boulevard. It looked grey and dark.

"George is a good-hearted chap," she said, almost thinking out loud. "Maybe he'll give me time to catch up with myself. That's not too much to ask, Mike, is it? I'm not asking him to take me on forever, just long enough to throw off the hangover of the past few years."

"I know George is fond of you, Biz. He'd put you in a castle if it were up to him. His heart is sound."

"You wouldn't think of taking me on, would you, Mike?" I could tell she was looking up at me, but I tried not to see. "I'm a terrible nuisance and I know I drink far too much, but I have always thought I had grit, deep down and hardly used at all."

"Biz, you know, I think I loved you the first moment I saw you at the Nègre de Toulouse. But I'm not the man for you. You're a bright meteor and I'm a pedestrian. I can't glow like you, Biz. I can't keep the bar at the Crillon spinning the way you can. You're a thoroughbred, I'm a cart horse. You're shimmering with colour and I'm like that church across the street. But, I'll tell you this, darling Lady Biz, I'll probably always love you. I'll never forget you."

The wind was still blowing, and Biz held my arm closer as we walked on. When I looked at her, her face was moist. She said it was the wind. I put my arms around her and kissed her under a huge doorway, out of the wind. I kissed her and held the back of her head and felt her close to me. I wanted to stay this close to her always, and I kissed her again and again and hoped that it said what I was feeling. But, in a few minutes, she pulled away and said something about catching up with the others. For a moment, I held her face close to mine, but it was no good. She was already thinking of the next thing even as she smiled at me with her sad, wet eyes.

"Yes, we should try to catch them," I said. Of course, there was hardly anyone to catch. The street was nearly empty, except for George, who was waiting at the corner of the rue de Montparnasse. Biz gave me a squeeze, then released me. When I saw her last, she was waiting by the ourb while George discussed a proposition with a taxi driver. Very few taxi drivers accept cheques in Paris.

It was a long way back to the rue Bonaparte. I walked past the building where Alice and Gertrude lived and skirted around the edge of the Luxembourg Gardens until I came to the square in front of St-Sulpice, with its fountains on one side and the police station on the other. Above there, the rue Bonaparte narrowed. I followed it and turned into my doorway just before it emptied out into St-Germain-des-Prés.

CHAPTER 29

It was just over a week later that I saw Waddington again. I didn't know then that it was to be for the last time. I was having dinner in the Nègre de Toulouse when I saw a taxi drive up and park just outside the window. As the door opened and a large back came out into the rain, I recognized it at once as Wad's. He was carrying a raincoat rolled up over his arm, as though his belief in the weather was not absolute. A figure in the taxi leaned towards him and he moved temporarily back under the shelter of the taxi's roof. They kissed and held one another while the taxi idled its engine. It was Julia in the back seat. When he pulled his head clear of the taxi a second time, he waved to her through the glass. As he turned away from the street and the departing car, he saw me looking at him through the window. He came into the restaurant and greeted M. Lavigne with a bear hug. Over the restaurateur's shoulder, he seemed to be adding me up. I don't know whether the sum turned me into a friend or a foe. On the surface, he was his old friendly self.

"Hello there!" His jacket was wet around the shoulders and the hat in his hand was dripping onto the sawdust on the floor. "Where have you been hiding, kid? I've missed you on the inside courts."

"Not much of a game for me inside, Wad. I like it when I can judge the sun and the wind."

He seemed stockier, more massive, than I remembered

him being. Maybe he'd started eating better. Maybe there had been more restaurant meals recently. Maybe he had come into money. I liked that idea. Waddington would know how to use money.

"You're off for your winter holiday soon, aren't you?"

"Tomorrow night, from the Gare de l'Est. You should come with us, you know, Michaeleen."

"Yes, I really should. I think I'd like the mountains."

"Then why not? You get along with Hash and Snick. You'll love the Montaphon Valley and Schruns. And you'll get a great kick out of some new people we've met. They've got a lot of *gelt* to throw around, but they're not stuffy about it. You could do yourself some good, kid."

"It's a tempting offer, but I've got the desk to run by myself until after the new year. You know what it's like to be the junior man."

"Why don't you chuck it? Come on to Austria. I can get the expenses for both of us, with a little luck. I'm expecting a big advance for one book and a modest one for the other."

"I thought you'd burned your bridges with Boni and Liveright?"

"I have, old boy, I have. But now I'm going to go with Scribners. Just as soon as I get formal notice that Liveright won't publish the Anderson parody."

"So, it was a contract-breaker, just as you said at the Dingo?"

"That was only half the story. That was to make Hal change his mind about shooting me."

"You haven't retired the Spanish book after all, have you?"

"It's the best thing I've ever done, Mike. I'm not crazy."

"They'll say you double-crossed them."

"You can't be held to what you promise at gunpoint, old man. Forget it. Max Perkins at Scribners is excited about it. I hope to win over the critics with a barrage of letters, and maybe I'll go to New York when it comes out."

"It sounds swell, Wad. You're on your way. Anson Tyler was right. You are going to make a name for yourself."

"Ah, McWardo, it's still me. I won't change." He gave me one of his playful jabs. It caught me on the shoulder.

"By the way, did you ever recover that suitcase full of your stories?"

"The one Hash lost on the train? Nope, I didn't."

"I thought that it had been recovered from Anson's barge. Commissaire Zamaron told me that —"

"You hear all sorts of things in the Quarter, Mike. That's another reason for getting away."

"I was pretty sure you had got the stories back, Wad."

"Naw, kid. Don't get your hopes up. It's a damned pity, I guess, losing two years of work like that. Almost a legend, really. But one thing I learned in the war is never discuss casualties." I had to agree with Wad: it did make a better story his way. As he said, a legend.

"It looks as if everything is working out for you the way you planned, Wad."

"Next time you see my name, it'll be in the *New York Times*." He slapped me on the back and gave me a grin. "Aw, come on, kid. Catch the train with us to Schruns. We'll have some great times skiing and mushing through the passes. And you know Julia. She'll be joining us too. It'll be like home with you on the scene. Bring your girl, if you've got one."

"Sorry, Wad. It just doesn't cut that way. We'll see you in the spring, okay?"

Wad took a deep breath before speaking. "Sure thing, kid," he said, with his face clouding over and the bounce going out of his voice. "Sure thing. We'll make it the spring, then."

"Give my love to Hash and Snick, you big galoot."

"You won't change your mind?" His moustache was lifted by his one-sided grin.

"Nope. Got things to do. You know how it is."

We had a *fine à l'eau* together, although it would have been more in keeping with the season to have taken a grog or a hot-buttered rum. When we finished, he made a gesture as though he were reaching into his pocket for his wallet, but he stopped before he got there.

"I'll get this last one," I said.

"Well, I'll match you for it in April. The next one is on me, Mike," he said. And he gathered up his coat and hat and strode out onto the boulevard.